Other books also by John Munro:

ELECTRICITY AND ITS USES, PIONEERS OF ELECTRICITY, HEROES
OF THE TELEGRAPH, ETC., AND JOINT AUTHOR OF MUNRO AND
JAMIESON'S POCKET-BOOK OF ELECTRICAL RULES AND TABLES

The Story Of Electricity

The Story Of Electricity

John Munro

THE STORY OF ELECTRICITY

Published in the United States by IndyPublish.com
McLean, Virginia

ISBN 1-4043-3098-4 (hardcover)
ISBN 1-4043-3099-2 (paperback)

PREFACE

A work on electricity needs little recommendation to stimulate the interest of the general reader. Electricity in its manifold applications is so large a factor in the comfort and convenience of our daily life, so essential to the industrial organization which embraces every dweller in a civilized land, so important in the development and extension of civilization itself, that a knowledge of its principles and the means through which they are directed to the service of mankind should be a part of the mental equipment of everyone who pretends to education in its truest sense. Let anyone stop to consider how he individually would be affected if all electrical service were suddenly to cease, and he cannot fail to appreciate the claims of electricity to attentive study.

The purpose of this little book is to present the essential facts of electrical science in a popular and interesting way, as befits the scheme of the series to which it belongs. Electrical phenomena have been observed since the first man viewed one of the most spectacular and magnificent of them all in the thunderstorm, but the services of electricity which we enjoy are the product solely of scientific achievement in the nineteenth century. It is to these services that the main part of the following discussion is devoted. The introductory chapters deal with various sources of electrical energy, in friction, chemical action, heat and magnetism. The rest of the book describes the applications of electricity in electroplating, communication by telegraph, telephone, and wireless telegraphy, the production of light and heat, the transmission of power, transportation over rails and in vehicles, and the multitude of other uses.

July, 1915.

CONTENTS

CHAPTER I.

THE ELECTRICITY OF FRICTION.

A schoolboy who rubs a stick of sealing-wax on the sleeve of his jacket, then holds it over dusty shreds or bits of straw to see them fly up and cling to the wax, repeats without knowing it the fundamental experiment of electricity. In rubbing the wax on his coat he has electrified it, and the dry dust or bits of wool are attracted to it by reason of a mysterious process which is called "induction."

Electricity, like fire, was probably discovered by some primeval savage. According to Humboldt, the Indians of the Orinoco sometimes amuse themselves by rubbing certain beans to make them attract wisps of the wild cotton, and the custom is doubtless very old. Certainly the ancient Greeks knew that a piece of amber had when rubbed the property of attracting light bodies. Thales of Miletus, wisest of the Seven Sages, and father of Greek philosophy, explained this curious effect by the presence of a "soul" in the amber, whatever he meant by that. Thales flourished 600 years before the Christian era, while Croesus reigned in Lydia, and Cyrus the Great, in Persia, when the renowned Solon gave his laws to Athens, and Necos, King of Egypt, made war on Josiah, King of Judah, and after defeating him at Megiddo, dedicated the corslet he had worn during the battle to Apollo Didymaeus in the temple of Branchidas, near Miletus.

Amber, the fossil resin of a pine tree, was found in Sicily, the shores of the Baltic, and other parts of Europe. It was a precious stone then as now, and an article of trade with the Phoenicians, those early merchants of the Mediterranean. The attractive power might enhance the value of the gem in the eyes of the supersti-

tious ancients, but they do not seem to have investigated it, and beyond the spec-
ulation of Thales, they have told us nothing more about it.

Towards the end of the sixteenth century Dr. Gilbert of Colchester, physician to
Queen Elizabeth, made this property the subject of experiment, and showed that,
far from being peculiar to amber, it was possessed by sulphur, wax, glass, and
many other bodies which he called electrics, from the Greek word elektron, sig-
nifying amber. This great discovery was the starting-point of the modern science
of electricity. That feeble and mysterious force which had been the wonder of the
simple and the amusement of the vain could not be slighted any longer as a curious freak of nature, but assuredly none dreamt that a day was dawning in which
it would transform the world.

Otto von Guericke, burgomaster of Magdeburg, was the first to invent a machine
for exciting the electric power in larger quantities by simply turning a ball of sulphur between the bare hands. Improved by Sir Isaac Newton and others, who
employed glass rubbed with silk, it created sparks several inches long. The ordinary frictional machine as now made is illustrated in figure i, where P is a disc of
plate glass mounted on a spindle and turned by hand. Rubbers of silk R, smeared
with an amalgam of mercury and tin, to increase their efficiency, press the rim of
the plate between them as it revolves, and a brass conductor C, insulated on glass
posts, is fitted with points like the teeth of a comb, which, as the electrified surface of the plate passes by, collect the electricity and charge the conductor with
positive electricity. Machines of this sort have been made with plates 7 feet in
diameter, and yielding sparks nearly 2 feet long.

The properties of the "electric fire," as it was now called, were chiefly investigated by Dufay. To refine on the primitive experiment let us replace the shreds by a
pithball hung from a support by a silk thread, as in figure 2. If we rub the glass
rod vigorously with a silk handkerchief and hold it near, the ball will fly toward
the rod. Similarly we may rub a stick of sealing wax, a bar of sulphur, indeed, a
great variety of substances, and by this easy test we shall find them electrified.
Glass rubbed with glass will not show any sign of electrification, nor will wax
rubbed on wax; but when the rubber is of a different material to the thing rubbed,
we shall find, on using proper precautions, that electricity is developed. In fact,
the property which was once thought peculiar to amber is found to belong to all
bodies. ANY SUBSTANCE, WHEN RUBBED WITH A DIFFERENT SUB-
STANCE, BECOMES ELECTRIFIED.

The electricity thus produced is termed frictional electricity. Of course there are
some materials, such as amber, glass, and wax, which display the effect much better than others, and hence its original discovery.

In dry frosty weather the friction of a tortoise-shell comb will electrify the hair and make it cling to the teeth. Sometimes persons emit sparks in pulling off their flannels or silk stockings. The fur of a cat, or even of a garment, stroked in the dark with a warm dry hand will be seen to glow, and perhaps heard to crackle. During winter a person can electrify himself by shuffling in his slippers over the carpet, and light the gas with a spark from his finger. Glass and sealing-wax are, however, the most convenient means for investigating the electricity of friction.

A glass rod when rubbed with a silk handkerchief becomes, as we have seen, highly electric, and will attract a pithball (fig. 2). Moreover, if we substitute the handkerchief for the rod it will also attract the ball (fig. 3). Clearly, then, the handkerchief which rubbed the rod as well as the rod itself is electrified. At first we might suppose that the handkerchief had merely rubbed off some of the electricity from the rod, but a little investigation will soon show that is not the case. If we allow the pithball to touch the glass rod it will steal some of the electricity on the rod, and we shall now find the ball REPELLED by the rod, as illustrated in figure 4. Then, if we withdraw the rod and bring forward the handkerchief, we shall find the ball ATTRACTED by it. Evidently, therefore, the electricity of the handkerchief is of a different kind from that of the rod.

Again, if we allow the ball to touch the handkerchief and rub off some of its electricity, the ball will be REPELLED by the handkerchief and ATTRACTED by the rod. Thus we arrive at the conclusion that whereas the glass rod is charged with one kind of electricity, the handkerchief which rubbed it is charged with another kind, and, judging by their contrary effects on the charged ball or indicator, they are of opposite kinds. To distinguish the two sorts, one is called POSITIVE and the other NEGATIVE electricity.

Further experiments with other substances will show that sometimes the rod is negative while the rubber is positive. Thus, if we rub the glass rod with cat's fur instead of silk, we shall find the glass negative and the fur positive. Again, if we rub a stick of sealing-wax with the silk handkerchief, we shall find the wax negative and the silk positive. But in every case one is the opposite of the other, and moreover, an equal quantity of both sorts of electricity is developed, one kind on the rod and the other on the rubber. Hence we conclude that EQUAL AND OPPOSITE QUANTITIES OF ELECTRICITY ARE SIMULTANEOUSLY DEVELOPED BY FRICTION.

If any two of the following materials be rubbed together, that higher in the list becomes positively and the other negatively electrified:—

POSITIVE (+).

Cats' fur.
Polished glass.
Wool.
Cork, at ordinary temperature.
Coarse brown paper.
Cork, heated.
White silk.
Black silk.
Shellac.
Rough glass.

NEGATIVE (-).

The list shows that quality, as well as kind, of material affects the production of electricity. Thus polished glass when rubbed with silk is positive, whereas rough glass is negative. Cork at ordinary temperature is positive when rubbed with hot cork. Black silk is negative to white silk, and it has been observed that the best radiator and absorber of light and heat is the most negative. Black cloth, for instance, is a better radiator than white, hence in the Arctic regions, where the body is much warmer than the surrounding air, many wild animals get a white coat in winter, and in the tropics, where the sunshine is hotter than the body, the European dons a white suit.

The experiments of figures 1, 2, and 3 have also shown us that when the pithball is charged with the positive electricity of the glass rod it is REPELLED by the like charge upon the rod, and ATTRACTED by the negative or unlike charge on the handkerchief. Again, when it is charged with the negative electricity of the hand-kerchief it is REPELLED by the like charge on the handkerchief and ATTRACT-ED by the positive or unlike charge on the rod. Therefore it is usual to say that LIKE ELECTRICITIES REPEL AND UNLIKE ELECTRICITIES ATTRACT EACH OTHER.

We have said that all bodies yield electricity under the friction of dissimilar bod-ies; but this cannot be proved for every body by simply holding it in one hand and rubbing it with the excitor, as may be done in the case of glass. For instance, if we take a brass rod in the hand and apply the rubber vigorously, it will fail to attract the pithball, for there is no trace of electricity upon it. This is because the metal differs from the glass in another electrical property, and they must therefore be differently treated. Brass, in fact, is a conductor of electricity and glass is not. In other words, electricity is conducted or led away by brass, so that, as soon as it is generated by the friction, it flows through the hand and body of the experimenter, which are also conductors, and is lost in the ground. Glass on the other hand, is an INSULATOR, and the electricity remains on the surface of it. If, however, we attach a glass handle to the rod and hold it by that whilst rubbing it, the electricity cannot then escape to the earth, and the brass rod will attract the pithball.

All bodies are conductors of electricity in some degree, but they vary so enormously in this respect that it has been found convenient to divide them into two extreme classes—conductors and insulators. These run into each other through an intermediate group, which are neither good conductors nor good insulators. The following are the chief examples of these classes:—

CONDUCTORS.—All the metals, carbon.

INTERMEDIATE (bad conductors and bad insulators).—Water, aqueous solutions, moist bodies; wood, cotton, hemp, and paper in any but a dry atmosphere; liquid acids, rarefied gases.

INSULATORS.—Paraffin (solid or liquid), ozokerit, turpentine, silk, resin, sealing-wax or shellac, india-rubber, gutta-percha, ebonite, ivory, dry wood, dry glass or porcelain, mica, ice, air at ordinary pressures.

It is remarkable that the best conductors of electricity, that is to say, the substances which offer least resistance to its passage, for instance the metals, are also the best conductors of heat, and that insulators made red hot become conductors. Air is an excellent insulator, and hence we are able to perform our experiments on frictional electricity in it. We can also run bare telegraph wires through it, by taking care to insulate them with glass or porcelain from the wooden poles which support them above the ground. Water, on the other hand, is a partial conductor, and a great enemy to the storage or conveyance of electricity, from its habit of soaking into porous metals, or depositing in a film of dew on the cold surfaces of insulators such as glass, porcelain, or ebonite. The remedy is to exclude it, or keep the insulators warm and dry, or coat them with shellac varnish, wax, or paraffin. Submarine telegraph wires running under the sea are usually insulated from the surrounding water by india-rubber or gutta-percha.

The distinction between conductors and non-conductors or insulators was first observed by Stephen Gray, a pensioner of the Charter-house. Gray actually trans-

mitted a charge of electricity along a pack-thread insulated with silk, to a distance
of several hundred yards, and thus took an important step in the direction of the
electric telegraph.

It has since been found that FRICTIONAL ELECTRICITY APPEARS ONLY
ON THE EXTERNAL SURFACE OF CONDUCTORS.

This is well shown by a device of Faraday resembling a small butterfly net insulated by a glass handle (fig. 5). If the net be charged it is found that the electrification is only outside, and if it be suddenly drawn outside in, as shown by the
dotted line, the electrification is still found outside, proving that the charge has
shifted from the inner to the outer surface. In the same way if a hollow conductor is charged with electricity, none is discoverable in the interior. Moreover, its
distribution on the exterior is influenced by the shape of the outer surface. On a
sphere or ball it is evenly distributed all round, but it accumulates on sharp edges
or corners, and most of all on points, from which it is easily discharged.

A neutral body can, as we have seen (fig. 4), be charged by CONTACT with an
electrified body: but it can also be charged by INDUCTION, or the influence of
the electrified body at a distance.

Thus if we electrify a glass rod positively (+) and bring it near a neutral or unelec-
trified brass ball, insulated on a glass support, as in figure 6, we shall find the side
of the ball next the rod no longer neutral but negatively electrified (-), and the
side away from the rod positively electrified (+).

If we take away the rod again the ball will return to its neutral or non-electric
state, showing that the charge was temporarily induced by the presence of the
electrified rod. Again, if, as in figure 7, we have two insulated balls touching each
other, and bring the rod up, that nearest the rod will become negative and that
farthest from it positive. It appears from these facts that electricity has the power
of disturbing or decomposing the neutral state of a neighbouring conductor, and
attracting the unlike while it repels the like induced charge. Hence, too, it is that
the electrified amber or sealing-wax is able to attract a light straw or pithball. The
effect supplies a simple way of developing a large amount of electricity from a
small initial charge. For if in figure 6 the positive side of the ball be connected for
a moment to earth by a conductor, its positive charge will escape, leaving the negative on the ball, and as there is no longer an equal positive charge to recombine
with it when the exciting rod is withdrawn, it remains as a negative charge on the
ball. Similarly, if we separate the two balls in figure 7, we gain two equal
charges—one positive, the other negative. These processes have only to be repeated by a machine in order to develop very strong charges from a feeble source.

Faraday saw that the intervening air played a part in this action at a distance, and proved conclusively that the value of the induction depended on the nature of the medium between the induced and the inducing charge. He showed, for example, that the induction through an intervening cake of sulphur is greater than through an equal thickness of air. This property of the medium is termed its INDUCTIVE CAPACITY.

The Electrophorus, or carrier of electricity, is a simple device for developing and conveying a charge on the principle of induction. It consists, as shown in figure 8, of a metal plate B having an insulating handle of glass H, and a flat cake of resin or ebonite R. If the resin is laid on a table and briskly rubbed with cat's fur it becomes negatively electrified. The brass plate is then lifted by the handle and laid upon the cake. It touches the electrified surface at a few points, takes a minute charge from these by contact. The rest of it, however, is insulated from the resin by the air. In the main, therefore, the negative charge of the resin is free to induce an opposite or positive charge on the lower surface and a negative charge on the upper surface of the plate. By touching this upper surface with the finger, as shown in figure 8, the negative charge will escape through the body to the ground or "earth," as it is technically called, and the positive charge will remain on the plate. We can withdraw it by lifting the plate, and prove its existence by drawing a spark from it with the knuckle. The process can be repeated as long as the negative charge continues on the resin.

These tiny sparks from the electrophorus, or the bigger discharges of an electrical machine, can be stored in a simple apparatus called a Leyden jar, which was discovered by accident. One day Cuneus, a pupil of Muschenbroeck, professor in the University of Leyden, was trying to charge some water in a glass bottle by connecting it with a chain to the sparkling knob of an electrical machine. Holding the bottle in one hand, he undid the chain with the other, and received a violent shock which cast the bottle on the floor. Muschenbroeck, eager to verify the phenomenon, repeated the experiment, with a still more lively and convincing result. His. nerves were shaken for two days, and he afterwards protested that he would not suffer another shock for the whole kingdom of France.

The Leyden jar is illustrated in figure 9, and consists in general of a glass bottle partly coated inside and out with tinfoil F, and having a brass knob K connecting with its internal coat. When the charged plate or conductor of the electrophorus touches the knob the inner foil takes a positive charge, which induces a negative charge in the outer foil through the glass. The corresponding positive charge induced at the same time escapes through the hand to the ground or "earth." The inner coating is now positively and the outer coating negatively electrified, and these two opposite charges bind or hold each other by mutual attraction. The bottle will therefore continue charged for a long time; in short, until it is purposely discharged or the two electricities combine by leakage over the surface of the glass.

To discharge the jar we need only connect the two foils by a conductor, and thus allow the separated charges to combine. This should be done by joining the OUTER to the INNER coat with a stout wire, or, better still, the discharging tongs T, as shown in the figure. Otherwise, if the tongs are first applied to the inner coat, the operator will receive the charge through his arms and chest in the manner of Cuneus and Muschenbroeck.

Leyden jars can be connected together in "batteries," so as to give very powerful effects. One method is to join the inner coat of one to the outer coat of the next. This is known as connecting in "series," and gives a very long spark. Another method is to join the inner coat of one to the inner coat of the next, and similarly all the outer coats together. This is called connecting "in parallel," or quantity, and gives a big, but not a long spark.

Of late years the principle of induction, which is the secret of the Leyden jar and electrophorus, has been applied in constructing "influence" machines for generating electricity. Perhaps the most effective of these is the Wimshurst, which we illustrate in figure 10, where PP are two circular glass plates which rotate in opposite directions on turning the handle. On the outer rim of each is cemented a row of radial slips of metal at equal intervals. The slips at opposite ends of a diameter are connected together twice during each revolution of the plates by wire brushes S, and collecting combs TT serve to charge the positive and negative conductors CC, which yield very powerful sparks at the knobs K above. The given theory of this machine may be open to question, but there can be no doubt of its wonderful performance. A small one produces a violent spark 8 or 10 inches long after a few turns of the handle.

The electricity of friction is so unmanageable that it has not been applied in practice to any great extent. In 1753 Mr. Charles Morrison, of Greenock, published the first plan of an electric telegraph in the Scots Magazine, and proposed to charge an insulated wire at the near end so as to make it attract printed letters of the alphabet at the far end. Sir Francis Ronalds also invented a telegraph actuated by this kind of electricity, but neither of these came into use. Morrison, an obscure genius, was before his age, and Ronalds was politely informed by the Government of his day that "telegraphs of any kind were wholly unnecessary." Little instruments for lighting gas by means of the spark are, however, made, and the noxious fumes of chemical and lead works are condensed and laid by the discharge from the Wimshurst machine. The electricity shed in the air causes the dust and smoke to adhere by induction and settle in flakes upon the sides of the flues. Perhaps the old remark that "smuts" or "blacks" falling to the ground on a sultry day are a sign of thunder is traceable to a similar action.

The most important practical result of the early experiments with frictional electricity was Benjamin Franklin's great discovery of the identity of lightning and the electric spark. One day in June, 1792, he went to the common at Philadelphia and flew a kite beneath a thundercloud, taking care to insulate his body from the cord. After a shower had wetted the string and made it a conductor, he was able to draw sparks from it with a key and to charge a Leyden jar. The man who had "robbed Jupiter of his thunderbolts" became celebrated throughout the world, and lightning rods or conductors for the protection of life and property were soon brought out. These, in their simplest form, are tapes or stranded wires of iron or copper attached to the walls of the building. The lower end of the conductor is soldered to a copper plate buried in the moist subsoil, or, if the ground is rather dry, in a pit containing coke. Sometimes it is merely soldered to the water mains of the house. The upper end rises above the highest chimney, turret, or spire of the edifice, and branches into points tipped with incorrosive metal, such as platinum. It is usual to connect all the outside metal of the house, such as the gutters and finials to the rod by means of soldered joints, so as to form one continuous metallic network or artery for the discharge.

When a thundercloud charged with electricity passes over the ground, it induces a charge of an opposite kind upon it. The cloud and earth with air between are analogous to the charged foils of the Leyden jar separated by the glass. The two electricities of the jar, we know, attract each other, and if the insulating glass is too weak to hold them asunder, the spark will pierce it. Similarly, if the insulating air cannot resist the attraction between the thundercloud and the earth, it will be ruptured by a flash of lightning. The metal rod, however, tends to allow the two charges of the cloud and earth to combine quietly or to shunt the discharge past the house.

CHAPTER II.

THE ELECTRICITY OF CHEMISTRY.

A more tractable kind of electricity than that of friction was discovered at the beginning of the present century. The story goes that some edible frogs were skinned to make a soup for Madame Galvani, wife of the professor of anatomy in the University of Bologna, who was in delicate health. As the frogs were lying in the laboratory of the professor they were observed to twitch each time a spark was drawn from an electrical machine that stood by. A similar twitching was also noticed when the limbs were hung by copper skewers from an iron rail. Galvani thought the spasms were due to electricity in the animal, and produced them at will by touching the nerve of a limb with a rod of zinc, and the muscle with a rod of copper in contact with the zinc. It was proved, however, by Alessanjra Volta, professor of physics in the University of Pavia, that the electricity was not in the animal but generated by the contact of the two dissimilar metals and the moisture of the flesh. Going a step further, in the year 1800 he invented a new source of electricity on this principle, which is known as "Volta's pile." It consists of plates or discs of zinc and copper separated by a wafer of cloth moistened with acidulated water. When the zinc and copper are joined externally by a wire, a CURRENT of electricity is found in the wire One pair of plates with the liquid between makes a "couple" or element; and two or more, built one above another in the same order of zinc, copper, zinc, copper, make the pile. The extreme zinc and copper plates, when joined by a wire, are found to deliver a current.

This form of the voltaic, or, as it is sometimes called, galvanic battery, has given place to the "cell" shown in figure II, where the two plates Z C are immersed in acidulated water within the vessel, and connected outside by the wire W. The zinc plate has a positive and the copper a negative charge. The positive current flows from the zinc to the copper inside the cell and from the copper to the zinc outside the cell, as shown by the arrows. It thus makes a complete round, which is called the voltaic "circuit," and if the circuit is broken anywhere it will not flow at all. The positive electricity of the zinc appears to traverse the liquid to the copper, from which it flows through the wire to the zinc. The effect is that the end of the wire attached to the copper is positive (+), and called the positive "pole" or electrode, while the end attached to the zinc is negative (-), and called the negative pole or electrode. "A simple and easy way to avoid confusion as to the direction of the current, is to remember that the POSITIVE current flows FROM the COPPER TO the ZINC at the point of METALLIC contact." The generation of this current is accompanied by chemical action in the cell. Experiment shows that the mere CONTACT of dissimilar materials, such as copper and zinc, electrifies them—zinc being positive and copper negative; but contact alone does not yield a continuous current of electricity. When we plunge the two metals, still in contact, either directly or through a wire, into water preferably acidulated, a chemical action is set up, the water is decomposed, and the zinc is consumed. Water, as is well known, consists of oxygen and hydrogen. The oxygen combines with the zinc to form oxide of zinc, and the hydrogen is set free as gas at the surface of the copper plate. So long as this process goes on, that is to say, as long as there is zinc and water left, we get an electric current in the circuit. The existence of such a current may be proved by a very simple experiment. Place a penny above and a dime below the tip of the tongue, then bring their edges into contact, and you will feel an acid taste in the mouth.

Figure 12 illustrates the supposed chemical action in the cell. On the left hand are the zinc and copper plates (Z C) disconnected in the liquid. The atoms of zinc are shown by small circles; the molecules of water, that is, oxygen, and hydrogen (H_2O) by lozenges of unequal size. On the right hand the plates are connected by a wire outside the cell; the current starts, and the chemical action begins. An atom of zinc unites with an atom of oxygen, leaving two atoms of hydrogen thus set free to combine with another atom of oxygen, which in turn frees two atoms of hydrogen. This interchange of atoms goes on until the two atoms of hydrogen which are freed last abide on the surface of the copper. The "contact electricity" of the zinc and copper probably begins the process, and the chemical action keeps it up. Oxygen, being an "electro-negative" element in chemistry, is attracted to the zinc, and hydrogen, being "electro-positive," is attracted to the copper.

The difference of electrical condition or "potential" between the plates by which the current is started has been called the electromotive force, or force which puts the electricity in motion. The obstruction or hindrance which the electricity overcomes in passing through its conductor is known as the RESISTANCE.

Obviously the higher the electromotive force and the lower the resistance, the stronger will be the current in the conductor. Hence it is desirable to have a cell which will give a high electromotive force and a low internal resistance.

Voltaic cells are grouped together in the mode of Leyden jars. Figure 13 shows how they are joined "in series," the zinc or negative pole of one being connected by wire to the copper or positive pole of the next. This arrangement multiplies alike the electromotive force and the resistance. The electromotive force of the battery is the sum of the electromotive forces of all the cells, and the resistance of the battery is the sum of the resistances of all the cells. High electromotive forces or "pressures" capable of overcoming high resistances outside the battery can be obtained in this way.

Figure 14 shows how the zincs are joined "in parallel," the zinc or negative pole of one being connected by wire to the zinc or negative pole of the rest, and all the copper or positive poles together. This arrangement does not increase the electro-motive force, but diminishes the resistance. In fact, the battery is equivalent to a single cell having plates equal in area to the total area of all the plates. Although unable to overcome a high resistance, it can produce a large volume or quantity of electricity.

Numerous voltaic combinations and varieties of cell have been found out. In gen-eral, where-ever two metals in contact are placed in a liquid which acts with more chemical energy on one than on the other, as sulphuric acid does on zinc in pref-erence to copper, there is a development of electricity. Readers may have seen how an iron fence post corrodes at its junction with the lead that fixes it in the stone. This decay is owing to the wet forming a voltaic couple with the two dissimilar metals and rusting the iron. In the following list of materials, when any two in contact are plunged in dilute acid, that which is higher in the order becomes the positive plate or negative pole to that which is lower:—

POSITIVE	Iron	Silver
Zinc	Nickel	Gold
Cadmium	Bismuth	Platinum
Tin	Antimony	Graphite
Lead	Copper	NEGATIVE

There being no chemical union between the hydrogen and copper in the zinc and copper couple, that gas accumulates on the surface of the copper plate, or is lib-erated in bubbles. Now, hydrogen is positive compared with copper, hence they tend to oppose each other in the combination. The hydrogen diminishes the value of the copper, the current grows weaker, and the cell is said to "polarise." It follows that a simple water cell is not a good arrangement for the supply of a steady current.

The Daniell cell is one of the best, and gives a very constant current. In this battery the copper plate is surrounded by a solution of sulphate of copper (Cu SO4), which the hydrogen decomposes, forming sulphuric acid (H2SO4), thus taking itself out of the way, and leaving pure copper (Cu) to be deposited as a fresh surface on the copper plate. A further improvement is made in the cell by surrounding the zinc plate with a solution of sulphate of zinc (Zn SO4), which is a good conductor. Now, when the oxide of zinc is formed by the oxygen uniting with the zinc, the free sulphuric acid combines with it, forming more sulphate of zinc, and maintaining the CONDUCTIVITY of the cell. It is only necessary to keep up the supply of zinc, water, and sulphate of copper to procure a steady current of electricity.

The Daniell cell is constructed in various ways. In the earlier models the two plates with their solutions were separated by a porous jar or partition, which allowed the solutions to meet without mixing, and the current to pass. Sawdust moistened with the solutions is sometimes used for this porous separator, for instance, on board ships for laying submarine cables, where the rolling of the waves would blend the liquids.

In the "gravity" Daniell the solutions are kept apart by their specific gravities, yet mingle by slow diffusion. Figure 15 illustrates this common type of cell, where Z is the zinc plate in a solution of sulphate of zinc, and C is the copper plate in a solution of sulphate of copper, fed by crystals of the "blue vitriol." The wires to connect the plates are shown at WW. It should be noticed that the zinc is cast like a wheel to expose a larger surface to oxidation, and to reduce the resistance of the cell, thus increasing the yield of current. The extent of surface is not so important in the case of the copper plate, which is not acted on, and in this case is merely a spiral of wire, helping to keep the solutions apart and the crystals down. The Daniell cell is much employed in telegraphy. The Bunsen cell consists of a zinc plate in sulphuric acid, and at carbon plate in nitric acid, with a porous separator between the liquids. During the action of the cell, hydrogen, which is liberated at the carbon plate, is removed by combining with the nitric acid. The Grove cell is a modification of the Bunsen, with platinum instead of carbon. The Smee cell is a zinc plate side by side with a "platinised" silver plate in dilute sulphuric acid. The silver is coated with rough platinum to increase the surface and help to dislodge the hydrogen as bubbles and keep it from polarising the cell. The Bunsen, Grove, and Smee batteries are, however, more used in the laboratory than elsewhere.

The Leclanche is a fairly constant cell, which requires little attention. It "polaris-es" in action but soon regains its normal strength when allowed to rest, and hence it is useful for working electric bells and telephones. As shown in figure 16, it consists of a zinc rod with its connecting wire Z, and a carbon plate C with its binding screw, between two cakes M M of a mixture of black oxide of manganese, sulphur, and carbon, plunged in a solution of sal-ammoniac. The oxide of manganese relieves the carbon plate of its hydrogen. The strength of the solution is maintained by spare crystals of sal-ammoniac lying on the bottom of the cell, which is closed to prevent evaporation, but has a venthole for the escape of gas.

The Bichromate of Potash cell polarises more than the Leclanche, but yields a more powerful current for a short time. It consists, as shown in figure 17, of a zinc plate Z between two carbon plates C C immersed in a solution of bichromate of potash, sulphuric acid (vitriol), and water. The zinc is always lifted out of the solution when the cell is not in use. The gas which collects in the carbons, and weakens the cell, can be set free by raising the plates out of the liquid when the cell is not wanted. Stirring the solution has a similar effect, and sometimes the constancy of the cell is maintained by a circulation of the liquid. In Fuller's bichromate cell the zinc is amalgamated with mercury, which is kept in a pool beside it by means of a porous pot.

De la Rue's chloride of silver cell (fig. 18) is, from its constancy and small size, well adapted for medical and testing purposes. The "plates" are a little rod or pencil of zinc Z, and a strip or wire of silver S, coated with chloride of silver and sheathed in parchment paper. They are plunged in a solution of ammonium chloride A, contained in a glass phial or beaker, which is closed to suppress evaporation. A tray form of the cell is also made by laying a sheet of silver foil on the bottom of the shallow jar, and strewing it with dry chloride of silver, on which is laid a jelly to support the zinc plate. The jelly is prepared by mixing a solution of chloride of ammonium with "agar-agar," or Ceylon moss. This type permits the use of larger plates, and adapts the battery for lighting small electric lamps. Skrivanoff has modified the De la Rue cell by substituting a solution of caustic potash for the ammonium chloride, and his battery has been used for "star" lights, that is to say, the tiny electric lamps of the ballet. The Schanschieff battery, consisting of zinc and carbon plates in a solution of basic sulphate of mercury, is suitable for reading, mining, and other portable lamps.

The Latimer Clark "standard" cell is used by electricians in testing, as a constant electromotive force. It consists of a pure zinc plate separated from a pool of mercury by a paste of mercurous proto-sulphate and saturated solution of sulphate of zinc. Platinum wires connect with the zinc and mercury and form the poles of the battery, and the mouth of the glass cell is plugged with solid paraffin. As it is apt to polarise, the cell must not be employed to yield a current, and otherwise much care should be taken of it.

Dry cells are more cleanly and portable than wet, they require little or no attention, and are well suited for household or medical purposes. The zinc plate forms the vessel containing the carbon plate and chemical reagents. Figure 19 represents a section of the "E. C. C." variety, where Z is the zinc standing on an insulating sole I, and fitted with a connecting wire or terminal T (-), which is the negative pole. The carbon C is embedded in black paste M, chiefly composed of manganese dioxide, and has a binding screw or terminal T (+), which is the positive pole. The black paste is surrounded by a white paste Z, consisting mainly of lime and sal-ammoniac. There is a layer of silicate cotton S C above the paste, and the mouth is sealed with black pitch P, through which a waste-tube W T allows the gas to escape.

The Hellesen dry cell is like the "E. C. C.," but contains a hollow carbon, and is packed with sawdust in a millboard case. The Leclanche-Barbier dry cell is a modification of the Leclanche wet cell, having a paste of sal-ammoniac instead of a solution.

All the foregoing cells are called "primary," because they are generators of electricity. There are, however, batteries known as "secondary," which store the current as the Leyden jar stores up the discharge from an electrical machine.

In the action of a primary cell, as we have seen, water is split into its constituent gases, oxygen and hydrogen. Moreover, it was discovered by Carlisle and Nicholson in the year 1800 that the current of a battery could decompose water in the outer part of the circuit. Their experiment is usually performed by the. apparatus shown in figure 20, which is termed a voltameter, and consists of a glass vessel V, containing water acidulated with a little sulphuric acid to render it a better conductor, and two glass test-tubes OH inverted over two platinum strips or electrodes, which rise up from the bottom of the vessel and are connected underneath it to wires from the positive and negative poles of the battery C Z. It will be understood that the current enters the water by the positive electrode, and leaves it by the negative electrode.

When the power of the battery is sufficient the water in the vessel is decomposed, and oxygen being the negative element, collects at the positive foil or electrode, which is covered by the tube O. The hydrogen, on the other hand, being positive,

collects at the negative foil under the tube H. These facts can be proved by dipping a red-hot wick or taper into the gas of the tube O and seeing it blaze in presence of the oxygen which feeds the combustion, then dipping the lighted taper
into the gas of the tube H and watching it burn with the blue flame of hydrogen.
The volume of gas at the CATHODE or negative electrode is always twice that
at the ANODE or positive electrode, as it should be according to the known composition of water.

Now, if we disconnect the battery and join the two platinum electrodes of the
voltameter by a wire, we shall find a current flowing out of the voltameter as
though it were a battery, but in the reverse direction to the original current which
decomposed the water. This "secondary" or reacting current is evidently due to
the polarisation of the foils—that is to say, the electro- positive and electro-negative gases collected on them.

Professor Groves constructed a gas battery on this principle, the plates being of
platinum and the two gases surrounding them oxygen and hydrogen, but the
most useful development of it is the accumulator or storage battery.

The first practicable secondary battery of Gaston Plante was made of sheet lead
plates or electrodes, kept apart by linen cloth soaked in dilute sulphuric acid, after
the manner of Volta's pile. It was "charged" by connecting the plates to a primary
battery, and peroxide of lead (PbO_2) was formed on one plate and spongy lead
(Pb) on the other. When the charging current was cut off the peroxide plate
became the positive and the spongy plate the negative pole of the secondary cell.

Faure improved the Plante cell by adding a paste of red lead or minium (Pb_2O_4)
and dilute sulphuric acid (H_2SO_4), by which a large quantity of peroxide and
spongy lead could be formed on the plates. Sellon and Volckmar increased its efficiency by putting the paste into holes cast in the lead. The "E. P. S." accumulator
of the Electrical Power Storage Company is illustrated in figure 21, and consists
of a glass or teak box containing two sets of leaden grids perforated with holes,
which are primed with the paste and steeped in dilute sulphuric acid. Alternate
grids are joined to the poles of a charging battery or generator, those connected
to the positive pole being converted into peroxide of lead and the others into
spongy lead. The terminal of the peroxide plates, being the positive pole of the
accumulator, is painted red, and that of the spongy plates or negative pole black.
Accumulators of this kind are highly useful as reservoirs of electricity for maintaining the electric light, or working electric motors in tramcars, boats, and other
carriages.

CHAPTER III.

THE ELECTRICITY OF HEAT.

In the year 1821 Professor Seebeck, of Berlin, discovered a third source of electricity. Volta had found that two dissimilar metals in contact will produce a current by chemical action, and Seebeck showed that heat might take the place of chemical action. Thus, if a bar of antimony A (fig. 22) and a bar of bismuth S are in contact at one end, and the junction is heated by a spirit lamp to a higher temperature than the rest of the bars, a difference in their electric state or potential will be set up, and if the other ends are joined by a wire W, a current will flow through the wire. The direction of the current, indicated by the arrow, is from the bismuth to the antimony across the joint, and from the antimony to the bismuth through the external wire. This combination, which is called a "thermo-electric couple," is clearly analogous to the voltaic couple, with heat in place of chemical affinity. The direction of the current within and without the couple shows that the bismuth is positive to the antimony. This property of generating a current of electricity by contact under the influence of heat is not confined to bismuth and antimony, or even to the metals, but is common to all dissimilar substances in their degree. In the following list of bodies each is positive to those beneath it, negative to those above it, and the further apart any two are in the scale the greater the effect. Thus bismuth and antimony give a much stronger current with the same heating than copper and iron. Bismuth and selenium produce the best result, but selenium is expensive and not easy to manipulate. Copper and German silver will make a cheap experimental couple:—

POSITIVE
Bismuth
Cobalt
Potassium
Nickel
Sodium
Lead
Tin
Copper
Platinum
Silver
Zinc
Cadmium
Arsenic
Iron
Red phosphorus
Antimony
Tellurium
Selenium
NEGATIVE

Other things being equal, the hotter the joint in comparison with the free ends of the bars the stronger the current of electricity. Within certain limits the current is, in fact, proportional to this difference of temperature. It always flows in the same direction if the joint is not overheated, or, in other words, raised above a certain temperature.

The electromotive force and current of a thermo-electric couple is very much smaller than that given by an ordinary voltaic cell. We can, however, multiply the effect by connecting a number of pairs together, and so forming a pile or battery. Thus figure 23 shows three couples joined "in series," the positive pole of one being connected to the negative pole of the next. Now, if all the junctions on the left are hot and those on the right are cool, we will get the united effect of the whole, and the total current will flow through the wire W, joining the extreme bars or positive and negative poles of the battery. It must be borne in mind that although the bismuth and antimony of this thermo-electric battery, like the zinc and copper of the voltaic or chemico-electric battery, are respectively positive and negative to each other, the poles or wires attached to these metals are, on the contrary, negative and positive. This peculiarity arises from the current starting between the bismuth and antimony at the heated junction.

The internal resistance of a "thermo-electric pile" is, of course, very slight, the metals being good conductors, and this fact gives it a certain advantage over the voltaic battery. Moreover, it is cleaner and less troublesome than the chemical battery, for it is only necessary to keep at the required difference of temperature between the hot and cold junctions in order to get a steady current. No solutions or salts are required, and there appears to be little or no waste of the metals. It is important, however, to avoid sudden heating and cooling of the joints, as this tends to destroy them. Clammond, Gulcher, and others have constructed useful thermo-piles for practical purposes. Figure 24 illustrates a Clammond thermo-pile of 75 couples or elements. The metals forming these pairs are an alloy of bismuth and antimony for one and iron for the other. Prisms of the alloy are cast on strips of iron to form the junctions. They are bent in rings, the junctions in a series making a zig-zag round the circle. The rings are built one over the other in a cylinder of couples, and the inner junctions are heated by a Bunsen gas-burner in the hollow core of the battery. A gas- pipe seen in front leads to the burner, and the wires WW connected to the extreme bars or poles are the electrodes of the pile.

Thermo-piles are interesting from a scientific point of view as a direct means of transforming heat into electricity. A sensitive pile is also a delicate detector of heat by virtue of the current set up, which can be measured with a galvanometer or current meter. Piles of antimony and bismuth are made which can indicate the heat of a lighted match at a distance of several yards, and even the radiation from certain of the stars.

Thermo-batteries have been used in France for working telegraphs, and they are capable of supplying small installations of the electric light or electric motors for domestic purposes.

The action of the thermo-pile, like that of a voltaic cell, can be reversed. By sending a current through the couple from the antimony to the bismuth we shall find the junction cooled. This "Peltier effect," as it is termed, after its discoverer, has been known to freeze water, but no practical application has been made of it.

A very feeble thermo-electric effect can be produced by heating the junction of two different pieces of the same substance, or even by making one part of the same conductor hotter than another. Thus a sensitive galvanometer will show a weak current if a copper wire connected in circuit with it be warmed at one point. Moreover, it has been found by Lord Kelvin that if an iron wire is heated at any point, and an electric current be passed through it, the hot point will shift along the wire in a direction contrary to that of the current.

CHAPTER IV.

THE ELECTRICITY OF MAGNETISM.

We have already seen how electricity was first produced by the simple method of rubbing one body on another, then by the less obvious means of chemical union, and next by the finer agency of heat. In all these, it will be observed, a substantial contact is necessary. We have now to consider a still more subtle process of generation, not requiring actual contact, which, as might be expected, was discovered later, that, mainly through the medium of magnetism.

The curious mineral which has the property of attracting iron was known to the Chinese several thousand years ago, and certainly to the Greeks in the times of Thales, who, as in the case of the rubbed amber, ascribed the property to its possession of a soul.

Lodestone, a magnetic oxide of iron ($FE3O4$), is found in various parts of China, especially at T'szchou in Southern Chihli, which was formerly known as the "City of the Magnet." It was called by the Chinese the love-stone or thsu-chy, and the stone that snatches iron or ny-thy-chy, and perchance its property of pointing out the north and south direction was discovered by dropping a light piece of the stone, if not a sewing needle made of it, on the surface of still water. At all events, we read in Pere Du Halde's Description de la Chine, that sometime in or about the year 2635 B.C. the great Emperor Hoang-ti, having lost his way in a fog whilst pursuing the rebellious Prince Tchiyeou on the plains of Tchou-lou, constructed a chariot which showed the cardinal points, thus enabling him to overtake and put the prince to death.

A magnetic car preceded the Emperors of China in ceremonies of state during the fourth century of our era. It contained a genius in a feather dress who pointed to the south, and was doubtless moved by a magnet floating in water or turning on a pivot. This rude appliance was afterwards refined into the needle compass for guiding mariners on the sea, and assisting the professors of feng- shui or geomancy in their magic rites.

Magnetite was also found at Heraclea in Lydia, and at Magnesium on the Meander or Magnesium at Sipylos, all in Asia Minor. It was called the "Heraclean Stone" by the people, but came at length to bear the name of "Magnet" after the city of Magnesia or the mythical shepherd Magnes, who was said to have discovered it by the attraction of his iron crook.

The ancients knew that it had the power of communicating its attractive property to iron, for we read in Plato's "Ion" that a number of iron rings can be supported in a chain by the Heraclean Stone. Lucretius also describes an experiment in which iron filings are made to rise up and "rave" in a brass basin by a magnet held underneath. We are told by other writers that images of the gods and goddesses were suspended in the air by lodestone in the ceilings of the temples of Diana of Ephesus, of Serapis at Alexandria, and others. It is surprising, however, that neither the Greeks nor Romans, with all their philosophy, would seem to have discovered its directive property.

During the dark ages pieces of Lodestone mounted as magnets were employed in the "black arts." A small natural magnet of this kind is shown in figure 25, where L is the stone shod with two iron "pole-pieces," which are joined by a "keeper" A or separable bridge of iron carrying a hook for supporting weights.

Apparently it was not until the twelfth century that the compass found its way into Europe from the East. In the Landnammabok of Ari Frode, the Norse historian, we read that Flocke Vildergersen, a renowned viking, sailed from Norway to discover Iceland in the year 868, and took with him two ravens as guides, for in those days the "seamen had no lodestone (that is, no lidar stein, or leading stone) in the northern countries." The Bible, a poem of Guiot de Provins, minstrel at the court of Barbarossa, which was written in or about the year 890, contains the first mention of the magnet in the West. Guiot relates how mariners have an "art which cannot deceive" of finding the position of the polestar, that does not move. After touching a needle with the magnet, "an ugly brown stone which draws iron to itself," he says they put the needle on a straw and float it on water so that its point turns to the hidden star, and enables them to keep their course. Arab traders had probably borrowed the floating needle from the Chinese, for Bailak Kibdjaki, author of the Merchant's Treasure, written in the thirteenth century, speaks of its use in the Syrian sea. The first Crusaders were probably instrumental in bringing it to France, at all events Jacobus de Vitry (1204-15) and Vincent de Beauvais (1250) mention its use, De Beauvais calling the poles of the needle by the Arab words aphron and zohran.

Ere long the needle was mounted on a pivot and provided with a moving card showing the principal directions. The variation of the needle from the true north and south was certainly known in China during the twelfth, and in Europe during the thirteenth century. Columbus also found that the variation changed its value as he sailed towards America on his memorable voyage of 1492. Moreover, in 1576, Norman, a compass maker in London, showed that the north- seeking end of the needle dipped below the horizontal.

In these early days it was supposed that lodestone in the pole- star, that is to say, the "lodestar" of the poets or in mountains of the far north, attracted the trembling needle; but in the year 1600, Dr. Gilbert, the founder of electric science, demonstrated beyond a doubt that the whole earth was a great magnet. A magnet, as is well known, has, like an electric battery, always two poles or centres of attraction, which are situated near its extremities. Sometimes, indeed, when the magnet is imperfect, there are "consequent poles" of weaker force between them. One of the poles is called the "north," and the other the "south," because if the magnet were freely pivotted like a compass needle, the former would turn to the north and the latter to the south.

Either pole will attract iron, but soft or annealed iron does not retain the magnetism nearly so well as steel. Hence a boy's test for the steel of his knife is only efficacious when the blade itself becomes magnetic after being touched with the magnet. A piece of steel is readily magnetised by stroking it from end to end in one direction with the pole of a magnet, and in this way compass needles and powerful bar magnets can be made.

The poles attract iron at a distance by "induction," just as a charge of electricity, be it positive or negative, will attract a neutral pith ball; and Dr. Gilbert showed that a north pole always repels another north pole and attracts a south pole, while, on the other hand, a south pole always repels a south pole and attracts a north pole. This can be proved by suspending a magnetic needle like a pithball, and approaching another towards it, as illustrated in figure 26, where the north pole N attracts the south S. Obviously there are two opposite kinds of magnetic poles, as of electricity, which always appear together, and like magnetic poles repel, unlike magnetic poles attract each other.

It follows that the magnetic pole of the compass needle which turns to the north must be unlike the north and like the south magnetic pole of the earth. Instead of calling it the "north," it would be less confusing to call it the "north-seeking" pole of the needle.

Gilbert made a "terella," or miniature of the earth, as a magnet, and not only demonstrated how the compass needle sets along the lines joining the north and south magnetic poles, but explained the variation and the dip. He imagined that the magnetic poles coincided with the geographical poles, but, as a matter of fact, they do not, and, moreover, they are slowly moving round the geographical poles, hence the declination of the needle, that is to say its angle of divergence from the true meridian or north and south line, is gradually changing. The north magnetic pole of the earth was actually discovered by Sir John Ross north of British America, on the coast of Boothia (latitude 70 degrees 5' N, longitude 96 degrees 46' W), where, as foreseen, the needle entirely lost its directive property and stood upright, or, so to speak, on its head. The south magnetic pole lies in the Prince Albert range of Victona Land, and was almost reached by Sir James Clark Ross.

The magnetism of the earth is such as might be produced by a powerful magnet inside, but its origin is unknown, although there is reason to believe that masses of lodestone or magnetic iron exist in the crust. Coulomb found that not only iron, but all substances are more or less magnetic, and Faraday showed in 1845 that while some are attracted by a magnet others are repelled. The former he called paramagnetic and the latter diamagnetic bodies.

The following is a list of these.—

Paramagnetic	Diamagnetic
Iron	Bismuth
Nickel	Phosphorus
Cobalt	Antimony
Aluminium	Zinc
Manganese	Mercury
Chromium	Lead
Cerium	Silver
Titanium	Copper
Platinum	Water
Many ores and	Alcohol
salts of the	Tellurium
above metals	Selenium
Oxygen	Sulphur

Thallium
Hydrogen
Air

We have theories of magnetism that reduce it to a phenomenon of electricity, though we are ignorant of the real nature of both. If we take a thin bar magnet and break it in two, we find that we have now two shorter magnets, each with its "north" and "south" poles, that is to say, poles of the same kind as the south and north—magnetic poles of the earth. If we break each of these again, we get four smaller magnets, and we can repeat the process as often as we like. It is supposed, therefore, that every atom of the bar is a little magnet in itself having its two opposite poles, and that in magnetising the bar we have merely partially turned all these atoms in one direction, that is to say, with their north poles pointing one way and their south poles the other way, as shown in figure 27. The polarity of the bar only shows itself at the ends, where the molecular poles are, so to speak, free.

There are many experiments which support this view. For example, if we heat a magnet red hot it loses its magnetism, perhaps because the heat has disarranged the particles and set the molecular poles in all directions. Again, if we magnetise a piece of soft iron we can destroy its magnetism by striking it so as to agitate its atoms and throw them out of line. In steel, which is iron with a small admixture of carbon, the atoms are not so free as in soft iron, and hence, while iron easily loses its magnetism, steel retains it, even under a shock, but not under a cherry red- heat. Nevertheless, if we put the atoms of soft iron under a strain by bend-ing it, we shall find it retain its magnetism more like a bit of steel.

It has been found, too, that the atoms show an indisposition to be moved by the magnetising force which is known as HYSTERESIS. They have a certain inertia, which can be overcome by a slight shock, as though they had a difficulty of turn-ing in the ranks to take up their new positions. Even if this molecular theory is true, however, it does not help us to explain why a molecule of matter is a tiny magnet. We have only pushed the mystery back to the atom. Something more is wanted, and electricians look for it in the constitution of the atom, and in the luminiferous ether which is believed to surround the atoms of matter, and to propagate not merely the waves of light, but induction from one electrified body to another.

We know in proof of this ethereal action that the space around a magnet is mag-netic. Thus, if we lay a horse-shoe magnet on a table and sprinkle iron filings round it, they will arrange themselves in curving lines between the poles, as shown in figure 28. Each filing has become a little magnet, and these set themselves end to end as the molecules in the metal are supposed to do. The "field" about the magnet is replete with these lines, which follow certain curves depending on the arrangement of the poles. In the horse- shoe magnet, as seen, they chiefly issue from one pole and sweep round to the other. They are never broken, and apparently they are lines of stress in the circumambient ether. A pivoted magnet tends to range itself along these lines, and thus the compass guides the sailor on the ocean by keeping itself in the line between the north and south magnetic poles of the earth. Faraday called them lines of magnetic force, and said that the stronger the magnet the more of these lines pass through a given space. Along them "magnetic induction" is supposed to be propagated, and a magnet is thus enabled to attract iron or any other magnetic substance. The pole induces an opposite pole to itself in the nearest part of the induced body and a like pole in the remote part. Consequently, as unlike poles attract and like repel, the soft iron is attracted by the inducing pole much as a pithball is attracted by an electric charge.

The resemblances of electricity and magnetism did not escape attention, and the derangement of the compass needle by the lightning flash, formerly so disastrous at sea, pointed to an intimate connection between them, which was ultimately disclosed by Professor Oersted, of Copenhagen, in the year 1820. Oersted was on the outlook for the required clue, and a happy chance is said to have rewarded him. His experiment is shown in figure 29, where a wire conveying a current of electricity flowing in the direction of the arrow is held over a pivoted magnetic needle so that the current flows from south to north. The needle will tend to set itself at right angles to the wire, its north or north-seeking pole moving towards the west. If the direction of the current is reversed, the needle is deflected in the opposite direction, its north pole moving towards the east. Further, if the wire is held below the needle, in the first place, the north pole will turn towards the east, and if the current be reversed it will move towards the west.

The direction of a current can thus be told with the aid of a compass needle. When the wire is wound many times round the needle on a bobbin, the whole forms what is called a galvanoscope, as shown in figure 30, where N is the needle and B the bobbin. When a proper scale is added to the needle by which its deflections can be accurately read, the instrument becomes a current measurer or galvanometer, for within certain limits the deflection of the needle is proportional to the strength of the current in the wire.

A rule commonly given for remembering the movement of the needle is as follows:—Imagine yourself laid along the wire so that the current flows from your feet to your head; then if you face the needle you will see its north pole go to the left and its south pole to the right. I find it simpler to recollect that if the current flows from your head to your feet a north pole will move round you from left to right in front. Or, again, if a current flows from north to south, a north pole will move round it like the sun round the earth.

The influence of the current on the needle implies a magnetic action, and if we dust iron filings around the wire we shall find they cling to it in concentric layers, showing that circular lines of magnetic force enclose it like the water waves caused by a stone dropped into a pond. Figure 31 represents the section of a wire carrying a current, with the iron filings arranged in circles round it. Since a magnetic pole tends to move in the direction of the lines of force, we now see why a north or south pole tends to move ROUND a current, and why a compass needle tries to set itself at right angles to a current, as in the original experiment of Oersted. The needle, having two opposite poles, is pulled in opposite directions by the lines, and being pivoted, sets itself tangentically to them. Were it free and flexible, it would curve itself along one of the lines. Did it consist of a single pole, it would revolve round the wire.

Action and re-action are equal and opposite, hence if the needle is fixed and the wire free the current will move round the magnet; and if both are free they will circle round each other. Applying the above rule we shall find that when the north pole moves from left to right the current moves from right to left. Ampere of Paris, following Oersted, promptly showed that two parallel wires carrying currents attracted each other when the currents flowed in the same direction, and repelled each other when they flowed in opposite directions. Thus, in figure 32, if A and B are the two parallel wires, and A is mounted on pivots and free to move in liquid "contacts" of mercury, it will be attracted or repelled by B according as the two currents flow in the same or in opposite directions. If the wires cross each other at right angles there is no attraction or repulsion. If they cross at an acute angle, they will tend to become parallel like two compass needles, when the currents are in one direction, and to open to a right angle and close up the other way when the currents are in opposite directions, always tending to arrange themselves parallel and flowing in the same direction. These effects arise from the circular lines of force around the wire. When the currents are similar the lines act as unlike magnetic poles and attract, but when the currents are dissimilar the lines act as like magnetic poles and repel each other.

Another important discovery of Ampere is that a circular current behaves like a magnet; and it has been suggested by him that the atoms are magnets because each has a circular current flowing round it. A series of circular currents, such as the spiral S in figure 33 gives, when connected to a battery C Z, is in fact a skeleton ELECTRO-MAGNET having its north and south poles at the extremities. If a rod or core of soft iron I be suspended by fibres from a support, it will be sucked towards the middle of the coil as into a vortex, by the circular magnetic lines of every spire or turn of the coil. Such a combination is sometimes called a solenoid, and is useful in practice.

When the core gains the interior of the coil it becomes a veritable electromagnet, as found by Arago, having a north pole at one end and a south pole at the other. Figure 34 illustrates a common poker magnetised in the same way, and supporting nails at both ends. The poker has become the core of the electromagnet. On reversing the direction of the current through the spiral we reverse the poles of the core, for the poker being of soft or wrought iron, does not retain its magnetism like steel. If we stop the current altogether it ceases to be a magnet, and the nails will drop away from it.

Ampere's experiment in figure 32 has shown us that two currents, more or less parallel, influence each other; but in 1831 Professor Faraday of the Royal Institution, London, also found that when a current is started and stopped in a wire, it induces a momentary and opposite current in a parallel wire. Thus, if a current is STARTED in the wire B (fig. 32) in direction of the arrow, it will induce or give rise to a momentary current in the wire A, flowing in a contrary direction to itself. Again, if the current in B be STOPEED, a momentary current is set up in the wire A in a direction the same as that of the exciting current in B. While the current in B is quietly flowing there is no induced current in A; and it is only at the start or the stoppage of the inducing or PRIMARY current that the induced or SECONDARY current is set up. Here again we have the influence of the magnetic field around the wire conveying a current.

This is the principle of the "induction coil" so much employed in medical electricity, and of the "transformer" or "converter" used in electric illumination. It consists essentially, as shown in figure 35, of two coils of wire, one enclosing the other, and both parallel or concentric. The inner or primary coil P C is of short thick wire of low resistance, and is traversed by the inducing current of a battery B. To increase its inductive effect a core of soft iron I C occupies its middle. The outer or secondary coil S C is of long thin wire terminating in two discharging points D1 D2. An interrupter or hammer "key" interrupts or "makes and breaks" the circuit of the primary coil very rapidly, so as to excite a great many induced currents in the secondary coil per second, and produce energetic sparks between the terminals D1 D2. The interrupter is actuated automatically by the magnetism of the iron core I C, for the hammer H has a soft iron head which is attracted by the core when the latter is magnetised, and being thus drawn away from the contact screw C S the circuit of the primary is broken, and the current is stopped. The iron core then ceases to be a magnet, the hammer H springs back to the contact screw, and the current again flows in the primary circuit only to be interrupted again as before. In this way the current in the primary coil is rapidly started and stopped many times a second, and this, as we know, induces corresponding currents in the secondary which appear as sparks at the discharging points. The effect of the apparatus is enhanced by interpolating a "condenser" C C in the primary circuit. A condenser is a form of Leyden jar, suitable for current electricity, and consists of layers of tinfoil separated from each other by sheets of paraffin paper, mica, or some other convenient insulator, and alternate foils are connected together. The wires joining each set of plates are the poles of the condenser, and when these are connected in the circuit of a current the condenser is charged. It can be discharged by joining its two poles with a wire, and letting the two opposite electricities on its plates rush together. Now, the sudden discharge of the condenser C C through the primary coil P C enhances the inductive effect of the current. The battery B, here shown by the conventional symbol [Electrical Symbol] where the thick dash is the negative and the thin dash the positive pole, is connected between the terminals T1 T2, and a COMMUTATOR or pole-changer R, turned with a handle, permits the direction of the current to be reversed at will.

Figure 36 represents the exterior of an ordinary induction coil of the Ruhmkorff pattern, with its two coils, one over the other C, its commutator R, and its sparkling points D1D2, the whole being mounted on a mahogany base, which holds the condenser.

The intermittent, or rather alternating, currents from the secondary coil are often applied to the body in certain nervous disorders. When sent through glass tubes filled with rarefied gases, sometimes called "Geissler tubes," they elicit glows of many colours, vieing in beauty with the fleeting tints of the aurora polaris, which, indeed, is probably a similar effect of electrical discharges in the atmosphere.

The action of the induction is reversible. We can not only send a current of low "pressure" from a generator of weak electromotive force through the primary coil, and thus excite a current of high pressure in the secondary coil, but we can send a current of high pressure through the secondary coil and provoke a current of low pressure in the primary coil The transformer or converter, a modified induction coil used in distributing electricity to electric lamps and motors, can not only transform a low pressure current into a high, but a high pressure current into a low. As the high pressure currents are best able to overcome the resistance of the wire convening them, it is customary to transmit high pressure currents from the generator to the distant place where they are wanted by means of small wires, and there transform them into currents of the pressure required to light the lamps or drive the motors.

We come now to another consequence of Oersted's great discovery, which is doubtless the most important of all, namely, the generation of electricity from magnetism, or, as it is usually called, magneto-electric induction. In the year 1831 the illustrious Michael Faraday further succeeded in demonstrating that when a magnet M is thrust into a hollow coil of wire C, as shown in figure 37, a current of electricity is set up in the coil whilst the motion lasts. When the magnet is withdrawn again another current is induced in the reverse direction to the first. If the coil be closed through a small galvanometer G the movements of the needle to one side or the other will indicate these temporary currents. It follows from the principle of action and reaction that if the magnet is kept still and the coil thrust over it similar currents will be induced in the coil. All that is necessary is for the wires to cut the lines of magnetic force around the magnet, or, in other words, the lines of force in a magnetic field We have seen already that a wire conveying a current can move a magnetic pole, and we are therefore prepared to find that a magnetic pole moved near a wire can excite a current in it.

Figure 38 illustrates the conditions of this remarkable effect, where N and S are two magnetic poles with lines of force between them, and W is a wire crossing these lines at right angles, which is the best position. If, now, this wire be moved so as to sink bodily through the paper away from the reader, an electric current flowing in the direction of the arrow will be induced in it. If, on the contrary, the wire be moved across the lines of force towards the reader, the induced current will flow oppositely to the arrow. Moreover, if the poles of the magnet N and S exchange places, the directions of the induced currents will also be reversed. This is the fundamental principle of the well known dynamo-electric machine, popularly called a dynamo.

Again, if we send a current from some external source through the wire in the direction of the arrow, the wire will move OF ITSELF across the lines of force away from the reader, that is to say, in the direction it would need to be moved in order to excite such a current; and if, on the other hand, the current be sent through it in the reverse direction to the arrow, it will move towards the reader. This is the principle of the equally well-known electric motor. Figure 39 shows a simple method of remembering these directions.

Let the right hand rest on the north pole of a magnet and the forefinger be extended in the direction of the lines of force, then the outstretched thumb will indicate the direction in which the wire or conductor moves and the bent middle finger the direction of the current. These three digits, as will be noticed, are all at right angles to each other, and this relation is the best for inducing the strongest current in a dynamo or the most energetic movement of the conductor in an electric motor.

Of course in a dynamo-electric generator the stronger the magnetic field, the less the resistance of the conductor, and the faster it is moved across the lines of force, that is to say, the more lines it cuts in a second the stronger is the current produced. Similarly in an electric motor, the stronger the current and magnetic field the faster will the conductor move.

The most convenient motion to give the conductor in practice is one of rotation, and hence the dynamo usually consists of a coil or series of coils of insulated wire termed the "armature," which is mounted on a spindle and rapidly rotated in a strong magnetic field between the poles of powerful magnets. Currents are generated in the coils, now in one direction then in another, as they revolve or cross different parts of the field; and, by means of a device termed a commutator, these currents can be collected or sifted at will, and led away by wires to an electric lamp, an accumulator, or an electric motor, as desired. The character of the electricity is precisely the same as that generated in the voltaic battery.

The commutator may only collect the currents as they are generated, and supply what is called an alternating current, that is to say, a current which alternates or changes its direction several hundred times a second, or it may sift the currents as they are produced and supply what is termed a continuous current, that is, a current always in the same direction, like that of a voltaic battery. Some machines are made to supply alternating currents, others continuous currents. Either class of current will do for electric lamps, but only continuous currents are used for electo-plating, or, in general, for electric motors.

In the "magneto-electric" machine the FIELD MAGNETS are simply steel bars permanently magnetised, but in the ordinary dynamo the field magnets are electro-magnets excited to a high pitch by means of the current generated in the moving conductor or armature. In the "series-wound" machine the whole of the current generated in the armature also goes through the coils of the field magnets. Such a machine is sketched in figure 40, where A is the armature, consisting of an iron core surrounded by coils of wire and rotating in the field of a powerful electro-magnet NS in the direction of the arrows. For the sake of simplicity only twelve coils are represented. They are all in circuit one with another, and a wire connects the ends of each coil to corresponding metal bars on the commutator C.

These bars are insulated from each other on the spindle X of the armature. Now, as each coil passes through the magnetic field in turn, a current is excited in it. Each coil therefore resembles an individual cell of a voltaic battery, connected in series. The current is drawn off from the ring by two copper "brushes" b, be which rub upon the bars of the commutator at opposite ends of a diameter, as shown. One brush is the positive pole of the dynamo, the other is the negative, and the current will flow through any wire or external circuit which may be connected with these, whether electric lamps, motors, accumulators, electro-plating baths, or other device. The small arrows show the movements of the current throughout the machine, and the terminals are marked (+) positive and (-) negative.

It will be observed that the current excited in the armature also flows through the coils of the electro-magnets, and thus keeps up their strength. When the machine is first started the current is feeble, because the field of the magnets in which the armature revolves is merely that due to the dregs or "residual magnetism" left in the soft iron cores of the magnet since the last time the machine was used. But this feeble current exalts the strength of the field-magnets, producing a stronger field, which in turn excites a still stronger current in the armature, and this process of give and take goes on until the full strength or "saturation" of the magnets is attained.

Such is the "series" dynamo, of which the well-known Gramme machine is a type. Figure 41 illustrates this machine as it is actually made, A being the armature revolving between the poles NS of the field-magnets M, M, M' M', on a spindle which is driven by means of a belt on the pulley P from a separate engine The brushes b b' of the commutator C collect the current, which in this case is continuous, or constant in its direction.

The current of the series machine varies with the resistance of the external or working circuit, because that is included in the circuit of the field magnets and the armature. Thus, if we vary the number of electric lamps fed by the machine, we shall vary the current it is capable of yielding. With arc lamps in series, by adding to the number in circuit we increase the resistance of the outer circuit, and therefore diminish the strength of the current yielded by the machine, because the current, weakened by the increase of resistance, fails to excite the field magnets as strongly as before. On the other hand, with glow lamps arranged in parallel, the reverse is the case, and putting more lamps in circuit increases the power of the machine, by diminishing the resistance of the outer circuit in providing more cross-cuts for the current. This, of course, is a drawback to the series machine in places where the number of lamps to be lighted varies from time to time. In the "shunt-wound" machine the field magnets are excited by diverting a small portion of the main current from the armature through them, by means of a "shunt" or loop circuit. Thus in figure 42 where C is the commutator and b b' the brushes, M is a shunt circuit through the magnets, and E is the external or working circuit of the machine.

The small arrows indicate the directions of the currents. With this arrangement the addition of more glow lamps to the external circuit E DIMINISHES the current, because the portion of it which flows through the by-path M, and excites the magnets, is less now that the alternative route for the current through E is of lower resistance than before. When fewer glow lamps are in the external circuit E, and its resistance therefore higher, the current in the shunt circuit M is greater than before, the magnets become stronger, and the electromotive force of the armature is increased. The Edison machine is of this type, and is illustrated in figure 43, where M M' are the field magnets with their poles N S, between which the armature A is revolved by means of the belt B, and a pulley seen behind. The leading wires W W convey the current from the brushes of the commutator to the external circuit. In this machine the conductors of the armature are not coils of wire, but separate bars of copper.

In shunt machines the variation of current due to a varying number of lamps in use occasions a rise and fall in the brightness of the lamps which is undesirable, and hence a third class of dynamo has been devised, which combines the principles of both the series and shunt machines. This is the "compound-wound" machine, in which the magnets are wound partly in shunt and partly in series with the armature, in such a manner that the strength of the field-magnets and the electromotive force of the current do not vary much, whatever be the number of lamps in circuit. In alternate current machines the electromotive force keeps constant, as the field- magnets are excited by a separate machine, giving a continuous current.

We have already seen that the action of the dynamo is reversible, and that just as a wire moved across a magnetic field supplies an electric current, so a wire at rest, but conducting a current across a magnetic field, will move. The electric motor is therefore essentially a dynamo, which on being traversed by an electric current from an external source puts itself in motion. Thus, if a current be sent through the armature of the Gramme machine, shown in figure 41, the armature will revolve, and the spindle, by means of a belt on the pulley P, can communicate its energy to another machine.

Hence the electric motor can be employed to work lathes, hoists, lifts, drive the screws of boats or the wheels of carriages, and for many other purposes. There are numerous types of electric motor as of the dynamo in use, but they are all modifications of the simple continuous or alternating current dynamo.

Obviously, since mechanical power can be converted into electricity by the dynamo, and reconverted into mechanical power by the motor, it is sufficient to connect a dynamo and motor together by insulated wire in order to transmit mechanical power, whether it be derived from wind, water, or fuel, to any reasonable distance.

CHAPTER V.

ELECTROLYSIS.

Having seen how electricity can be generated and stored in considerable quantity, let us now turn to its practical uses. Of these by far the most important are based on its property of developing light and heat as in the electric spark, chemical action as m the voltameter, and magnetism as in the electromagnet.

The words "current," "pressure," and so on point to a certain analogy between electricity and water, which helps the imagination to figure what can neither be seen nor handled, though it must not be traced too far. 'Water, for example, runs by the force of gravity from a place of higher to a place of lower level. The pressure of the stream is greater the more the difference of level or "head of water" The strength of the current or quantity of water flowing per second is greater the higher the pressure, and the less the resistance of its channel. The power of the water or its rate of doing mechanical work is greater the higher the pressure and the stronger the current. So, too, electricity flows by the electromotive force from a place of higher to a place of lower electric level or potential. The electric pressure is greater the more the difference of potential or electromotive force. The strength of the electric current or quantity of electricity flowing per second is greater the higher the pressure or electromotive force and the less the resistance of the circuit The power of the electricity or its rate of doing work is greater the higher the electromotive force and the stronger the current.

It follows that a small quantity of water or electricity at a high pressure will give us the same amount of energy as a large quantity at a low pressure, and our choice of one or the other will depend on the purpose we have in view. As a rule, however, a large current at a comparatively low or moderate pressure is found the more convenient in practice.

The electricity of friction belongs to the former category, and the electricity of chemistry, heat, and magnetism to the latter. The spark of a factional or influence machine can be compared to a highland cataract of lofty height but small volume, which is more picturesque than useful, and the current from a voltaic battery, a thermopile, or a dynamo to a lowland river which can be dammed to turn a mill. It is the difference between a skittish gelding and a tame carthorse.

Not the spark from an induction coil or Leyden jar, but a strong and steady current at a low pressure, is adapted for electrolysis or electrodeposition, and hence the voltaic battery or a special form of dynamo is usually employed in this work. A flash of lightning is the very symbol of terrific power, and yet, according to the illustrious Faraday, it contains a smaller amount of electricity than the feeble current required to decompose a single drop of rain.

In our simile of the mill dam and the battery or dynamo, the dam corresponds to the positive pole and the river or sea below the mill to the negative pole. The mill-race will stand for the wire joining the poles, that is to say, the external circuit, and the mill-wheel for the work to be done in the circuit, whether it be a chemical for decomposition, a telegraph instrument, an electric lamp, or any other appliance. As the current in the race depends on the "head of water," or difference of level between the dam and the sea as well as on the resistance of the channel, so the current in the circuit depends on the "electromotive force," or difference of potential between the positive and negative poles, as well as on the resistance of the circuit. The relation between these is expressed by the well-known law of Ohm, which runs: A current of electricity is directly proportional to the electromotive force and inversely proportional to the resistance of the circuit.

In practice electricity is measured by various units or standards named after celebrated electricians. Thus the unit of quantity is the coulomb, the unit of current or quantity flowing per second is the ampere, the unit of electromotive force is the volt, and the unit of resistance is the ohm.

The quantity of water or any other "electrolyte" decomposed by electricity is proportional to the strength of the current. One ampere decomposes .00009324 gramme of water per second, liberating .000010384 gramme of hydrogen and .00008286 gramme of oxygen.

The quantity in grammes of any other chemical element or ion which is liberated from an electrolyte or body capable of electrochemical decomposition in a second by a current of one ampere is given by what is called the electrochemical equivalent of the ion. This is found by multiplying its ordinary chemical equivalent or combining weight by .000010384, which is the electrochemical equivalent of hydrogen. Thus the weight of metal deposited from a solution of any of its salts by a current of so many amperes in so many seconds is equal to the number of amperes multiplied by the number of seconds, and by the electrochemical equivalent of the metal.

The deposition of a metal from a solution of its salt is very easily shown in the case of copper. In fact, we have already seen that in the Daniell cell the current decomposes a solution of sulphate of copper and deposits the pure metal on the copper plate. If we simply make a solution of blue vitriol in a glass beaker and dip the wires from a voltaic cell into it, we shall find the wire from the negative pole become freshly coated with particles of new copper. The sulphate has been broken up, and the liberated metal, being positive, gathers on the negative electrode. Moreover, if we examine the positive electrode we shall find it slightly eaten away, because the sulphuric acid set free from the sulphate has combined with the particles of that wire to make new sulphate. Thus the copper is deposited on one electrode, namely, the cathode, by which the current leaves the bath, and at the expense of the other electrode, that is to say, the anode, by which the current enters the bath.

The fact that the weight of metal deposited in this way from its salts is proportional to the current, has been utilised for measuring the strength of currents with a fine degree of accuracy. If, for example, the tubes of the voltameter described on page 38 were graduated, the volume of gas evolved would be a measure of the current. Usually, however, it is the weight of silver or copper deposited from their salts in a certain time which gives the current in amperes.

Electro-plating is the principal application of this chemical process. In 1805 Brugnatelli took a silver medal and coated it with gold by making it the cathode in a solution of a salt of gold, and using a plate of gold for the anode. The shops of our jewellers are now bright with teapots, salt cellars, spoons, and other articles of the table made of inferior metals, but beautified and preserved from rust in this way.

Figure 44 illustrates an electro-plating bath in which a number of spoons are being plated. A portion of the vat V is cut away to show the interior, which contains a solution S of the double cyanide of gold and potassium when gold is to be laid, and the double cyanide of silver and potassium when silver is to be deposited. The electrodes are hung from metal rods, the anode A being a plate of gold or silver G, as the case may be, and the cathode C the spoons in question. When the current of the battery or dynamo passes through the bath from the anode to the cathode, gold or silver is deposited on the spoons, and the bath recuperates its strength by consuming the gold or silver plate.

Enormous quantities of copper are now deposited in a similar way, sulphate of copper being the solution and a copper plate the anode. Large articles of iron, such as the parts of ordnance, are sometimes copper-plated to preserve them from the action of the atmosphere. Seamless copper pipes for conveying steam, and wires of pure copper for conducting electricity, are also deposited, and it is not unlikely that the kettle of the future will be made by electrolysis.

Nickel-plating is another extensive branch of the industry, the white nickel forming a cloak for metals more subject to corrosion. Nickel is found to deposit best from a solution of the double sulphate of nickel and ammonia. Aluminium, however, has not yet been successfully deposited by electricity.

In 1836 De la Rue observed that copper laid in this manner on another surface took on its under side an accurate impression of that surface, even to the scratches on it, and three years later Jacobi, of St. Petersburg, and Jordan, of London, applied the method to making copies or replicas of medals and woodcuts. Even non-metallic surfaces could be reproduced in copper by taking a cast of them in wax and lining the mould with fine plumbago, which, being a conductor, served as a cathode to receive the layer of metal. It is by the process of electrotyping or galvano- plastics that the copper faces for printing woodcuts are prepared, and copies made of seals or medals.

Natural objects, such as flowers, ferns, leaves, feathers, insects, and lizards, can be prettily coated with bronze or copper, not to speak of gold and silver, by a similar process. They are too delicate to be coated with black lead in order to receive the skin of metal, but they can be dipped in solutions, leaving a film which can be reduced to gold or silver. For instance, they may be soaked in an alcoholic solution of nitrate of silver, made by shaking 2 parts of the crystals in 100 parts of alcohol in a stoppered bottle. When dry, the object should be suspended under a glass shade and exposed to a stream of sulphuretted hydrogen gas; or it may be immersed in a solution of 1 part of phosphorus in 15 parts of bisulphide of carbon, 1 part of bees-wax, 1 part of spirits of turpentine, 1 part of asphaltum, and 1/8 part of caoutchouc dissolved in bisulphide of carbon. This leaves a superficial film which is metallised by dipping in a solution of 20 grains of nitrate of silver to a pint of water. On this metallic film a thicker layer of gold and silver in different shades can be deposited by the current, and the silver surface may also be "oxidised" by washing it in a weak solution of platinum chloride.

Electrolysis is also used to some extent in reducing metals from their ores, in bleaching fibre, in manufacturing hydrogen and oxygen from water, and in the chemical treatment of sewage.

CHAPTER VI.

THE TELEGRAPH AND TELEPHONE.

Like the "philosopher's stone," the "elixir of youth," and "perpetual motion," the telegraph was long a dream of the imagination. In the sixteenth century, if not before, it was believed that two magnetic needles could be made sympathetic, so that when one was moved the other would likewise move, however far apart they were, and thus enable two distant friends to communicate their minds to one another.

The idea was prophetic, although the means of giving effect to it were mistaken. It became practicable, however, when Oersted discovered that a magnetic needle could be swung to one side or the other by an electric current passing near it.

The illustrious Laplace was the first to suggest a telegraph on this principle. A wire connecting the two poles of a battery is traversed, as we know, by an electric current, which makes the round of the circuit, and only flows when that circuit is complete. However long the wire may be, however far it may run between the poles, the current will follow all its windings, and finish its course from pole to pole of the battery. You may lead the wire across the ocean and back, or round the world if you will, and the current will travel through it.

The moment you break the wire or circuit, however, the current will stop. By its electromotive force it can overcome the resistance of the many miles of conductor; but unless it be unusually strong it cannot leap across even a minute gap of air, which is one of the best insulators.

If, then, we have a simple device easily manipulated by which we can interrupt the circuit of the battery, in accordance with a given code, we shall be able to send a series of currents through the wire and make sensible signals wherever we choose. These signs can be produced by the deviation of a magnetic needle, as Laplace pointed out, or by causing an electro-magnet to attract soft iron, or by chemical decomposition, or any other sensible effect of the current.

Ampere developed the idea of Laplace into a definite plan, and in 1830 or thereabout Ritchie, in London, and Baron Schilling, in St. Petersburg, exhibited experimental models. In 1833 and afterwards Professors Gauss and Weber installed a private telegraph between the observatory and the physical cabinet of the University of Gottingen. Moreover, in 1836 William Fothergill Cooke, a retired surgeon of the Madras army, attending lectures on anatomy at the University of Heidelberg, saw an experimental telegraph of Professor Moncke, which turned all his thoughts to the subject. On returning to London he made the acquaintance of Professor Wheatstone, of King's College, who was also experimenting in this direction, and in 1836 they took out a patent for a needle telegraph. It was tried successfully between the Euston terminus and the Camden Town station of the London and North-Western Railway on the evening of July 25th, 1837, in presence of Mr. Robert Stephenson, and other eminent engineers. Wheatstone, sitting in a small room near the booking-office at Euston, sent the first message to Cooke at Camden Town, who at once replied. "Never," said Wheatstone, "did I feel such a tumultuous sensation before, as when, all alone in the still room, I heard the needles click, and as I spelled the words I felt all the magnitude of the invention pronounced to be practicable without cavil or dispute."

The importance of the telegraph in working railways was manifest, and yet the directors of the company were so purblind as to order the removal of the apparatus, and it was not until two years later that the Great Western Railway Company adopted it on their line from Paddington to West Drayton, and subsequently to Slough. This was the first telegraph for public use, not merely in England, but the world. The charge for a message was only a shilling, nevertheless few persons availed themselves of the new invention, and it was not until its fame was spread abroad by the clever capture of a murderer named Tawell that it began to prosper. Tawell had killed a woman at Slough, and on leaving his victim took the train for Paddington. The police, apprised of the murder, telegraphed a description of him to London. The original "five needle instrument," now in the museum of the Post Office, had a dial in the shape of a diamond, on which were marked the letters of the alphabet, and each letter of a word was pointed out by the movements of a pair of needles. The dial had no letter "q," and as the man was described as a quaker the word was sent "kwaker." When the tram arrived at Paddington he was shadowed by detectives, and to his utter astonishment was quietly arrested in a tavern near Cannon Street.

In Cooke and Wheatstone's early telegraph the wire travelled the whole round of the circuit, but it was soon found that a "return" wire in the circuit was unnecessary, since the earth itself could take the place of it. One wire from the sending station to the receiving station was sufficient, provided the apparatus at each end were properly connected to the ground. This use of the earth not only saved the expense of a return wire, but diminished the resistance of the circuit, because the earth offered practically no resistance.

Figure 45 is a diagram of the connections in a simple telegraph circuit. At each of the stations there is a battery B B', an interruptor or sending key K K'to make and break the continuity of the circuit, a receiving instrument R R'to indicate the signal currents by their sensible effects, and connections with ground or "earth plates" E E' to engage the earth as a return wire. These are usually copper plates buried in the moist subsoil or the water pipes of a city. The line wire is commonly of iron supported on poles, but insulated from them by earthenware "cups" or insulators.

At the station on the left the key is in the act of SENDING a message, and at the post on the right it is conformably in the position for receiving the message. The key is so constructed that when it is at rest it puts the line in connection with the earth through the RECEIVING INSTRUMENT and the earth plate.

The key K consists essentially of a spring-lever, with two platinum contacts, so placed that when the lever is pressed down by the hand of the telegraphist it breaks contact with the receiver R, and puts the line-wire L in connection with the earth E through the battery B, as shown on the left. A current then flows into the line and traverses the receiver R' at the distant station, returning or seeming to return to the sending battery by way of the earth plate E' on the right and the intermediate ground.

The duration of the current is at the will of the operator who works the sending-key, and it is plain that signals can be made by currents of various lengths. In the "Morse code" of signals, which is now universal, only two lengths of current are employed— namely, a short, momentary pulse, produced by instant contact of the key, and a jet given by a contact about three times longer. These two signals are called "dot" and "dash," and the code is merely a suitable combination of them to signify the several letters of the alphabet. Thus e, the commonest letter in

English, is telegraphed by a single "dot," and the letter t by a single "dash," while the letter a is indicated by a "dot" followed after a brief interval or "space" by a dash.

Obviously, if two kinds of current are used, that is to say, if the poles of the battery are reversed by the sending-key, and the direction of the current is consequently reversed in the circuit, there is no need to alter the length of the signal currents, because a momentary current sent in one direction will stand for a "dot" and in the other direction for a "dash." As a matter of fact, the code is used in both ways, according to the nature of the line and receiving instrument. On submarine cables and with needle and "mirror" instruments, the signals are made by reversing currents of equal duration, but on land lines worked by "Morse" instruments and "sounders," they are produced by short and long currents.

The Morse code is also used in the army for signalling by waving flags or flashing lights, and may also be serviceable in private life. Telegraph clerks have been known to "speak" with each other in company by winking the right and left eye, or tapping with their teaspoon on a cup and saucer. Any two distinct signs, however made, can be employed as a telegraph by means of the Morse code, which runs as shown in figure 46.

The receiving instruments R R' may consist of a magnetic needle pivotted on its centre and surrounded by a coil of wire, through which the current passes and deflects the needle to one side or the other, according to the direction in which it flows. Such was the pioneer instrument of Cooke and Wheatstone, which is still employed in England in a simplified form as the "single" and "double" needle-instrument on some of the local lines and in railway telegraphs. The signals are made by sending momentary currents in opposite directions by a "double current" key, which (unlike the key K in figure 45) reverses the poles

A .-	J -.-.
B -...	K -.-
C ...	L —
D -..	M - -
E .	N -.
F .-.	O . .
G —.	Q ..-.
H . ..	R . ..
I ..	

S ...	1 .—.
T -	2 ..-..
U ..-	3 ...-.
V ...-	4 ....-
W .-	5 ——
X .-..	6 ......
Y	7 —..
Z	8 -.. ..
& . ..	9 -..-
Period ..—..	0 ———
Comma .-.-	

The International (Morse) code used elsewhere is the same as the above, with the following exceptions:

C -.-.	Q —.-
F . -.	R .-.
J .——	X -..-
L .-..	Y -.—
O —-	Z —..
P .—.	

FIG. 46.—Morse Signal Alphabet.

of the battery, in putting the line to one or the other, and thus making the "dot" signal with the positive and the "dash" signal with the negative pole. It follows that if the "dot" is indicated by a throw of the needle to the right side, a "dash" will be given by a throw to the left.

Most of the telegraph instruments for land lines are based on the principle of the electro-magnet. We have already seen (page 59) how Ampere found that a spiral of wire with a current flowing in it behaved like a magnet and was able to suck a piece of soft iron into it. If the iron is allowed to remain there as a core, the combination of coil and core becomes an electro-magnet, that is to say, a magnet which is only a magnet so long as the current passes. Figure 47 represents a simple "horse-shoe" electro-magnet as invented by Sturgeon. A U-shaped core of soft iron is wound with insulated wire W, and when a current is sent through the wire, the core is found to become magnetic with a "north" pole in one end and a "south" pole in the other. These poles are therefore able to attract a separate piece of soft iron or armature A. When the current is stopped, however, the core ceases to be a magnet and the armature drops away. In practice the electromagnet usually takes the form shown in figure 48, where the poles are two bobbins or sole-noids of wire 61 having straight cores of iron which are united by an iron bar B, and A is the armature.

Such an electromagnet is a more powerful device than a swinging needle, and bet-ter able to actuate a mechanism. It became the foundation of the recording instru-ment of Samuel Morse, the father of the telegraph in America. The Morse, or, rather, Morse and Vail instrument, actually marks the signals in "dots" and "dash-es" on a ribbon of moving paper. Figure 49 represents the Morse instrument, in which an electromagnet M attracts an iron armature A when a current passes through its bobbins, and by means of a lever L connected with the armature rais-es the edge of a small disc out of an ink-pot I against the surface of a travelling slip of paper P, and marks a dot or dash upon it as the case may be. The rest of the apparatus consists of details and accessories for its action and adjustment, together with the sending-key K, which is used in asking for repetitions of the words, if necessary.

A permanent record of the message is of course convenient, nevertheless the oper-ators prefer to "read" the signals by the ear, rather than the eye, and, to the annoy-ance of Morse, would listen to the click of the marking disc rather than decipher the marks on the paper. Consequently Alfred Vail, the collaborator of Morse, who really invented the Morse code, produced a modification of the recording instru-ment working solely for the ear. The "sounder," as it is called, has largely driven the "printer" from the field. This neat little instrument is shown in figure 50, where M is the electromagnet, and A is the armature which chatters up and down between two metal stops, as the current is made and broken by the sending-key, and the operator listening to the sounds interprets the message letter by letter and word by word.

The motion of the armature in both of these instruments takes a sensible time, but Alexander Bain, of Thurso, by trade a watchmaker, and by nature a genius, invented a chemical telegraph which was capable of a prodigious activity. The instrument of Bain resembled the Morse in marking the signals on a tape of mov-ing paper, but this was done by electrolysis or electro-chemical decomposition. The paper was soaked in a solution of iodide of potassium in starch and water, and the signal currents were passed through it by a marking stylus or pencil of iron. The electricity decomposed the solution in its passage and left a blue stain on the paper, which corresponded to the dot and dash of the Morse apparatus. The Bain telegraph can record over 1000 words a minute as against 40 to 50 by the Morse or sounder, nevertheless it has fallen into disuse, perhaps because the solution was troublesome.

It is stated that a certain blind operator could read the signals by the smell of the chemical action; and we can well believe it. In fact, the telegraph appeals to every sense, for a deaf clerk can feel the movements of a sounder, and the signals of the current can be told without any instrument by the mere taste of the wires inserted in the mouth.

A skilful telegraphist can transmit twenty-five words a minute with the single-current key, and nearly twice as many by the double-current key, and if we remember that an average English word requires fifteen separate signals, the number will seem remarkable; but by means of Wheatstone's automatic sender 150 words or more can be sent in a minute.

Among telegraphs designed to print the message in Roman type, that of Professor David Edward Hughes is doubtless the fittest, since it is now in general use on the Continent, and conveys our Continental news. In this apparatus the electromagnet, on attracting its armature, presses the paper against a revolving type wheel and receives the print of a type, so that the message can be read by a novice. To this effect the type wheel at the receiving station has to keep in perfect time as it revolves, so that the right letter shall be above the paper when the current passes. Small varieties of the type-printer are employed for the distribution of news and prices in most of the large towns, being located in hotels, restaurants, saloons, and other public places, and reporting prices of stocks and bonds, horse races, and sporting and general news. The "duplex system," whereby two messages, one in either direction, can be sent over one wire simultaneously without interfering, and the quadruplex system, whereby four messages, two in either direction, are also sent at once, have come into use where the traffic over the lines is very great. Both of these systems and their modifications depend on an ingenious arrangement of the apparatus at each end of the line, by which the signal currents sent out from one station do not influence the receivers there, but leave them free to indicate the currents from the distant station. When the Wheatstone Automatic Sender is employed with these systems about 500 words per minute can be sent through the line. Press news is generally sent by night, and it is on record, that during a great debate in Parliament, as many as half a million words poured out of the Central Telegraph Station at St. Martin's-le-Grand in a single night to all parts of the country.

Errors occur now and then through bad penmanship or the similarity of certain signals, and amusing telegrams have been sent out, as when the nomination of Mr. Brand for the Speakership of the Commons took the form of "Proposed to brand Speaker"; and an excursion party assured their friends at home of their security by the message, "Arrived all tight."

Telegraphs, in the literal sense of the word, which actually write the message as with a pen, and make a copy or facsimile of the original, have been invented from time to time. Such are the "telegraphic pen" of Mr. E. A. Cowper, and the "telautographs" of Mr. J. H. Robertson and Mr. Elisha Gray. The first two are based on a method of varying the strength of the current in accordance with the curves of the handwriting, and making the varied current actuate by means of magnetism a writing pen or stylus at the distant station. The instrument of Gray, which is the most successful, works by intermittent currents or electrical impulses, that excite electro-magnets and move the stylus at the far end of the line. They are too complicated for description here, and are not of much practical importance.

Telegraphs for transmitting sketches and drawings have also been devised by D'Ablincourt and others, but they have not come into general use. Of late another step forward has been taken by Mr. Amstutz, who has invented an apparatus for transmitting photographic pictures to a distance by means of electricity. The system may be described as a combination of the photograph and telegraph. An ordinary negative picture is taken, and then impressed on a gelatine plate sensitised with bichromate of potash. The parts of the gelatine in light become insoluble, while the parts in shade can be washed away by water. In this way a relief or engraving of the picture is obtained on the gelatine, and a cross section through the plate would, if looked at edgeways, appear serrated, or up and down, like a section of country or the trace of the stylus in the record of a phonograph. The gelatine plate thus carved by the action of light and water is wrapped round a revolving drum or barrel, and a spring stylus or point is caused to pass over it as the barrel revolves, after the manner of a phonographic cylinder. In doing so the stylus rises and falls over the projections in the plate and works a lever against a set of telegraph keys, which open electric contacts and break the connections of an electric battery which is joined between the keys and the earth. There are four keys, and when they are untouched the current splits up through four by-paths or bobbins of wire before it enters the line wire and passes to the distant station. When any of the keys are touched, however, the corresponding by-path or bobbin is cut out of circuit. The suppression of a by-path or channel for the current has the effect of adding to the "resistance" of the line, and therefore of diminishing the strength of the current. When all the keys are untouched the resistance is least and the current strongest. On the other hand, when all the keys but the last are touched, the resistance is greatest and the current weakest. By this device it is easy to see that as the stylus or tracer sinks into a hollow of the gelatine, or rises over a height, the current in the line becomes stronger or weaker. At the distant station the current passes through a solenoid or hollow coil of wire connected to the earth and magnetises it, so as to pull the soft iron plug or "core" with greater or less force into its hollow interior. The up and down movement of the plug actuates a graving stylus or point through a lever, and engraves a copy of the original gelatine trace on the surface of a wax or gelatine plate overlying another barrel or drum, which revolves at a rate corresponding to that of the barrel at the transmitting station. In this way a facsimile of the gelatine picture is produced at the distant station, and an electrotype or cliche of it can be made for printing purposes. The method is, in fact, a species of electric line graving, and Mr. Amstutz hopes to apply it to engraving on gold, silver, or any soft metal, not necessarily at a distance.

We know that an electric current in one wire can induce a transient current in a neighbouring wire, and the fact has been utilised in the United States by Phelps and others to send messages from moving trains. The signal currents are intermittent, and when they are passed through a conductor on the train they excite corresponding currents in a wire run along the track, which can be interpreted by the hum they make in a telephone. Experiments recently made by Mr. W. H. Preece for the Post Office show that with currents of sufficient strength and proper apparatus messages can be sent through the air for five miles or more by this method of induction.

We come now to the submarine telegraph, which differs in many respects from the overland telegraph. Obviously, since water and moist earth is a conductor, a wire to convey an electric current must be insulated if it is intended to lie at the bottom of the sea or buried underground. The best materials for the purpose yet discovered are gutta-percha and india-rubber, which are both flexible and very good insulators.

The first submarine cable was laid across the Channel from Dover to Calais in 1851, and consisted of a copper strand, coated with gutta-percha, and protected from injury by an outer sheath of hemp and iron wire. It is the general type of all the submarine cables which have been deposited since then in every part of the world. As a rule, the armour or sheathing is made heavier for shore water than it is for the deep sea, but the electrical portion, or "core," that is to say, the insulated conductor, is the same throughout.

The first Atlantic cable was laid in 1858 by Cyrus W. Field and a company of British capitalists, but it broke down, and it was not until 1866 that a new and successful cable was laid to replace it. Figure 51 represents various cross-sections of an Atlantic cable deposited in 1894.

The inner star of twelve copper wires is the conductor, and the black circle round it is the gutta-percha or insulator which keeps the electricity from escaping into the water. The core in shallow water is protected from the bites of teredoes by a brass tape, and the envelope or armour consists of hemp and iron wire preserved from corrosion by a covering of tape and a compound of mineral pitch and sand.

The circuit of a submarine line is essentially the same as that of a land line, except that the earth connection is usually the iron sheathing of the cable in lieu of an earth-plate. On a cable, however, at least a long cable, the instruments for sending and receiving the messages are different from those employed on a land line. A cable is virtually a Leyden jar or condenser, and the signal currents in the wire induce opposite currents in the water or earth. As these charges hold each other the signals are retarded in their progress, and altered from sharp sudden jets to lagging undulations or waves, which tend to run together or coalesce. The result is that the separate signal currents which enter a long cable issue from it at the other end in one continuous current, with pulsations at every signal, that is to say, in a lapsing stream, like a jet of water flowing from a constricted spout. The receiving instrument must be sufficiently delicate to manifest every pulsation of the current. Its indicator, in fact, must respond to every rise and fall of the current, as a float rides on the ripples of a stream.

Such an instrument is the beautiful "mirror" galvanometer of Lord Kelvin, Ex-President of the Royal Society, which we illustrate in figure 52, where C is a coil of wire with a small magnetic needle suspended in its heart, and D is a steel magnet supported over it. The needle (M figure 53) is made of watch spring cemented to the back of a tiny mirror the size of a half-dime which is hung by a single fibre of floss silk inside an air cell or chamber with a glass lens G in front, and the coil C surrounds it. A ray of light from a lamp L (figure 52) falls on the mirror, and is reflected back to a scale S, on which it makes a bright spot. Now, when the coil C is connected between the end of the cable and the earth, the signal current passing through it causes the tiny magnet to swing from side to side, and the mirror moving with it throws the beam up and down the scale. The operator sitting by watches the spot of light as it flits and flickers like a fire-fly in the darkness, and spells out the mysterious message.

A condenser joined in the circuit between the cable and the receiver, or between the receiver and the earth, has the effect of sharpening the waves of the current, and consequently of the signals. The double-current key, which reverses the poles of the battery and allows the signal currents to be of one length, that is to say, all "dots," is employed to send the message.

Another receiving instrument employed on most of the longer cables is the siphon recorder of Lord Kelvin, shown in figure 54, which marks or writes the message on a slip of travelling paper. Essentially it is the inverse of the mirror instrument, and consists of a light coil of wire S suspended in the field between the poles of a strong magnet M. The coil is attached to a fine siphon (T5) filled with ink, and sometimes kept in vibration by an induction coil so as to shake the ink in fine drops upon a slip of moving paper. The coil is connected between the cable and the earth, and, as the signal current passes through, it swings to one side or the other, pulling the siphon with it. The ink, therefore, marks a wavy line on the paper, which is in fact a delineation of the rise and fall of the signal current and a record of the message. The dots in this case are represented by the waves above, and the "dashes" by the waves below the middle line, as may be seen in the following alphabet, which is a copy of one actually written by the recorder on a long submarine cable.

Owing to induction, the speed of signalling on long cables is much slower than on land lines of the same length, and only reaches from 25 to 45 words a minute on the Atlantic cables, or 30 to 50 words with an automatic sending-key; but this rate is practically doubled by employing the Muirhead duplex system of sending two messages, one from each end, at the same time.

The relation of the telegraph to the telephone is analogous to that of the lower animals and man. In a telegraph circuit, with its clicking key at one end and its chattering sounder at the other, we have, in fact, an apish forerunner of the exquisite telephone, with its mysterious microphone and oracular plate. Nevertheless, the telephone descended from the telegraph in a very indirect manner, if at all, and certainly not through the sounder. The first practical suggestion of an electric telephone was made by M. Charles Bourseul, a French telegraphist, in 1854, but to all appearance nothing came of it. In 1860, however, Philipp Reis, a German schoolmaster, constructed a rudimentary telephone, by which music and a few spoken words were sent. Finally, in 1876, Mr. Alexander Graham Bell, a Scotchman, residing in Canada, and subsequently in the United States, exhibited a capable speaking telephone of his invention at the Centennial Exhibition, Philadelphia.

Figure 56 represents an outside view and section of the Bell telephone as it is now made, where M is a bar magnet having a small bobbin or coil of fine insulated wire C girdling one pole. In front of this coil there is a circular plate of soft iron capable of vibrating like a diaphragm or the drum of the ear. A cover shaped like a mouthpiece O fixes the diaphragm all round, and the wires W W serve to connect the coil in the circuit.

The soft iron diaphragm is, of course, magnetised by the induction of the pole, and would be attracted bodily to the pole were it not fixed by the rim, so that only its middle is free to move. Now, when a person speaks into the mouthpiece the sonorous waves impinge on the diaphragm and make it vibrate in sympathy with them. Being magnetic, the movement of the diaphragm to and from the bobbin excites corresponding waves of electricity in the coil, after the famous experiment of Faraday (page 64). If this undulatory current is passed through the coil of a similar telephone at the far end of the line, it will, by a reverse action, set the diaphragm in vibration and reproduce the original sonorous waves. The result is, that when another person listens at the mouthpiece of the receiving telephone, he will hear a faithful imitation of the original speech.

The Bell telephone is virtually a small magneto-electric generator of electricity, and when two are joined in circuit we have a system for the transmission of energy. As the voice is the motive power, its talk, though distinct, is comparatively feeble, and further improvements were made before the telephone became as serviceable as it is now.

Edison, in 1877, was the first to invent a working telephone, which, instead of generating the current, merely controlled the strength of it, as the sluice of a mill-dam regulates the flow of water in the lead. Du Moncel had observed that powder of carbon altered in electrical resistance under pressure, and Edison found that lamp-black was so sensitive as to change in resistance under the impact of the sonorous waves. His transmitter consisted of a button or wafer of lamp-black behind a diaphragm, and connected in the circuit. On speaking to the diaphragm the sonorous waves pressed it against the button, and so varied the strength of the current in a sympathetic manner. The receiver of Edison was equally ingenious, and consisted of a cylinder of prepared chalk kept in rotation and a brass stylus rubbing on it. When the undulatory current passed from the stylus to the chalk, the stylus slipped on the surface, and, being connected to a diaphragm, made it vibrate and repeat the original sounds. This "electro- motograph" receiver was, however, given up, and a combination of the Edison transmitter and the Bell receiver came into use.

At the end of 1877 Professor D. E. Hughes, a distinguished Welshman, inventor of the printing telegraph, discovered that any loose contact between two conductors had the property of transmitting sounds by varying the strength of an electric current passing through it. Two pieces of metal—for instance, two nails or ends of wire—when brought into a loose or crazy contact under a slight pressure, and traversed by a current, will transmit speech. Two pieces of hard carbon are still better than metals, and if properly adjusted will make the tread of a fly quite audible in a telephone connected with them. Such is the famous "microphone," by which a faint sound can be magnified to the ear.

Figure 57 represents what is known as the "pencil" microphone, in which M is a pointed rod of hard carbon, delicately poised between two brackets of carbon, which are connected in circuit with a battery B and a Bell telephone T. The joints of rod and bracket are so sensitive that the current flowing across them is affected in strength by the slightest vibration, even the walking of an insect. If, therefore, we speak near this microphone, the sonorous waves, causing the pencil to vibrate, will so vary the current in accordance with them as to reproduce the sounds of the voice in the telephone.

The true nature of the microphone is not yet known, but it is evident that the air or ether between the surfaces in contact plays an important part in varying the resistance, and, therefore, the current. In fact, a small "voltaic arc," not luminous, but dark, seems to be formed between the points, and the vibrations probably alter its length, and, consequently, its resistance. The fact that a microphone is reversible and can act as a receiver, though a poor one, tends to confirm this theory. Moreover, it is not unlikely that the slipping of the stylus in the electromotograph is due to a similar cause. Be this as it may, there can be no doubt that carbon powder and the lamp-black of the Edison button are essentially a cluster of microphones.

Many varieties of the Hughes microphone under different names are now employed as transmitters in connection with the Bell telephone. Figure 58 represents a simple micro-telephone circuit, where M is the Hughes microphone transmitter, T the Bell telephone receiver, JB the battery, and E E the earth-plates; but sometimes a return wire is used in place of the "earth." The line wire is usually of copper and its alloys, which are more suitable than iron, especially for long distances. Just as the signal currents in a submarine cable induce corresponding currents in the sea water which retard them, so the currents in a land wire induce corresponding currents in the earth, but in aerial lines the earth is generally so far away that the consequent retardation is negligible except in fast working on long lines. The Bell telephone, however, is extremely sensitive, and this induction affects it so much that a conversation through one wire can be overheard on a neighbouring wire. Moreover, there is such a thing as "self-induction" in a wire— that is to say, a current in a wire tends to induce an opposite current in the same wire, which is practically equivalent to an increase of resistance in the wire. It is particularly observed at the starting and stopping of a current, and gives rise to what is called the "extra-spark" seen in breaking the circuit of an induction coil. It is also active in the vibratory currents of the telephone, and, like ordinary induction, tends to retard their passage. Copper being less susceptible of self-induction than iron, is preferred for trunk lines. The disturbing effect of ordinary induction is avoided by using a return wire or loop circuit, and crossing the going and coming wires so as to make them exchange places at intervals. Moreover, it is found that an induction coil in the telephone circuit, like a condenser in the cable circuit, improves the working, and hence it is usual to join the battery and transmitter with the primary wire, and the secondary wire with the line and the receiver. The longest telephone line as yet made is that from New York to Chicago, a distance of 950 miles. It is made of thick copper wire, erected on cedar poles 35 feet above the ground.

Induction is so strong on submarine cables of 50 or 100 miles in length that the delicate waves of the telephone current are smoothed away, and the speech is either muffled or entirely stifled. Nevertheless, a telephone cable 20 miles long was laid between Dover and Calais in 1891, and another between Stranraer and Donaghadee more recently, thus placing Great Britain on speaking terms with France and other parts of the Continent.

Figure 59 shows a form of telephone apparatus employed in the United Kingdom. In it the transmitter and receiver, together with a call-bell, which are required at each end of the line, are neatly combined. The transmitter is a Blake microphone, in which the loose joint is a contact of platinum on hard carbon. It is fitted up inside the box, together with an induction coil, and M is the mouthpiece for speaking to it. The receiver is a pair of Bell telephones T T, which are detached from their hooks and held to the ear. A call-bell B serves to "ring up" the correspondent at the other end of the line.

Excepting private lines, the telephone is worked on the "exchange system"—that is to say, the wires running to different persons converge in a central exchange, where, by means of an apparatus called a "switch board," they are connected together for the purpose of conversation

A telephone exchange would make an excellent subject for the artist. He delights to paint us a row of Venetian bead stringers or a band of Sevilhan cigarette makers, but why does he shirk a bevy of industrious girls working a telephone exchange? Let us peep into one of these retired haunts, where the modern Fates are cutting and joining the lines of electric speech between man and man in a great city.

The scene is a long, handsome room or gallery, with a singular piece of furniture in the shape of an L occupying the middle. This is the switchboard, in which the wires from the offices and homes of the subscribers are concentrated like the nerves in a ganglion. It is known as the "multiple switchboard," an American invention, and is divided into sections, over which the operators preside. The lines of all the subscribers are brought to each section, so that the operator can cross connect any two lines in the whole system without leaving her chair. Each section of the board is, in fact, an epitome of the whole, but it is physically impossible for a single operator to make all the connections of a large exchange, and the work is distributed amongst them. A multiplicity of wires is therefore needed to connect, say, two thousand subscribers. These are all concealed, however, at the back of the board, and in charge of the electricians. The young lady operators have nothing to do with these, and so much the better for them, as it would puzzle their minds a good deal worse than a ravelled skein of thread. Their duty is to sit in front of the board in comfortable seats at a long table and make the needful connections. The call signal of a subscriber is given by the drop of a disc bearing his number. The operator then asks the subscriber by telephone what he wants, and on hearing the number of the other subscriber he wishes to speak with, she takes up a pair of brass plugs coupled by a flexible conductor and joins the lines of the subscribers on the switchboard by simply thrusting the plugs into holes corresponding to the wires. The subscribers are then free to talk with each other undisturbed, and the end of the conversation is signalled to the operator. Every instant the call discs are dropping, the connecting plugs are thrust into the holes, and the girls are asking "Hullo! hullo!" "Are you there?" "Who are you?" "Have you finished?" Yet all this constant activity goes on quietly, deftly —we might say elegantly—and in comparative silence, for the low tones of the girlish voices are soft and pleasing, and the harsher sounds of the subscriber are unheard in the room by all save the operator who attends to him.

CHAPTER VII.

ELECTRIC LIGHT AND HEAT.

The electric spark was, of course, familiar to the early experimenters with electricity, but the electric light, as we know it, was first discovered by Sir Humphrey Davy, the Cornish philosopher, in the year 1811 or thereabout. With the magic of his genius Davy transformed the spark into a brilliant glow by passing it between two points of carbon instead of metal. If, as in figure 60, we twist the wires (+ and—) which come from a voltaic battery, say of 20 cells, about two carbon pencils, and bring their tips together in order to start the current, then draw them a little apart, we shall produce an artificial or mimic star. A sheet of dazzling light, which is called the electric arc, is seen to bridge the gap. It is not a true flame, for there is little combustion, but rather a nebulous blaze of silvery lustre in a bluish veil of heated air. The points of carbon are white-hot, and the positive is eaten away into a hollow or crater by the current, which violently tears its particles from their seat and whirls them into the fierce vortex of the arc. The negative remains pointed, but it is also worn away about half as fast as the positive. This wasting of the carbons tends to widen the arc too much and break the current, hence in arc lamps meant to yield the light for hours the sticks are made of a good length, and a self- acting mechanism feeds them forward to the arc as they are slowly consumed, thus maintaining the splendour of the illumination.

Many ingenious lamps have been devised by Serrin, Dubosq, Siemens, Brockie, and others, some regulating the arc by clockwork and electro-magnetism, or by thermal and other effects of the current. They are chiefly used for lighting halls and railway stations, streets and open spaces, search-lights and lighthouses. They are sometimes naked, but as a rule their brightness is tempered by globes of ground or opal glass. In search-lights a parabolic mirror projects all the rays in any one direction, and in lighthouses the arc is placed in the focus of the condensing lenses, and the beam is visible for at least twenty or thirty miles on clear nights. Very powerful arc lights, equivalent to hundreds of thousands of candles, can be seen for 100 or 150 miles.

Figure 61 illustrates the Pilsen lamp, in which the positive Carbon G runs on rollers rr through the hollow interior of two solenoids or coils of wire MM' and carries at its middle a spindle-shaped piece of soft iron C. The current flows through the solenoid M on its way to the arc, but a branch or shunted portion of it flows through the solenoid M', and as both of these solenoids act as electro-magnets on the soft iron C, each tending to suck it into its interior, the iron rests between them when their powers are balanced. When, however, the arc grows too wide, and the current therefore becomes too weak, the shunt solenoid M' gains a purchase over the main solenoid M, and, pulling the iron core towards it, feeds the positive carbon to the arc. In this way the balance of the solenoids is read-justed, the current regains its normal strength, the arc its proper width, and the light its brilliancy.

Figure 62 is a diagrammatic representation of the Brush arc lamp. X and Y are the line terminals connecting the lamp in circuit. On the one hand, the current splits and passes around the hollow spools H H', thence to the rod N through the car-bon K, the arc, the carbon K', and thence through the lamp frame to Y. On the other hand, it runs in a resistance fine-wire coil around the magnet T, thence to Y. The operation of the lamp is as follows: K and K' being in contact, a strong current starts through the lamp energising H and H', which suck in their core pieces N and S, lifting C, and by it the "washer-clutch" W and the rod N and car-bon K, establishing the arc. K is lifted until the increasing resistance of the length-ening arc weakens the current in H H' and a balance is established. As the car-bons burn away, C gradually lowers until a stop under W holds it horizontal and allows N to drop through W, and the lamp starts anew. If for any reason the resist-ance of the lamp becomes too great, or the circuit is broken, the increased current through T draws up its armature, closing the contacts M, thus short-circuiting the lamp through a thick, heavy wire coil on T, which then keeps M closed, and pre-vents the dead lamp from interfering with the others on its line. Numerous mod-ifications of this lamp are in very general use.

Davy also found that a continuous wire or stick of carbon could be made white-hot by sending a sufficient current through it, and this fact is the basis of the incandescent lamp now so common in our homes.

Wires of platinum, iridium, and other inoxidisable metals raised to incandescence by the current are useful in firing mines, but they are not quite suitable for yielding a light, because at a very high temperature they begin to melt. Every solid body becomes red-hot—that is to say, emits rays of red light, at a temperature of about 1000 degrees Fahrenheit, yellow rays at 1300 degrees, blue rays at 1500 degrees, and white light at 2000 degrees. It is found, however, that as the temperature of a wire is pushed beyond this figure the light emitted becomes far more brilliant than the increase of temperature would seem to warrant. It therefore pays to elevate the temperature of the filament as high as possible. Unfortunately the most refractory metals, such as platinum and alloys of platinum with iridium, fuse at a temperature of about 3450 degrees Fahrenheit. Electricians have therefore forsaken metals, and fallen back on carbon for producing a light. In 1845 Mr. Staite devised an incandescent lamp consisting of a fine rod or stick of carbon rendered white-hot by the current, and to preserve the carbon from burning in the atmosphere, he enclosed it in a glass bulb, from which the air was exhausted by an air pump. Edison and Swan, in 1878, and subsequently, went a step further, and substituted a filament or fine thread of carbon for the rod. The new lamp united the advantages of wire in point of form with those of carbon as a material. The Edison filament was made by cutting thin slips of bamboo and charring them, the Swan by carbonising linen fibre with sulphuric acid. It was subsequently found that a hard skin could be given to the filament by "flashing" it— that is to say, heating it to incandescence by the current in an atmosphere of hydrocarbon gas. The filament thus treated becomes dense and resilient.

Figure 63 represents an ordinary glow lamp of the Edison-Swan type, where E is the filament, moulded into a loop, and cemented to two platinum wires or electrodes P penetrating the glass bulb L, which is exhausted of air.

Platinum is chosen because it expands and contracts with temperature about the same as glass, and hence there is little chance of the glass cracking through unequal stress. The vacuum in the bulb is made by a mercurial air pump of the Sprengel sort, and the pressure of air in it is only about one-millionth of an atmosphere. The bulb is fastened with a holder like that shown in figure 64, where two little hooks H connected to screw terminals T T are provided to make contact with the platinum terminals of the lamp (P, figure 63), and the spiral spring, by pressing on the bulb, ensures a good contact.

Fig. 65 is a cut of the ordinary Edison lamp and socket. One end of the filament is connected to the metal screw ferule at the base. The other end is attached to the metal button in the centre of the extreme bottom of the base. Screwing the lamp into the socket automatically connects the filament on one end to the screw, on the other to an insulated plate at the bottom of the socket.

The resistance of such a filament hot is about 200 ohms, and to produce a good light from it the battery or dynamo ought to give an electromotive force of at least 100 volts. Few voltaic cells or accumulators have an electromotive force of more than 2 volts, therefore we require a battery of 50 cells joined in series, each cell giving 2 volts, and the whole set 100 volts. The strength of current in the circuit must also be taken into account. To yield a good light such a lamp requires or "takes" about 1/2 an ampere. Hence the cells must be chosen with regard to their size and internal resistance as well as to their kind, so that when the battery, in series, is connected to the lamp, the resistance of the whole circuit, including the filament or lamp, the battery itself, and the connecting wires shall give by Ohm's law a current of 1\2 an ampere. It will be understood that the current has the same strength in every part of the circuit, no matter how it is made up. Thus, if 1/2 of an ampere is flowing in the lamp, it is also flowing in the battery and wires. An Edison-Swan lamp of this model gives a light of about 15 candles, and is well adapted for illuminating the interior of houses. The temperature of the carbon filament is about 3450 degrees Fahr—that is to say, the temperature at which platinum melts. Similar lamps of various sizes and shapes are also made, some equivalent to as many as 100 candles, and fitted for large halls or streets, others emitting a tiny beam like the spark of a glow-worm, and designed for medical examinations, or lighting flowers, jewels, and dresses in theatres or ball-rooms.

The electric incandescent lamp is pure and healthy, since it neither burns nor pollutes the air. It is also cool and safe, for it produces little heat, and cannot ignite any inflammable stuffs near it. Hence its peculiar merit as a light for colliers working in fiery mines. Independent of air, it acts equally well under water, and is therefore used by divers. Moreover, it can be fixed wherever a wire can be run, does not tarnish gilding, and lends itself to the most artistic decoration.

Electric lamps are usually connected in circuit on the series, parallel, and three wire system.

The series system is shown in figure 66, where the lamps L L follow each other in a row like beads on a string. It is commonly reserved for the arc lamp, which has a resistance so low that a moderate electromotive force can overcome the added resistance of the lamps, but, of course, if the circuit breaks at any point all the lamps go out.

The parallel system is illustrated in figure 67, where the lamps are connected between two main conductors cross-wise, like the steps of a ladder. The current is thus divided into cross channels, like water used for irrigating fields, and it is obvious that, although the circuit is broken at one point, say by the rupture of a filament, all the lamps do not go out.

Fig. 68 exhibits the Edison three-wire system, in which two batteries or dynamos are connected together in series, and a third or central main conductor is run from their middle poles. The plan saves a return wire, for if two generators had been used separately, four mains would have been necessary.

The parallel and three-wire systems in various groups, with or without accumulators as local reservoirs, are chiefly employed for incandescent lamps.

The main conductors conveying the current from the dynamos are commonly of stout copper insulated with air like telegraph wires, or cables coated with india-rubber or gutta-percha, and buried underground or suspended overhead. The branch and lamp conductors or "leads" are finer wires of copper, insulated with india-rubber or silk.

The current of an installation or section of one is made and broken at will by means of a "switch" or key turned by hand. It is simply a series of metal contacts insulated from each other and connected to the conductors, with a sliding contact connected to the dynamo which travels over them. To guard against an excess of current on the lamps, "cut-outs," or safety-fuses, are inserted between the switch and the conductors, or at other leading points in the circuit. They are usually made of short slips of metal foil or wire, which melt or deflagrate when the current is too strong, and thus interrupt the circuit.

There is some prospect of the luminosity excited in a vacuum tube by the alternating currents from a dynamo or an induction coil becoming an illuminant. Crookes has obtained exquisitely beautiful glows by the phosphorescence of gems and other minerals in a vacuum bulb like that shown in figure 69, where A and B are the metal electrodes on the outside of the glass. A heap of diamonds from various countries emit red, orange, yellow, green, and blue rays. Ruby, sapphire, and emerald give a deep red, crimson, or lilac phosphorescence, and sulphate of zinc a magnificent green glow. Tesla has also shown that vacuum bulbs can be lit inside without any outside connection with the current, by means of an apparatus like that shown in figure 70, where D is an alternating dynamo, C a condenser, P S the primary and secondary coils of a sparking transformer, T T two metal sheets or plates, and SB the exhausted bulbs. The alternating or see-saw current in this case charges the condenser and excites the primary coil P, while the induced current in the secondary coil 5 charges the terminal plates T T. So long as the bulbs or tubes are kept within the space between the plates, they are filled with a soft radiance, and it is easy to see that if these plates covered the opposite walls of a room, the vacuum lamps would yield a light in any part of it.

Electric heating bids fair to become almost as important as electric illumination. When the arc was first discovered it was noticed that platinum, gold, quartz, ruby, and diamond—in fine, the most refractory minerals—were melted in it, and ran like wax. Ores and salts of the metals were also vapourised, and it was clear that a powerful engine of research had been placed in the hands of the chemist. As a matter of fact, the temperature of the carbons in the arc is comparable to that of the Sun. It measures 5000 to 10,000 degrees Fahrenheit, and is the highest artificial heat known. Sir William Siemens was among the first to make an electric furnace heated by the arc, which fused and vapourised metallic ores, so that the metal could be extracted from them. Aluminium, chromium, and other valuable metals are now smelted by its means, and rough brilliants such as those found in diamond mines and meteoric stones have been crystallised from the fumes of carbon, like hoar frost in a cold mist.

The electric arc is also applied to the welding of wires, boiler plates, rails, and other metal work, by heating the parts to be joined and fusing them together.

Cooking and heating by electricity are coming more and more into favour, owing to their cleanliness and convenience. Kitchen ranges, including ovens and grills, entirely heated by the electric current, are finding their way into the best houses and hotels. Most of these are based on the principle of incandescence, the current heating a fine wire or other conductor of high resistance in passing through it. Figure 71 represents an electric kettle of this sort, which requires no outside fire to boil it, since the current flows through fine wires of platinum or some highly resisting metal embedded in fireproof insulating cement in its bottom. Figures 72 and 73 are a sauce-pan and a flat-iron heated in the same way. Figure 74 is a cigar-lighter for smoking rooms, the fusee F consisting of short platinum wires, which become red-hot when it is unhooked, and at the same time the lamp Z is automatically lit. Figure 75 is an electric radiator for heating rooms and passages, after the manner of stoves and hot water pipes. Quilts for beds, warmed by fine wires inside, have also been brought out, a constant temperature being maintained by a simple regulator, and it is not unlikely that personal clothing of the kind will soon be at the service of invalids and chilly mortals, more especially to make them comfortable on their travels.

An ingenious device places an electric heater inside a hot water bag, thus keeping it at a uniform temperature for sick-room and hospital use.

CHAPTER VIII.

ELECTRIC POWER.

On the discovery of electromagnetism (Chap. IV.), Faraday, Barlow, and others devised experimental apparatus for producing rotary motion from the electric current, and in 1831, Joseph Henry, the famous American electrician, invented a small electromagnetic engine or motor. These early machines were actuated by the current from a voltaic battery, but in the middle of the century Jacobi found that a dynamo-electric generator can also work as a motor, and that by coupling two dynamos in circuit—one as a generator, the other as a motor—it was possible to transmit mechanical power to any distance by means of electricity. Figure 76 is a diagram of a simple circuit for the transmission of power, where D is the technical symbol for a dynamo as a generator, having its poles (+ and -) connected by wire to the poles of M, the distant dynamo, as a motor. The generator D is driven by mechanical energy from any convenient source, and transforms it into electric energy, which flows through the circuit in the direction of the arrows, and, in traversing the motor M, is re-transformed into mechanical energy. There is, of course, a certain waste of energy in the process, but with good machines and conductors, it is not more than 10 to 25 per cent., or the "efficiency" of the installation is from 75 to 90 per cent—that is to say, for every 100 horse-power put into the generator, from 75 to 90 horse-power are given out again by the motor.

It was not until 1870, when Gramme had improved the dynamo, that power was practically transmitted in this way, and applied to pumping water, and other work. Since then great progress has been made, and electricity is now recognised, not only as a rival of steam, but as the best means of distributing steam, wind, water, or any other power to a distance, and bringing it to bear on the proper point.

The first electric railway, or, rather, tramway, was built by Dr. Werner von Siemens at Berlin in 1879, and was soon followed by many others. The wheels of the car were driven by an electric motor drawing its electricity from the rails, which were insulated from the ground, and being connected to the generator, served as conductors. It was found very difficult to insulate the rails, and keep the electricity from leaking to the ground, however, and at the Pans Electrical Exhibition of 1881, von Siemens made a short tramway in which the current was drawn from a bare copper conductor running on poles, like a telegraph wire, along the line.

The system will be understood from figure 77, where L is the overhead conductor joined to the positive pole of the dynamo or generator in the power house, and C is a rolling contact or trolley wheel travelling with the car and connected by the wire W to an electric motor M under the car, and geared to the axles. After passing through the motor the current escapes to the rail R by a brush or sliding contact C', and so returns to the negative pole of the generator. A very general way is to allow the return current to escape to the rails through the wheels. Many tramways, covering thousands of miles, are now worked on this plan in the United States. At Bangor, Maine, a modification of it is in use whereby the conductor is divided into sections, alternately connected to the positive and negative poles of two generators, coupled together as in the "three-wire system" of electric lighting (page 119), their middle poles being joined to the earth —that is to say, the rails. It enables two cars to be run on the same line at once, and with a considerable saving of copper.

To make the car independent of the conductor L for a short time, as in switching, a battery of accumulators B may be added and charged from the conductor, so that when the motor is disconnected from the conductor, the discharge from the accumulator may still work it and drive the wheels.

Attempts have been made to run tramcars with the electricity supplied by accumulators alone, but the system is not economical owing to the dead weight of the cells, and the periodical trouble of recharging them at the generating station.

On heavy railroads worked by electricity the overhead conductor is replaced by a third rail along the middle of the track, and insulated from the ground In another system the middle conductor is buried underground, and the current is tapped at intervals by the motor connecting with it for a moment by means of spring contacts as the car travels In each case, however, the outer rails serve as the return conductors

Another system puts one or both the conductors in a conduit underground, the trolley pole entering through a narrow slot similar to that used on cable roads

The first electric carriages for ordinary roads were constructed in 1889 by Mr. Magnus Volk of Brighton. Figure 78 represents one of these made for the Sultan of Turkey, and propelled by a one- horse-power Immisch electric motor, geared to one of the hind wheels by means of a chain. The current for the motor was supplied by thirty "EPS" accumulators stowed in the body of the vehicle, and of sufficient power to give a speed of ten miles an hour. The driver steers with a hand lever as shown, and controls the speed by a switch in front of him.

Vans, bath chairs, and tricycles are also driven by electric motors, but the weight of the battery is a drawback to their use.

In or about the year 1839, Jacobi sailed an electric boat on the Neva, with the help of an electromagnetic engine of one horse- power, fed by the current from a battery of Grove cells, and in 1882 a screw launch, carrying several passengers, and propelled by an electric motor of three horse-power, worked by forty-five accumulators, was tried on the Thames. Being silent and smokeless in its action, the electric boat soon came into favour, and there is now quite a flotilla on the river, with power stations for charging the accumulators at various points along the banks.

Figure 79 illustrates the interior of a handsome electric launch, the Lady Cooper, built for the "E P S," or Electric Power Storage Company. An electric motor in the after part of the hull is coupled directly to the shaft of the screw propeller, and fed by "E P S" accumulators in teak boxes lodged under the deck amidships. The screw is controlled by a switch, and the rudder by an ordinary helm. The cabin is seven feet long, and lighted by electric lamps. Alarm signals are given by an electric gong, and a search-light can be brought into operation whenever it is desirable. The speed attained by the Lady Cooper is from ten to fifteen knots.

M. Goubet, a Frenchman, has constructed a submarine boat for discharging torpedoes and exploring the sea bottom, which is propelled by a screw and an electric motor fed by accumulators. It can travel entirely under water, below the agitation of the waves, where sea-sickness is impossible, and the inventor hopes that vessels of the kind will yet carry passengers across the Channel.

The screw propeller of the Edison and Sim's torpedo is also driven by an electric motor. In this case the current is conveyed from the ship or fort which discharges the torpedo by an insulated conductor running off a reel carried by the torpedo, the "earth" or return half of the circuit being the sea-water.

All sorts of machinery are now worked by the electric motor—for instance, cranes, elevators, capstans, rivetters, lathes, pumps, chaff-cutters, and saws. Of domestic appliances, figure 80 shows an air propeller or ventilation fan, where F is a screw-like fan attached to the spindle of the motor M, and revolving with its armature. Figure 81 represents a Trouve motor working a sewing- machine, where N is the motor which gears with P the driving axle of the machine. Figure 82 represents a fine drill actuated by a Griscom motor. The motor M is suspended from a bracket A B C by the tackle D E, and transmits the rotation of its armature by a flexible shaft S T to the terminal drill O, which can be applied at any point, and is useful in boring teeth.

Now that electricity is manufactured and distributed in towns and villages for the electric light, it is more and more employed for driving the lighter machinery. Steam, however, is more economical on a large scale, and still continues to be used in great factories for the heavier machinery. Nevertheless a day is coming when coal, instead of being carried by rail to distant works and cities, will be burned at the pit mouth, and its heat transformed by means of engines and dynamos into electricity for distribution to the surrounding country. I have shown elsewhere that peat can be utilised in a similar manner, and how the great Bog of Allen is virtually a neglected gold field in the heart of Ireland. [Footnote: The Nineteenth Century for December 1894.] The sunshine of deserts, and perhaps the electricity of the atmosphere, but at all events the power of winds, waves, and waterfalls are also destined to whirl the dynamo, and yield us light, heat, or motion. Much has already been done in this direction. In 1891 the power of turbines driven by the Falls of Neckar at Lauffen was transformed into electricity, and transmitted by a small wire to the Electrical Exhibition of Frankfort-on-the-Main, 117 miles away. The city of Rome is now lighted from the Falls of Tivoli, 16 miles distant. The finest cataract in Great Britain, the Falls of Foyers, in the Highlands, which persons of taste and culture wished to preserve for the nation, is being sacrificed to the spirit of trade, and deprived of its waters for the purpose of generating electricity to reduce aluminium from its ores.

The great scheme recently completed for utilizing the power of Niagara Falls by means of electricity is a triumph of human enterprise which outrivals some of the bold creations of Jules Verne.

When in 1678 the French missionaries La Salle and Hennepin discovered the stupendous cataract on the Niagara River between Lake Ontario and Lake Erie, the science of electricity was in its early infancy, and little more was known about the mysterious force which is performing miracles in our day than its manifestation on rubbed amber, sealing-wax, glass, and other bodies. Nearly a hundred years had still to pass ere Franklin should demonstrate the identity of the electric fire with lightning, and nearly another hundred before Faraday should reveal a mode of generating it from mechanical power. Assuredly, neither La Salle nor his contemporaries ever dreamed of a time when the water-power of the Falls would be distributed by means of electricity to produce light or heat and serve all manner of industries in the surrounding district. The awestruck Iroquois Indians had named the cataract "Oniagahra," or Thunder of the Waters, and believed it the dwelling-place of the Spirit of Thunder. This poetical name is none the less appropriate now that the modern electrician is preparing to draw his lightnings from its waters and compel the genius loci to become his willing bondsman.

The Falls of Niagara are situated about twenty-one miles from Lake Erie, and fourteen miles from Lake Ontario. At this point the Niagara River, nearly a mile broad, flowing between level banks, and parted by several islands, is suddenly shot over a precipice 170 feet high, and making a sharp bend to the north, pursues its course through a narrow gorge towards Lake Ontario. The Falls are divided at the brink by Goat Island, whose primeval woods are still thriving in their spray. The Horseshoe Fall on the Canadian side is 812 yards, and the American Falls on the south side are 325 yards wide. For a considerable distance both above and below the Falls the river is turbulent with rapids.

The water-power of the cataract has been employed from olden times. The French fur-traders placed a mill beside the upper rapids, and the early British settlers built another to saw the timber used in their stockades. By-and-by, the Stedman and Porter mills were established below the Falls; and subsequently, others which derived their water-supply from the lower rapids by means of raceways or leads. Eventually, an open hydraulic canal, three- fourths of a mile long, was cut across the elbow of land on the American side, through the town of Niagara Falls, between the rapids above and the verge of the chasm below the Falls, where, since 1874, a cluster of factories has arisen, which discharge their spent water over the cliff in a series of cascades almost rivalling Niagara itself. This canal, which only taps a mere drop from the ocean of power that is running to waste, has been utilised to the full; and the decrease of water-privileges in the New England States, owing to the clearing of the forests and settlement of the country, together with the growth of the electrical industries, have led to a further demand on the resources of Niagara.

With the example of Minneapolis, which draws the power for its many mills from the Falls of St. Anthony, in the Mississippi River, before them, a group of far-seeing and enterprising citizens of Niagara Falls resolved to satisfy this requirement by the foundation of an industrial city in the neighbourhood of the Falls. They perceived that a better site could nowhere be found on the American Continent. Apart from its healthy air and attractive scenery, Niagara is a kind of half-way house between the East and West, the consuming and the producing States. By the Erie Canal at Tonawanda it commands the great waterway of the Lakes and the St. Lawrence. A system of trunk railways from different parts of the States and Canada are focussed there, and cross the river by the Cantilever and Suspension bridges below the Falls. The New York Central and Hudson River, the Lehigh Valley, the Buffalo, Rochester, and Pittsburgh, the Michigan Central, and the Grand Trunk of Canada, are some of these lines. Draining as it does the great lakes of the interior, which have a total area of 92,000 square miles, with an aggregate basin of 290,000 square miles, the volume of water in the Niagara River passing over the cataract every second is something like 300,000 cubic feet; and this, with a fall of 276 feet from the head of the upper rapids to the whirlpool rapids below, is equivalent to about nine million, or, allowing for waste in the turbines, say, seven million horse- power. Moreover, the great lakes discharging—into each other form a chain of immense reservoirs, and the level of the river being little affected by flood or drought, the supply of pure water is practically constant all the year round. Mr. R. C. Reid has shown that a rainfall of three inches in twenty-four hours over the basin of Lake Superior would take ninety days to run off into Lake Huron, which, with Lake Michigan, would take as long to overflow into Lake Erie; and, therefore, six months would elapse before the full effect of the flood was expended at the Falls.

The first outcome of the movement was the Niagara River Hydraulic Power and Sewer Company, incorporated in 1886, and succeeded by the Niagara Falls Power Company. The old plan of utilising the water by means of an open canal was unsuited to the circumstances, and the company adopted that of the late Mr. Thomas Evershed, divisional engineer of the New York State Canals. Like the other, it consists in tapping the river above the Falls, and using the pressure of the water to drive the number of turbines, then restoring the water to the river below the Falls; but instead of a surface canal, the tail-race is a hydraulic tunnel or underground conduit. To this end some fifteen hundred acres of spare land, having a frontage just above the upper rapids, was quietly secured at the low price of three hundred dollars an acre; and we believe its rise in value owing to the progress of the works is such that a yearly rental of two hundred dollars an acre can even now be got for it. This land has been laid out as an industrial city, with a residential quarter for the operatives, wharves along the river, and sidings or short lines to connect with the trunk railways. In carrying out their purpose the company has budded and branched into other companies—one for the purchase of the land; another for making the railways; and a third, the Cataract Construction Company, which is charged with the carrying out of the engineering works, for the utilisation of the water-power, and is therefore the most important of all. A subsidiary company has also been formed to transmit by electricity a portion of the available power to the city of Buffalo, at the head of the Niagara River, on Lake Erie, some twenty miles distant. All these affiliated bodies are, however, under the directorate of the Cataract Construction Company; and amongst those who have taken the most active part in the work we may mention the president, Mr. E. D. Adams; Professor Coleman Sellers, the consulting engineer; and Professor George Forbes, F. R. S., the consulting electrical engineer, a son of the late Principal Forbes of Edinburgh.

In securing the necessary right of way for the hydraulic tunnel or in the acquisit-om of land, the Company has shown consummate tact. A few proprietors declined to accept its terms, and the Company selected a parallel route. Having obtained the right of way for the latter, it informed the refractory owners on the first line of their success, and intimated that the Company could now dispense with that. On this the sticklers professed their willingness to accept the original terms, and the bargain was concluded, thus leaving the Company in possession of the rights of way for two tunnels, both of which they propose to utilise.

The liberal policy of the directors is deserving of the highest commendation. They have risen above mere "chauvinism," and instead of narrowly confining the work to American engineers, they have availed themselves of the best scientific counsel which the entire world could afford. The great question as to the best means of distributing and applying the power at their command had to be settled; and in 1890, after Mr. Adams and Dr. Sellers had made a visit of inspection to Europe, an International Commission was appointed to consider the various methods submitted to them, and award prizes to the successful competitors. Lord Kelvin (then Sir William Thomson) was the president, and Professor W. C. Unwin, the well-known expert in hydraulic engineering, the secretary, while other members were Professor Mascart of the Institute, a leading French electrician; Colonel Turretini of Geneva, and Dr. Sellers. A large number of schemes were sent in, and many distinguished engineers gave evidence before the Commission. The relative merits of compressed air and electricity as a means of distributing the power were discussed, and on the whole the balance of opinion was in favour of electricity. Prizes of two hundred and two hundred and fifty pounds were awarded to a number of firms who had submitted plans, but none of these were taken up by the

Company. The impulse turbines of Messrs. Faesch & Piccard, of Geneva, who gained a prize of two hundred and fifty pounds, have, however, been adopted since. It is another proof of the determination of the Company to procure the best information on the subject, regardless of cost, that Professor Forbes had carte blanche to go to any part of the world and make a report on any system of electrical distribution which he might think fit.

With the selection of electricity another question arose as to the expediency of employing continuous or alternating currents. At that time continuous currents were chiefly in vogue, and it speaks well for the sagacity and prescience of Professor Forbes that he boldly advocated the adoption of alternating currents, more especially for the transmission of power to Buffalo. His proposals encountered strong opposition, even in the highest quarters; but since then, partly owing to the striking success of the Lauffen to Frankfort experiment in transmitting power by alternating currents over a bare wire on poles a distance of more than a hundred miles, the directors and engineers have come round to his view of the matter, and alternating currents have been employed, at all events for the Buffalo line, and also for the chief supply of the industrial city. Continuous currents, flowing always in the same direction, like the current of a battery, can, it is true, be stored in accumulators, but they cannot be converted to higher or lower pressure in a transformer. Alternating currents, on the other hand, which see-saw in direction many times a second, cannot be stored in accumulators, but they can be sent at high pressure along a very fine wire, and then converted to higher or lower pressures where they are wanted, and even to continuous currents. Each kind, therefore, has its peculiar advantages, and both will be employed to some extent.

With regard to the engineering works, the hydraulic tunnel starts from the bank of the river where it is navigable, at a point a mile and a half above the Falls, and after keeping by the shore, it cuts across the bend beneath the city of Niagara Falls, and terminates below the Suspension Bridge under the Falls at the level of the water. It is 6700 yards long, and of a horseshoe section, 19 feet wide by 21 feet high. It has been cut 160 feet below the surface through the limestone and shale, but is arched with brick, having rubble above, and at the outfall is lined on the invert or under side with iron. The gradient is 36 feet in the mile, and the total fall is 205 feet, of which 140 feet are available for use. The capacity of the tunnel is 100,000 horse- power. In the lands of the company it is 400 feet from the margin of the river, to which it is connected by a canal, which is over 1500 feet long, 500 feet wide at the mouth, and 12 feet deep.

Out of this canal, head-races fitted with sluices conduct the water to a number of wheel-pits 160 feet deep, which have been dug near the edge of the canal, and communicate below with the tunnel. At the bottom of each wheel-pit a 5000 horse-power Girard double turbine is mounted on a vertical shaft, which drives a propeller shaft rising to the surface of the ground; a dynamo of 5000 horse-power is fixed on the top of this shaft, and so driven by it. The upward pressure of the water is ingeniously contrived to relieve the foundation of the weight of the turbine shaft and dynamo. Twenty of these turbines, which are made by the I. P. Morris Company of Philadelphia, from the designs of Messrs. Faesch and Piccard, will be required to utilize the full capacity of the tunnel.

The company possesses a strip of land extending two miles along the shore; and in excavating the tunnel a coffer-dam was made with the extracted rock, to keep the river from flooding the works. This dam now forms part of a system by which a tract of land has been reclaimed from the river. Part of it has already been acquired by the Niagara Paper Pulp Company, which is building gigantic factories, and will employ the tailrace or tunnel of the Cataract Construction Company. Wharfs for the use of ships and canal boats will also be constructed on this frontage. By land and water the raw materials of the West will be conveyed to the industrial town which is now coming into existence; grain from the prairies of Illinois and Dakota; timber from the forests of Michigan and Wisconsin; coal and copper from the mines of Lake Superior; and what not. It is expected that one industry having a seat there will attract others. Thus, the pulp mills will bring the makers of paper wheels and barrels; the smelting of iron will draw foundries and engine works; the electrical refining of copper will lead to the establishment of wire-works, cable factories, dynamo shops, and so on. Aluminum, too, promises to create an important industry in the future. In the meantime, the Cataract Construction Company is about to start an electrical factory of its own, which will give employment to a large number of men. It has also undertaken the water supply of the adjacent city of Niagara Falls. The Cataract Electric Company of Buffalo has obtained the exclusive right to use the electricity transmitted to that city, and the line will be run in a subway. This underground line will be more expensive to make than an overhead line, but it will not require to be renewed every eight to fifteen years, and it will not be liable to interruption from the heavy gales that sweep across the lakes, or the weight of frozen sleet: moreover, it will be more easily inspected, and quite safe for the public. We should also add that, in addition to the contemplated duplicate tunnel of 100,000 horse-power, the Cataract Construction Company owns a concession for utilising 250,000 horse-power from the Horseshoe Falls on the Canadian side in the same manner. It has thus a virtual monopoly of the available water-power of Niagara, and the promoters have not the least doubt that the enterprise will be a great financial success. Already the Pittsburg Reduction Company have begun to use the electricity in reducing aluminum from the mineral known as bauxite, an oxide of the metal, by means of the electric furnace.

Another portion of the power is to be used to produce carbide of calcium for the manufacture of acetylene gas. At a recent electrical exhibition held in New York city a model of the Niagara plant was operated by an electric current brought from Niagara, 450 miles distant; and a collection of telephones were so connected that the spectator could hear the roar of the real cataract.

Thanks to the foresight of New York State and Canada, the scenery of the Falls has been preserved by the institution of public parks, and the works in question will do nothing to spoil it, especially as they will be free from smoke. Mr. Bogarts, State Engineer of New York, estimates that the water drawn from the river will only lower the mean depth of the Falls about two inches, and will therefore make no appreciable difference in the view. Altogether, the enterprise is something new in the history of the world. It is not only the grandest application of electrical power, but one of the most remarkable feats in an age when romance has become science, and science has become romance.

CHAPTER IX.

MINOR USES OF ELECTRICITY.

The electric "trembling bell," now in common use, was first invented by John Mirand in 1850. Figure 83 shows the scheme of the circuit, where

B is a small battery, say two or three "dry" or Leclanche cells, joined by insulated wire to P, a press-button or contact key, and G an electromagnetic gong or bell. On pressing the button P, a spring contact is made, and the current flowing through the circuit strikes the bell. The action of the contact key will be understood from figure 84, where P is the press-button removed to show the underlying mechanism, which is merely a metal spring A over a metal plate B. The spring is connected by wire to a pole of the battery, and the plate to a terminal or binding screw of the bell, or vice versa. When the button P is pressed by the finger the spring is forced against the plate, the circuit is made, and the bell rings. On releasing the button it springs back, the circuit is broken, and the bell stops.

Figure 85 shows the inner mechanism of the bell, which consists of a double-poled electromagnet M, having a soft iron armature A hinged on a straight spring or tongue S, with one end fixed, and the other resting against a screw contact T. The hammer H projects from the armature beside the edge of the gong E.

In passing through the instrument the current proceeds from one terminal, say that on the right, by the wire W to the screw contact T, and thence by the spring S through the bobbins of the electromagnet to the other terminal. The electromagnet attracts the armature A, and the hammer H strikes the gong; but in the act the spring S is drawn from the contact T, and the circuit is broken. Consequently the electromagnet, no longer excited, lets the armature go, and the spring leaps back against the contact T, withdrawing the hammer from the gong. But the instrument is now as it was at first, the current again flows, and the hammer strikes the gong, only to fly back a second time. In this way, as long as the button is pressed by the operator, the hammer will continue to tap the bell and give a ringing sound. Press-buttons are of various patterns, and either affixed to the wall or inserted in the handle of an ordinary bell-pull, as shown in figure 86.

The ordinary electric bell actuated by a battery is liable to get out of order owing to the battery spending its force, or to the contacts becoming dirty. Magnetoelectric bells have, therefore, been introduced of late years. With these no battery or interrupting contacts are required, since the bell-pull or press-button is made in the form of a small dynamo which generates the current when it is pulled or pushed. Figure 87 illustrates a form of this apparatus, where M P is the bell-pull and B the bell, these being connected by a double wire W, to convey the current. The bell-pull consists of a horseshoe magnet M, having a bobbin of insulated wire between its poles, and mounted on a spindle. When the key P is turned round by the hand, the bobbin moves in the magnetic field between the poles of the magnet, and the current thus generated circulates in the wires W, and passing through an electromagnet under the bell, attracts its armature, and strikes the hammer on the bell. Of course the bell may be placed at any distance from the generator. In other types the current is generated and the bell rung by the act of pulling, as in a common house-bell.

Electric bells in large houses and hotels are usually fitted up with indicators, as shown in figure 88, which tell the room from which the call proceeds. They are serviceable as instantaneous signals, annunciators, and alarms in many different ways. An outbreak of fire can be announced by causing the undue rise of temperature to melt a piece of tallow or fusible metal, and thus release a weight, which tails on a press-button, and closes the circuit of an electric bell. Or, the rising temperature may expand the mercury in a tube like that of a thermometer until it connects two platinum wires fused through the glass and in circuit with a bell. Some employ a curving bi-metallic spring to make the necessary contact. The spring is made by soldering strips of brass and iron back to back, and as these metals expand unequally when heated, the spring is deformed, and touches the contact which is connected in the circuit, thus permitting the current to ring the bell. A still better device, however, is a small box containing a thin metallic diaphragm, which expands with the heat, and sagging in the centre, touches a contact screw, thus completing the circuit, and allowing the current to pass.

These automatic or self-acting fire-alarms can, of course, be connected in the circuit of the ordinary street fire-alarms, which are usually worked by pulling a handle to make the necessary contact.

From what has been said, it will be easy to understand how the stealthy entrance of burglars into a house can be announced by an electric bell or warning lamp. If press-buttons or contact-keys are placed on the sashes of the windows, the posts of the door, or the treads of the stair, so that when the window or door is opened, or the tread bends under the footstep, an electric circuit is closed, the alarm will be given. Of course, the connections need only be arranged when the device is wanted. Shops and offices can be guarded by making the current show a red light from a lamp hung in front of the premises, so that the night watchman can see it on his beat. This can readily be done by adjusting an electromagnet to drop a screen of red glass before the flame of the lamp. Safes and showcases forcibly opened can be made to signal the fact, and recently in the United States a thief was photographed by a flashlight kindled in this way, and afterwards captured through the likeness.

The level of water in cisterns and reservoirs, can be told in a similar manner by causing a float to rise with the water and make the required contact. The degree of frost in a conservatory can also be announced by means of the mercury "thermostat," already described, or some equivalent device. There are, indeed, many actual or possible applications of a similar kind.

The Massey log is an instrument for telling the speed of a ship by the revolutions of a "fly" as it is towed through the water, and by making the fly complete a circuit as it revolves the number of turns a second can be struck by a bell on board. In one form of the "electric log," the current is generated by the chemical action of zinc and copper plates attached to the log, and immersed in the sea water, and in others provided by a battery on the ship.

Captain M'Evoy has invented an alarm for torpedoes and torpedo boats, which is a veritable watchdog of the sea. It consists of an iron bell-jar inverted in the water, and moored at a depth below the agitation of the waves. In the upper part of the jar, where the pressure of the air keeps back the water, there is a delicate needle contact in circuit with a battery and an electric bell or lamp, as the case may be, on the shore. Waves of sound passing through the water from the screw propeller of the torpedo, or, indeed, any ship, make and break the sensitive contact, and ring the bell or light the lamp. The apparatus is intended to alarm a fleet lying at anchor or a port in time of war.

Electricity has also been employed to register the movements of weathercocks and anemometers. A few years ago it was applied successfully to telegraph the course marked by a steering compass to the navigating officer on the bridge. This was done without impeding the motion of the compass card by causing an electric spark to jump from a light pointer on the card to a series of metal plates round the bowl of the compass, and actuate an electric alarm.

The "Domestic Telegraph," an American device, is a little dial apparatus by which a citizen can signal for a policeman, doctor, messenger, or carriage, as well as a fire engine, by the simple act of setting a hand on the dial.

Alexander Bain was the first to drive a clock with electricity instead of weights, by employing a pendulum having an iron bob, which was attracted to one side and the other by an electromagnet, but as its rate depends on the constancy of the current, which is not easy to maintain, the invention has not come into general use. The "butterfly clock" of Lemoine, which we illustrate in figure 89, is an improved type, in which the bob of soft iron P swings to and fro over the poles of a double electro magnet M in circuit with a battery and contact key. When the rate is too slow the key is closed, and a current passing through the electromagnet pulls on the pendulum, thus correcting the clock. This is done by the ingenious device of Hipp, shown in figure 90, where M is the electromagnet, P the iron bob, from which projects a wire bearing a light vane B of mica in the shape of a butterfly. As the bob swings the wire drags over the hump of the metal spring S, and when the bob is going too slowly the wire thrusts the spring into contact with another spring T below, thus closing the circuit, and sending a current through the magnet M, which attracts the bob and gives a fillip to the pendulum.

Local clocks controlled from a standard clock by electricity have been more successful in practice, and are employed in several towns—for example, Glasgow. Behind local dials are electromagnets which, by means of an armature working a frame and ratchet wheel, move the hands forward every minute or half-minute as the current is sent from the standard clock.

The electrical chronograph is an instrument for measuring minute intervals of time by means of a stylus tracing a line on a band of travelling paper or a revolving barrel of smoked glass. The current, by exciting an electromagnet, jerks the stylus, and the interval between two jerks is found from the length of the trace between them and the speed of the paper or smoked surface. Retarded clocks are sometimes employed as electric meters for registering the consumption of electricity. In these the current to be measured flows through a coil beneath the bob of the pendulum, which is a magnet, and thus affects the rate. In other meters the current passes through a species of galvanometer called an ampere meter, and controls a clockwork counter. In a third kind of meter the chemical effect of the current is brought into play— that of Edison, for example, decomposing sulphate of copper, or more commonly of zinc.

The electric light is now used for signalling and advertising by night in a variety of ways. Incandescent lamps inside a translucent balloon, and their light controlled by a current key, as in a telegraph circuit, so as to give long and short flashes, according to the Morse code, are employed in the army. Signals at sea are also made by a set of red and white glow-lamps, which are combined according to the code in use. The powerful arc lamp is extremely useful as a "search light," especially on men of war and fortifications, and it has also been tried in signalling by projecting the beam on the clouds by way of a screen, and eclipsing it according to a given code.

In 1879, Professor Graham Bell, the inventor of the speaking telephone, and Mr Summer Tamter, brought out an ingenious apparatus called the photophone, by which music and speech were sent along a beam of light for several hundred yards. The action of the photophone is based on the peculiar fact observed in 1873 by Mr J E Mayhew, that the electrical resistance of crystalline selenium diminishes when a ray of light falls upon it. Figure 91 shows how Bell and Tamter utilised this property in the telephone. A beam of sun or electric light, concentrated by a lens L, is reflected by a thin mirror M, and after traversing another lens L, travels to the parabolic reflector R, in the focus of which there is a selenium resistance in circuit with a battery S and two telephones T T'. Now, when a person speaks into the tube at the back of the mirror M, the light is caused to vibrate with the sounds, and a wavering beam falls on the selenium, changing its resistance to the current. The strength of the current is thus varied with the sonorous waves, and the words spoken by the transmitter are heard in the telephones by the receiver. The photophone is, however, more of a scientific toy than a practical instrument.

Becquerel, the French chemist, found that two plates of silver freshly coated with silver from a solution of chloride of silver and plunged into water, form a voltaic cell which is sensitive to light. This can be seen by connecting the plates through a galvanometer, and allowing a ray of light to fall upon them. Other combinations of the kind have been discovered, and Professor Minchin, the Irish physicist, has used one of these cells to measure the intensity of starlight.

The "induction balance" of Professor Hughes is founded on the well-known fact that a current passing in one wire can induce a sympathetic current in a neighbouring wire. The arrangement will be understood from figure 92, where P and

P1 are two similar coils or bobbins of thick wire in circuit with a battery B and a microphone M, while S and S1 are two similar coils or bobbins of fine wire in circuit with a telephone T. It need hardly be said that when the microphone M is disturbed by a sound, the current in the primary coils P P1 will induce a corresponding current in the secondary coils S S1; but the coils S S1 are so wound that the induction of P on S neutralises the induction of P1 on S1; and no current passes in the secondary circuit, hence no sound is heard in the telephone. When, however, this balance of induction is upset by bringing a piece of metal—say, a coin—near one or other of the coils S S1, a sound will be heard in the telephone.

The induction balance has been used as a "Sonometer" for measuring the sense of hearing, and also for telling base coins. The writer devised a form of it for "divining" the presence of gold and metallic ores which has been applied by Captain M'Evoy in his "submarine detector" for exploring the sea bottom for lost anchors and sunken treasure. When President Garfield was shot, the position of the bullet was ascertained by a similar arrangement.

The microphone as a means of magnifying feeble sounds has been employed for localising the leaks in water pipes and in medical examinations. Some years ago it saved a Russian lady from premature burial by rendering the faint beating of her heart audible.

Edison's electric pen is useful in copying letters. It works by puncturing a row of minute holes along the lines of the writing, and thus producing a stencil plate, which, when placed over a clean sheet of paper and brushed with ink, gives a duplicate of the writing by the ink penetrating the holes to the paper below. It is illustrated in figure 93, where P is the pen, consisting of a hollow stem in which a fine needle actuated by the armature of a small electromagnet plies rapidly up and down and pierces the paper. The current is derived from a small battery B, and an inking roller like that used in printing serves to apply the ink.

In 1878 Mr. Edison announced his invention of a machine for the storage and reproduction of speech, and the announcement was received with a good deal of incredulity, notwithstanding the partial success of Faber and others in devising mechanical articulators. The simplicity of Edison's invention when it was seen and heard elicited much admiration, and although his first instrument was obviously imperfect, it was nevertheless regarded as the germ of something better. If the words spoken into the instrument were heard in the first place, the likeness of the reproduction was found to be unmistakable. Indeed, so faithful was the replica, that a member of the Academy of Sciences, Paris, stoutly maintained that it was due to ventriloquism or some other trickery. It was evident, however, that before the phonograph could become a practical instrument, further improvements in the nicety of its articulation were required. The introduction of the electric light diverted Mr. Edison from the task of improving it, although he does not seem to have lost faith in his pet invention. During the next ten years he accumulated a large fortune, and was the principal means of introducing both electric light and power to the world at large. This done, however, he returned to his earlier love, and has at length succeeded in perfecting it so as to redeem his past promises and fulfill his hopes regarding it.

The old instrument consisted, as is well known, of a vibrating tympan or drum, from the centre of which projected a steel point or stylus, in such a manner that on speaking to the tympan its vibrations would urge the stylus to dig into a sheet of tinfoil moving past its point. The foil was supported on a grooved barrel, so that the hollow of the groove behind it permitted the foil to give under the point of the stylus, and take a corrugated or wavy surface corresponding to the vibrations of the speech. Thus recorded on a yielding but somewhat stiff material, these undulations could be preserved, and at a future time made to deflect the point of a similar stylus, and set a corresponding diaphragm or tympan into vibration, so as to give out the original sounds, or an imitation of them.

Tinfoil, however, is not a very satisfactory material on which to receive the vibrations in the first place. It does not precisely respond to the movements of the marking stylus in taking the impression, and does not guide the receiving stylus sufficiently well in reproducing sounds. Mr. Edison has therefore adopted wax in preference to it; and instead of tinfoil spread on a grooved support, he now employs a cylinder of wax to take the print of the vibrations. Moreover, he no longer uses the same kind of diaphragm to print and receive the sounds, but employs a more delicate one for receiving them. The marking cylinder is now kept in motion by an electric motor, instead of by hand-turning, as in the earlier instrument.

The new phonograph, which we illustrate in figure 94, is about the size of an ordinary sewing machine, and is of exquisite workmanship, the performance depending to a great extent on the perfection and fitness of the mechanism. It consists of a horizontal spindle S, carrying at one end the wax cylinder C, on which the sonorous vibrations are to be imprinted. Over the cylinder is supported a diaphragm or tympan T, provided with a conical mouthpiece M for speaking into. Under the tympan there is a delicate needle or stylus, with its point projecting from the centre of the tympan downwards to the surface of the wax cylinder, so that when a person speaks into the mouthpiece, the voice vibrates the tympan and drives the point of the stylus down into the wax, making an imprint more or less deep in accordance with the vibrations of the voice. The cylinder is kept revolving in a spiral path, at a uniform speed, by means of an electric motor E, fitted with a sensitive regulator and situated at the base of the machine. The result is that a delicate and ridgy trace is cut in the surface of wax along a spiral line. This is the sound record, and by substituting a finer tympan for the one used in producing it, the ridges and inequalities of the trace can be made to agitate a light stylus resting on them, and cause it to set the delicate tympan into vibrations corresponding very accurately to those of the original sounds. The tympan employed for receiving is made of gold-beater's skin, having a stud at its centre and a springy stylus of steel wire. The sounds emitted by this device are almost a whisper as compared to the original ones, but they are faithful in articulation, which is the main object, and they are conveyed to the ear by means of flexible hearing-tubes.

These tympans are interchangeable at will, and the arm which carries them is also provided with a turning tool for smoothing the wax cylinder prior to its receiving the print. The cylinders are made of different sizes, from 1 to 8 inches long and 4 inches in diameter. The former has a storage capacity of 200 words. The next in size has twice that, or 400 words, and so on. Mr. Edison states that four of the large 8-inch cylinders can record all "Nicholas Nickleby," which could therefore be automatically read to a private invalid or to a number of patients in a hospital simultaneously, by means of a bunch of hearing-tubes. The cylinders can be readily posted like letters, and made to deliver their contents viva voce in a duplicate phonograph, every tone and expression of the writer being rendered with more or less fidelity. The phonograph has proved serviceable in recording the languages and dialects of vanishing races, as well as in teaching pronunciation.

The dimensions, form, and consequent appearance of the present commercial American phonograph are quite different from that above described, but the underlying principles and operations are identical.

A device for lighting gas by the electric spark is shown in figure 95, where A is a flat vulcanite box, containing the apparatus which generates the electricity, and a stem or pointer L, which applies the spark to the gas jet. The generator consists of a small "influence" machine, which is started by pressing the thumb- key C on the side of the box. The rotation of a disc inside the box produces a supply of static electricity, which passes in a stream of sparks between two contact-points in the open end of the stem D. The latter is tubular, and contains a wire insulated from the metal of the tube, and forming with the tube the circuit for the electric discharge. The handle enables the contrivance to be readily applied. The apparatus is one of the few successful practical applications of static electricity.

Other electric gas-lighters consist of metal points placed on the burner, so that the electric spark from a small induction coil or dynamo kindles the jet.

A platinum wire made white-hot by the passage of a current is sometimes used to light lamps, as shown in figure 96, where W is a small spiral of platinum connected in circuit with a generator by the terminals T T. When the lamp L is pressed against the button B the wire glows and lights it.

Explosives, such as gunpowder and guncotton, are also ignited by the electric spark from an induction coil or the incandescence of a wire. Figure 97 shows the interior of an ordinary electric fuse for blasting or exploding underground mines. It consists of a box of wood or metal primed with gunpowder or other explosive, and a platinum wire P soldered to a pair of stout copper wires W, insulated with gutta-percha. When the current is sent along these wires, the platinum glows and ignites the explosive. Detonating fuses are primed with fulminate of mercury.

Springs for watches and other purposes are tempered by heating them with the current and quenching them in a bath of oil.

Electrical cautery is performed with an incandescent platinum wire in lieu of the knife, especially for such operations as the removal of the tongue or a tumour.

It was known to the ancients that a fish called a torpedo existed in the Mediterranean which was capable of administering a shock to persons and benumbing them. The torpedo, or "electric ray," is found in the Atlantic as well as the Mediterranean, and is allied to the skate. It has an electric organ composed of 800 or 1000 polygonal cells in its head, and the discharge, which appears to be a vibratory current, passes from the back or positive pole to the belly or negative pole through the water. The gymotus, or Surinam eel, which attains a length of five or six feet, has an electric organ from head to tail, and can give a shock sufficient to kill a man. Humboldt has left a vivid picture of the frantic struggles of wild horses driven by the Indians of Venezuela into the ponds of the savannahs infested by these eels, in order to make them discharge their thunderbolts and be readily caught.

Other fishes—the silurus, malapterurus, and so on—are likewise endowed with electric batteries for stunning and capturing their prey. The action of the organs is still a mystery, as, indeed, is the whole subject of animal electricity. Nobili and Matteucci discovered that feeble currents are generated by the excitation of the nerves and the contraction of the muscles in the human subject.

Electricity promises to become a valuable remedy, and currents— continuous, intermittent, or alternating—are applied to the body in nervous and muscular affections with good effect; but this should only be done under medical advice, and with proper apparatus.

In many cases of severe electric shock or lightning stroke, death is merely apparent, and the person may be brought back to life by the method of artificial respiration and rhythmic traction of the tongue, as applied to the victims of drowning or dead faint.

A good lightning conductor should not have a higher electrical resistance than 10 ohms from the point to the ground, including the "earth" contact. Exceptionally good conductors have only about 5 ohms. A high resistance in the rod is due either to a flaw in the conductor or a bad earth connection, and in such a case the rod may be a source of danger instead of security, since the discharge is apt to find its way through some part of the building to the ground, rather than entirely by the rod. It is, therefore, important to test lightning conductors from time to time, and the magneto-electric tester of Siemens, which we illustrate in figures 98 and 99, is very serviceable for the purpose, and requires no battery. The apparatus consists of a magneto-electric machine AT, which generates the testing current by turning a handle, and a Wheatstone bridge. The latter comprises a ring of German silver wire, forming two branches. A contact lever P moves over the ring, and is used as a battery key. A small galvanometer G shows the indications of the testing current. A brass sliding piece S puts the galvanometer needle in and out of action. There are also several connecting terminals, b b', l, &c., and a comparison resistance R (figure 98). A small key K is fixed to the terminal l (figure 99), and used to put the current on the lightning-rod, or take it off at will. A leather bag A at one side of the wooden case (figure 99) holds a double conductor leading wire, which is used for connecting the magneto-electric machine to the bridge. On turning the handle of M the current is generated, and on closing the key K it circulates from the terminals of the machine through the bridge and the lightning-rod joined with the latter. The needle of the galvanometer is deflected by it, until the resistance in the box R is adjusted to balance that in the rod. When this is so, the galvanometer needle remains at rest. In this way the resistance of the rod is told, and any change in it noted. In order to effect the test, it is necessary to have two earth plates, E1 and E2, one (El) that of the rod, and the other (E2) that for connecting to the testing apparatus by the terminal b1 (figure 99). The whole instrument only weighs about 9 lbs. In order to test the "earth" alone, a copper wire should be soldered to the rod at a convenient height above the ground, and terminal screws fitted to it, as shown at T (figure 99), so that instead of joining the whole rod in circuit with the apparatus, only that part from T downwards is connected. The Hon. R. Abercrombie has recently drawn attention to the fact that there are three types of thunderstorm in Great Britain. The first, or squall thunderstorms, are squalls associated with thunder and lightning. They form on the sides of primary cyclones. The second, or commonest thunderstorms, are associated with secondary cyclones, and are rarely accompanied by squalls The third, or line thunderstorms, take the form of narrow bands of rain and thunder—for example, 100 miles long by 5 to 10 miles broad. They cross the country rapidly, and nearly broadside on. These are usually preceded by a violent squall, like that which capsized the Eurydice.

The gloom of January, 1896, with its war and rumours of war, was, at all events, relieved by a single bright spot. Electricity has surprised the world with a new marvel, which confirms her title to be regarded as the most miraculous of all the sciences. Within the past twenty years she has given us the telephone of Bell, enabling London to speak with Paris, and Chicago with New York; the microphone of Hughes, which makes the tread of a fly sound like the "tramp of an elephant," as Lord Kelvin has said; the phonograph of Edison, in which we can hear again the voices of the dead; the electric light which glows without air and underwater, electric heat without fire, electric power without fuel, and a great deal more beside. To these triumphs we must now add a means of photographing unseen objects, such as the bony skeletons in the living body, and so revealing the invisible.

Whether it be that the press and general public are growing more enlightened in matters of science, or that Professor Rontgen's discovery appeals in a peculiar way to the popular imagination, it has certainly evoked a livelier and more sudden interest than either the telephone, microphone, or phonograph. I was present when Lord Kelvin first announced the invention of the telephone to a British audience, and showed the instrument itself, but the intelligence was received so apathetically that I suspect its importance was hardly realised. It fell to my own lot, a few years afterwards, to publish the first account of the phonograph in this country, and I remember that, between incredulity on the one hand, and perhaps lack of scientific interest on the other, a considerable time elapsed before the public at large were really impressed by the invention. Perhaps the uncanny and mysterious results of Rontgen's discovery, which seem to link it with the "black arts," have something to do with the quickness of its reception by all manner of people.

Like most, if not all, discoveries and inventions, it is the outcome of work already done by other men. In the early days of electricity it was found that when an electric spark from a frictional machine was sent through a glass bulb from which the air had been sucked by an air pump, a cloudy light filled the bulb, which was therefore called an "electric egg". Hittorf and others improved on this effect by employing the spark from an induction coil and large tubes, highly exhausted of air, or containing a rare infusion of other gases, such as hydrogen. By this means beautiful glows of various colours, resembling the tender hues of the tropical sky, or the fleeting tints of the aurora borealis, were produced, and have become familiar to us in the well-known Geissler tubes.

Crookes, the celebrated English chemist, went still further, and by exhausting the bulbs with an improved Sprengel air-pump, obtained an extremely high vacuum, which gave remarkable effects (page 120). The diffused glow or cloudy light of the tube now shrank into a single stream, which joined the sparking points inserted through the ends of the tube as with a luminous thread A magnet held near the tube bent the streamer from its course; and there was a dark space or gap in it near the negative point or cathode, from which proceeded invisible rays, having the property of impressing a photographic plate, and of rendering matter in general on which they impinged phosphorescent, and, in course of time, red-hot. Where they strike on the glass of the tube it is seen to glow with a green or bluish phosphorescence, and it will ultimately soften with heat.

These are the famous "cathode rays" of which we have recently heard so much. Apparently they cannot be produced except in a very high vacuum, where the pressure of the air is about 1-100th millionth of an atmosphere, or that which it is some 90 or 100 miles above the earth. Mr Crookes regards them as a stream of airy particles electrified by contact with the cathode or negative discharging point, and repelled from it in straight lines. The rarity of the air in the tube enables these particles to keep their line without being jostled by the other particles of air in the tube. A molecular bombardment from the cathode is, in his opinion, going on, and when the shots, that is to say, the molecules of air, strike the wall of the tube, or any other body within the tube, the shock gives rise to phosphorescence or fluorescence and to heat. This, in brief, is the celebrated hypothesis of "radiant matter," which has been supported in the United Kingdom by champions such as Lord Kelvin, Sir Gabriel Stokes, and Professor Fitzgerald, but questioned abroad by Goldstem, Jaumann, Wiedemann, Ebert, and others.

Lenard, a young Hungarian, pupil of the illustrious Heinrich Hertz, was the first to inflict a serious blow on the hypothesis, by showing that the cathode rays could exist outside the tube in air at ordinary pressure. Hertz had found that a thin foil of aluminium was penetrated by the rays, and Lenard made a tube having a "window" of aluminium, through which the rays darted into the open air. Their path could be traced by the bluish phosphorescence which they excited in the air, and he succeeded in getting them to penetrate a thin metal box and take a photograph inside it. But if the rays are a stream of radiant matter which can only exist in a high vacuum, how can they survive in air at ordinary pressure? Lenard's experiments certainly favour the hypothesis of their being waves in the luminiferous ether.

Professor Rontgen, of Wirzburg, profiting by Lenard's results, accidentally discovered that the rays coming from a Crookes tube, through the glass itself, could photograph the bones in the living hand, coins inside a purse, and other objects covered up or hid in the dark. Some bodies, such as flesh, paper, wood, ebonite, or vulcanised fibre, thin sheets of metal, and so on, are more or less transparent, and others, such as bones, carbon, quartz, thick plates of metal, are more or less opaque to the rays. The human hand, for example, consisting of flesh and bones, allows the rays to pass easily through the flesh, but not through the bones. Consequently, when it is interposed between the rays and a photographic plate, the skeleton inside is photographed on the plate. A lead pencil photographed in this way shows only the black lead, and a razor with a horn handle only the blade.

Thanks to the courtesy of Mr. A. A. Campbell Swinton, of the firm of Swinton & Stanton, the well-known electrical engineers, of Victoria Street, Westminster, a skilful experimentalist, who was the first to turn to the subject in England, I have witnessed the taking of these "shadow photographs," as they are called, somewhat erroneously, for "radiographs" or "cryptographs" would be a better word, and shall briefly describe his method. Rontgen employs an induction coil insulated in oil to excite the Crookes tube and yield the rays, but Mr. Swinton uses a "high frequency current," obtained from apparatus similar to that of Tesla, and shown in figure 100, namely, a high frequency induction coil insulated by means of oil and excited by the continuous discharge of twelve half-gallon Leyden jars charged by an alternating current at a pressure of 20,000 volts produced by an ordinary large induction coil sparking across its high pressure terminals.

A vacuum bulb connected between the discharge terminals of the high frequency coil, as shown in figure 101, was illuminated with a pink glow, which streamed from the negative to the positive pole—that is to say, the cathode to the anode, and the glass became luminous with bluish phosphorescence and greenish fluorescence. Immediately under the bulb was placed my naked hand resting on a photographic slide containing a sensitive bromide plate covered with a plate of vulcanised fibre. An exposure of five or ten minutes is sufficient to give a good picture of the bones, as will be seen from the frontispiece.

The term "shadow" photograph requires a word of explanation. The bones do not appear as flat shadows, but rounded like solid bodies, as though the active rays passed through their substance. According to Rontgen, these "x" rays, as he calls them, are not true cathode rays, partly because they are not deflected by a magnet, but cathode rays transformed by the glass of the tube; and they are probably not ultra-violet rays, because they are not refracted by water or reflected from surfaces. He thinks they are the missing "longitudinal" rays of light whose existence has been conjectured by Lord Kelvin and others—that is to say, waves in which the ether sways to and fro along the direction of the ray, as in the case of sound vibrations, and not from side to side across it as in ordinary light.

Be this as it may, his discovery has opened up a new field of research and invention. It has been found that the immediate source of the rays is the fluorescence and phosphorescence of the glass, and they are more effective when the fluorescence is greenish-yellow or canary colour. Certain salts—for example, the sulphates of zinc and of calcium, barium platino-cyanide, tungstate of calcium, and the double sulphate of uranyle and potassium—are more active than glass, and even emit the rays after exposure to ordinary light, if not also in the dark. Salvioni of Perugia has invented a "cryptoscope," which enables us to see the hidden object without the aid of photography by allowing the rays to fall on a plate coated with one of these phosphorescent substances. Already the new method has been applied by doctors in examining malformations and diseases of the bones or internal organs, and in localising and extracting bullets, needles, or other foreign matters in the body. There is little doubt that it will be very useful as an adjunct to hospitals, especially in warfare, and, if the apparatus can be reduced in size, it will be employed by ordinary practitioners. It has also been used to photograph the skeleton of a mummy, and to detect true from artificial gems. However, one cannot now easily predict its future value, and applications will be found out one after another as time goes on.

CHAPTER X.

THE WIRELESS TELEGRAPH.

Magnetic waves generated in the ether (see pp. 53-95) by an electric current flowing in a conductor are not the only waves which can be set up in it by aid of electricity. A merely stationary or "static" charge of electricity on a body, say a brass ball, can also disturb the ether; and if the strength of the charge is varied, ether oscillations or waves are excited. A simple way of producing these "electric waves" in the ether is to vary the strength of charge by drawing sparks from the charged body. Of course this can be done according to the Morse code; and as the waves after travelling through the ether with the speed of light are capable of influencing conductors at a distance, it is easy to see that signals can be sent in this way. The first to do so in a practical manner was Signer Marconi, a young Italian hitherto unknown to fame. In carrying out his invention, Marconi made use of facts well known to theoretical electricians, one of whom, Dr, Oliver J. Lodge, had even sent signals with them in 1894; but it often happens in science as in literature that the recognised professors, the men who seem to have everything in their favour—knowledge, even talent—the men whom most people would expect to give us an original discovery or invention, are beaten by an outsider whom nobody heard of, who had neither learning, leisure, nor apparatus, but what he could pick up for himself.

Marconi produces his waves in the ether by electric sparks passing between four brass balls, a device of Professor Righi, following the classical experiments of Heinrich Hertz. The balls are electrified by connecting them to the well-known instrument called an induction coil, sometimes used by physicians to administer gentle shocks to invalids; and as the working of the coil is started and stopped by an ordinary telegraph key for interrupting the electric current, the sparking can be controlled according to the Morse code. In our diagram, which explains the apparatus, the four balls are seen at D, the inner and larger pair being partly immersed in vaseline oil, the outer and smaller pair being connected to the secondary or induced circuit of the induction coil C, which is represented by a wavy line. The primary or inducing circuit of the coil is connected to a battery B through a telegraph signalling key K, so that when this key is opened and closed by the telegraphist according to the Morse code, the induction coil is excited for a longer or shorter time by the current from the battery, in agreement with the longer and shorter signals of the message. At the same time longer or shorter series of sparks corresponding to these signals pass across the gaps between the four balls, and give rise to longer or shorter series of etheric waves represented by the dotted line. So much for the "Transmitter." But how does Marconi transform these invisible waves into visible or audible signals at the distant place? He does this by virtue of a property discovered by Mr. S. A. Varley as far back as 1866, and investigated by Mr. E. Branly in 1889. They found that powder of metals, carbon, and other conductors, while offering a great resistance to the passage of an electric current when in a loose state, coheres together when electric waves act upon it, and opposes much less resistance to the electric current. It follows that if a Morse telegraph instrument at the distant place be connected in circuit with a battery and some loose metal dust, it can be adjusted to work when the etheric waves pass through the dust, and only then. In the diagram R is this Morse "Receiver" joined in circuit with a battery B1; and a thin layer of nickel and silver dust, mixed with a trace of mercury, is placed between two cylindrical knobs or "electrodes" of silver fused into the glass tube d, which is exhausted of air like an electric glow lamp. Now, when the etheric waves proceeding from the transmitting station traverse the glass of the tube and act upon the metal dust, the current of the battery B1 works the Morse receiver, and marks the signals in ink on a strip of travelling paper. Inasmuch as the dust tends to stick together after a wave passes through it, however, it requires to be shaken loose after each signal, and this is done by a small round hammer head seen on the right, which gives a slight tap to the tube. The hammer is worked by a small electromagnet E, connected to the Morse instrument, and another battery b in what is called a "relay" circuit; so that after the Morse instrument marks a signal, the hammer makes a tap on the tube. As this tap has a bell-like sound, the telegraphist can also read the signals of the message by his ear.

Two "self-induction bobbins," L Ll, a well-known device of electricians for opposing resistance to electric waves, are included in the circuit of the Morse instrument the better to confine the action of the waves to the powder in the tube.

Further, the tube d is connected to two metal conductors V VI, which may be compared to resonators in music. They can be adjusted or attuned to the electric waves as a string or pipe is to sonorous waves. In this way the receiver can be made to work only when electric waves of a certain rate are passing through the tube, just as a tuning-fork resounds to a certain note; it being understood that the length of the waves can be regulated by adjusting the balls of the transmitter. As the etheric waves produced by the sparks, like ripples of water caused by dropping a stone into a pool, travel in all directions from the balls, a single transmitter can work a number of receivers at different stations, provided these are "tuned" by adjusting the conductors V VI to the length of the waves.

This indeed was the condition of affairs at the time when the young Italian transmitted messages from France to England in March, 1899, and it is a method that since has been found useful over limited distances. But to the inventor there seemed no reason why wireless telegraphy should be limited by any such distances. Accordingly he immediately developed his method and his apparatus, having in mind the transmission of signals over considerable intervals. The first question that arose was the effect of the curvature of the Earth and whether the waves follow the surface of the Earth or were propagated in straight lines, which would require the erection of aerial towers and wires of considerable height. Then there was the question of the amount of power involved and whether generators or other devices could be used to furnish waves of sufficient intensity to traverse considerable distances.

Little by little progress was made and in January, 1901, wireless communication was established between the Isle of Wight and Lizard in Cornwall, a distance of 186 miles with towers less than 300 feet in height, so that it was demonstrated that the curvature of the Earth did not seriously affect the transmission of the waves, as towers at least a mile high would have been required in case the waves were so cut off. This was a source of considerable encouragement to Marconi, and his apparatus was further improved so that the resonance of the circuit and the variation of the capacity of the primary circuit of the oscillation transformer made for increased efficiency. The coherer was still retained and by the end of 1900 enough had been accomplished to warrant Marconi in arranging for trans-Atlantic experiments between Poldhu, Cornwall and the United States, stations being located on Cape Cod and in Newfoundland. The trans-Atlantic transmission of signals was quite a different matter from working over 100 miles or so in Great Britain. The single aerial wire was supplanted by a set of fifty almost vertical wires, supported at the top by a horizontal wire stretched between two masts 157 1/2 feet high and 52 1/2 feet apart, converging together at the lower end in the shape of a large fan. The capacity of the condenser was increased and instead of the battery a small generator was employed so that a spark 1 1/2 inches in length would be discharged between spheres 3 inches in diameter. At the end of the year 1901 temporary stations at Newfoundland were established and experiments were carried on with aerial wires raised in the air by means of kites. It was here realized that various refinements in the receiving apparatus were necessary, and instead of the coherer a telephone was inserted in the secondary circuit of the oscillation transformer, and with this device on February 12th the first signals to be transmitted across the Atlantic were heard. These early experiments were seriously affected by the fact that the antennae or aerial wires were constantly varying in height with the movement of the kites, and it was found that a permanent arrangement of receiving wires, independent of kites or balloons, was essential. Yet it was demonstrated at this time that the transmission of electric waves and their detection over distances of 2000 miles was distinctly possible.

A more systematic and thorough test occurred in February, 1902, when a receiving station was installed on the steamship Philadelphia, proceeding from Southampton to New York. The receiving aerial was rigged to the mainmast, the top of which was 197 feet above the level of the sea, and a syntonic receiver was employed, enabling the signals to be recorded on the tape of an ordinary Morse recorder. On this voyage readable messages were received from Poldhu up to a distance of 1551 miles, and test letters were received as far as 2099 miles. It was on this voyage that Marconi made the interesting discovery of the effect of sunlight on the propagation of electric waves over great distances. He found that the waves were absorbed during the daytime much more than at night and he eventually reached the conclusion that the ultraviolet light from the sun ionized the gaseous molecules of the air, and ionized air absorbs the energy of the electric waves, so that the fact was established that clear sunlight and blue skies, though transparent to light, serve as a fog to the powerful Hertzian waves of wireless telegraphy. For that reason the transmission of messages is carried on with greater facility on the shores of England and Newfoundland across the North Atlantic than in the clearer atmosphere of lower latitudes. But atmospheric conditions do not affect all forms of waves the same, and long waves with small amplitudes are far less subject to the effect of daylight than those of large amplitude and short wave length, and generators and circuits were arranged to produce the former. But the difficulty did not prove insuperable, as Marconi found that increasing the energy of the transmitting station during the daytime would more than make up for the loss of range.

The experiments begun at Newfoundland were transferred to Nova Scotia, and at Glace Bay in 1902 was established a station from which messages were transmitted and experimental work carried on until its work was temporarily interrupted by fire in 1909. Here four wooden lattice towers, each 210 feet in height, were built at the corner of a square 200 feet on a side, and a conical arrangement of 400 copper wires supported on stays between the tops of the towers and connected in the middle at the generating station was built. Additional machinery was installed and at the same time a station at Cape Cod for commercial work was built. In December, 1902, regular communication was established between Glace Bay and Poldhu, but it was only satisfactory from Canada to England as the apparatus at the Poldhu station was less powerful and efficient than that installed in Canada. The transmission of a message from President Roosevelt to King Edward marked the practical beginning of trans-Atlantic wireless telegraphy. By this time a new device for the detection of messages was employed, as the coherer we have described even in its improved forms was found to possess its limitations of sensitiveness and did not respond satisfactorily to long distance signals. A magnetic detector was devised by Marconi while other inventors had contrived electrolytic, mercurial, thermal, and other forms of detector, used for the most part with a telephone receiver in order to detect minute variations in the current caused by the reception of the electro-magnetic waves. With one of Marconi's magnetic detectors signals from Cape Cod were read at Poldhu.

In 1903 wireless telegraphy had reached such a development that the transmission of news messages was attempted in March and April of that year. But the service was suspended, owing to defects which manifested themselves in the apparatus, and in the meantime a new station in Ireland was erected. But there was no cessation of the practical experiments carried on, and in 1903 the Cunard steamship Lucania received, during her entire voyage across from New York to Liverpool, news transmitted direct from shore to shore. In the meantime intercommunication between ships had been developed and the use of wireless in naval operations was recognized as a necessity.

Various improvements from time to time were made in the aerial wires, and in 1905 a number of horizontal wires were connected to an aerial of the inverted cone type previously used. The directional aerial with the horizontal wires was tried at Glace Bay, and adopted for all the long distance stations, affording considerable strengthening of the received signals at Poldhu stations. Likewise improvements in the apparatus were effected at both trans-Atlantic stations, consisting of the adoption of air condensers composed of insulated metallic plate suspended in the air, which were found much better than the condensers where glass was previously used to separate the plates. For producing the energy employed for transmitting the signals a high tension continuous current dynamo is used. An oscillatory current of high potential is produced in a circuit which consists of rapidly rotating disks in connection with the dynamo and suitable condensers.

The production of electric oscillations can be accomplished in several ways and waves of the desired frequency and amplitude produced. Thus in 1903 it was found by Poulsen, elaborating on a principle first discovered by Duddell, that an oscillatory current may be derived from an electric arc maintained under certain conditions and that undamped high frequency waves so produced were suitable for wireless telegraphy. This discovery was of importance, as it was found that the waves so generated were undamped, that is, capable of proceeding to their destination without loss of amplitude. On this account they were especially suitable for wireless telephony where they were early applied, as it was found possible so to arrange a circuit with an ordinary microphone transmitter that the amplitude of the waves would be varied in harmony with the vibrations of the human voice. These waves so modulated could be received by some form of sensitive wave detector at a distant station and reproduced in the form of sound with an ordinary telephone receiver. With undamped waves from the arc and from special forms of generators wireless telephony over distances as great as 200 miles has been accomplished and over shorter distances, especially at sea and for sea to shore, communication has found considerable application. It is, however, an art that is just at the beginning of its usefulness, standing in much the same relation to wireless telegraphy that the ordinary telephone does to the familiar system employing metallic conductors.

On the spark and arc systems various methods of wireless telegraphy have been developed and improved so that Marconi no longer has any monopoly of methods or instruments. Various companies and government officials have devised or modified systems so that to-day wireless is practically universal and is governed by an international convention to which leading nations of the world subscribe.

One of the recent features of wireless telegraphy of interest is the success of various directional devices. As we have seen, various schemes were tried by Marconi ranging from metallic reflectors used by Hertz in his early experiments with the electric waves to the more successful arrangement of aerial conductors. In Europe Bellini and Tosi have developed a method for obtaining directed aerial waves which promises to be of considerable utility, enabling them to be projected in a single direction just as a searchlight beam and thus restrict the number of points at which the signals could be intercepted and read. Likewise an arrangement was perfected which enabled a station to determine the direction in which the waves were being projected and consequently the bearing of another vessel or lighthouse or other station. The fundamental principle was the arrangement of the antennae, two triangular systems being provided on the same mast, but in one the current is brought down in a perpendicular direction. The action depends upon the difference of the current in the two triangles.

Wireless telegraph apparatus is found installed in almost every seagoing passenger vessel of large size engaged in regular traffic, and as a means of safety as well as a convenience its usefulness has been demonstrated. Thus on the North Atlantic the largest liners are never out of touch with land on one side of the ocean or the other, and news is supplied for daily papers which are published on shipboard. Every ship in this part of the ocean equipped with the Marconi system, for example, is in communication on an average with four vessels supplied with instruments of the same system every twenty-four hours. In case of danger or disaster signals going out over the sea speedily can bring succour, as clearly was demonstrated in the case of the collision between the White Star steamship Republic and the steamship Florida on January 26, 1909. Here wireless danger messages were sent out as long as the Republic was afloat and its wireless apparatus working. These brought aid from various steamers in the vicinity and the passengers were speedily transferred from the sinking Republic. On April 15, 1912, the White Star liner Titanic, the largest ship afloat, sank off Newfoundland, after colliding with an iceberg. Wireless SOS calls for help brought several steamships to the scene, and 703 persons from a total of 2,206, were rescued. On October 9, 1913, the Uranium liner Volturno caught fire in mid- ocean, and her wireless calls brought ten steamships to her aid, which, despite a heavy sea, rescued 532 persons from a total of 657. Again, on November 14, 1913, the Spanish steamship Balmes caught fire off Bermuda, and at her wireless call the Cunard liner Pannonia saved all of her passengers—103. The Titanic horror led the principal maritime nations to take immediate steps to perfect their wireless systems, and the installation of apparatus and operators soon became a prime requisite of the equipment of the world's shipping. Wireless telegraphy has been developed to great efficiency in all the leading navies, and powerful plants are installed on all warships. The United States, Great Britain, and Germany, most noticeably, have established shore stations, by which they can "talk all around the world" from any ship or station. In operation secrecy is most important. For in the navy practically all important messages are sent in code or cipher under all conditions while in commercial work the tapping of land wires or the stealing of messages while illegal is physically possible for the evil disposed yet has never proved in practice a serious evil. The problem of interference, however, seems to have been fairly solved by the large systems though the activity of amateurs is often a serious disturbance for government and other stations.

Despite the progress of wireless telegraphy it has not yet supplanted the submarine cable and the land wire, and in conservative opinion it will be many years before it will do so. In fact, since Marconi's work there has been no diminution in the number or amount of cables laid and the business handled, nor is there prospect of such for years to come. While the cable has answered admirably for telegraphic purposes yet for telephony over considerable distances it has failed entirely so that wireless telephony over oceans starts with a more than favorable outlook. But wireless telegraphy to a large extent has made its own field and here its work has been greatly successful. Thus when Peary's message announcing his discovery of the North Pole came out of the Frozen North, it was by way of the wireless station on the distant Labrador coast that it reached an anxious and interested civilization. It is this same wireless that watches the progress of the fishing fleets at stations where commercial considerations would render impossible the maintenance of a submarine cable. It is the wireless telegraph that maintains communication in the interior of Alaska and between islands in the Pacific and elsewhere where conditions of development do not permit of the more expensive installation of submarine cable or climatic or other conditions render impossible overland lines. At sea its advantages are obvious. Everywhere the ether responds to the impulses of the crackling sparks, and even from the airship we soon may expect wireless messages as the few untrodden regions of our globe are explored.

CHAPTER XI.

ELECTRO-CHEMISTRY AND ELECTRO-METALLURGY.

In no department of the application of electricity to practical work has there been a greater development than in electro- metallurgy and electro-chemistry. To-day there are vast industries depending upon electrical processes and the developments of a quarter of a century have been truly remarkable. Already more than one-half of the copper used in the arts is derived by electrolytic refining. The production of aluminum depends entirely on electricity, the electric furnace as a possible rival to the blast furnace for the production of iron and steel is being seriously considered, and many other metallurgical processes are being undertaken on a large scale. We have seen in our chapter on Electrolysis how a metal may be deposited from a solution of its salt and how this process could be used for deriving a pure metal or for plating or coating with the desired metal the surface of another metal or one covered with graphite. In the following pages it is intended to take up some of the more notable accomplishments in this field achieved by electricity, which have been developed to a state of commercial importance.

The electric arc not only supplies light, but heat of great intensity which the electrical engineer as well as the pure scientist has found so valuable for many practical operations. It is of course obvious that for most chemical operations, and especially in the field of metallurgy, heat is required for the separation of combinations of various elements, for their purification, as well as for the combination with other elements into alloys or compounds of direct utility. The usual method of generating heat is by the combustion of some fuel, such as coal, coke, gas or oil, and this has been utilized for hundreds of years in smelting metals and ores and in refining the material from a crude state. Now it may happen that a nation or region may be rich in metalliferous ores, but possess few, if any, coal deposits. Accordingly the ore must be mined and transported considerable distances for treatment and the advantages of manufacturing industries are lost to the neighborhood of its original production. But if water power is available, as it is in many mountainous countries where various ores are found, then this power can be transformed into electricity which is available as power not only in various manufacturing operations, but for primary metallurgical work in smelting the ores and obtaining the metal therefrom. A striking instance of this is the kingdom of Sweden, which contains but little coal, yet is rich in minerals and in water power, so that its waterfalls have been picturesquely alluded to as the country's "white coal." Likewise, at Niagara Falls a portion of the vast water power developed there has been used in the manufacture of aluminum, calcium carbide, carborundum, and other materials, while at other points in the United States and Canada, not to mention Europe, large industries where electricity is used for metallurgical or chemical work are carried on and the erection of new plants is contemplated.

The application of electricity to metallurgical and chemical work has been, in nearly all cases, the result of scientific research, and elaborate experimental laboratories are maintained by the various corporations interested in the present or future use of electrical processes. It is recognized by many of the older workers in this field that electrical developments are bound to come in the near future, and while they have not installed such appliances in their works yet they are keeping close watch of present developments, and in many cases experimental investigation and research is being carried on where electrical methods have not yet been introduced generally into the plant.

Prior to 1886 the refining of copper was the only electro- metallurgical industry and at that time it was carried on on a very limited scale. To-day the production of electrolytic copper as an industry is second in importance only to the actual production of that metal. From the small refinery started by James Elkington at Pembury in South Wales, a vast industry has developed in which there has been a change in the size of operations and in the details of methods rather than in the fundamental process. For a solution of copper sulphate is employed as the electrolyte, blocks of raw copper as the anodes, and thin sheets of pure copper as the cathodes. The passage of the electric current, as we have seen on page 79, in the chapter on Electrolysis, is able to decompose the copper in the electrolyte and to precipitate chemically pure copper on the cathode, the copper of the solution being replenished from the raw material used as the anode by which the current is passed into the bath. At this Welsh factory 250 tons yearly were produced, and small earthenware pots sufficed for the electrolyte. Thirty years later one

American factory alone was able to produce at least 350 tons of electrolytic copper in twenty-four hours, and over 400,000 tons is the aggregate output of the refineries of the world, which is about 53 per cent, of the total raw copper production. Of this amount 85 per cent, comes from American refineries, whose output has more than doubled since 1900.

The chief reason for this increased output of electrolytic copper has been the great demand for its use in the electrical industries where not only a vast amount is consumed, but where copper of high purity, to give the maximum conductivity required by the electrical engineer, is demanded. When it is realized that every dynamo is wound with copper wire and that the same material is used for the trolley wire and for the distribution wires in electric lighting, it will be apparent how the demand for copper has increased in the last quarter of a century. Electrolytic methods not only supply a purer article and are economical to operate, especially if there is water power in the vicinity, but the copper ores contain varying amounts of silver and gold which can be recovered from the slimes obtained in the electrolytic process. Wherever possible machinery has been substituted for hand labor, the raw copper anodes have been cast, and the charging and discharging of the vats is carried on by the most modern mechanical methods in which efficiency and economy are secured. On the chemical side of the process attempts have been made to improve the electrolyte, notably by the addition of a small amount of hydrochloric acid to prevent the loss of silver in the slimes, and this part of the work is watched with quite as much care as the other stages. Electric furnaces have also been constructed for smelting copper ores, but these have not found wide application, and the problem is one of the future. For the most part the copper electrically refined is produced in an ordinary smelter. The mints of the United States are now all equipped with electrolytic refining plants to produce the pure metal needed for coinage and they have proved most satisfactory and economical.

As the electrolytic production of copper is an industry of great present importance, so the production of iron and steel by electricity promises to be of the greatest future importance. Electric furnaces for making steel are now maintained, and the industry has passed beyond an experimental condition. But it has not reached the point where it is competing with the Bessemer or the open hearth process of the manufacture of steel, while for the smelting of iron ores the electric furnace has not yet been found practical from an economic standpoint. Before 1880 Sir William Siemens showed that an electric arc could be used to melt iron or steel in a crucible, and he patented an electric crucible furnace which was the first attempt to use electricity in iron and steel manufacture. He stated that the process would not be too costly and that it had a great future before it. This was an application of the intense heat of the arc, which supplies a higher temperature than any source known except that of the sun. This heat is used to melt the metal, in which condition various impurities can be removed and necessary ingredients added. Siemens' furnace did not find extensive application, largely on account of the great metallurgical developments then taking place in the iron industry and the thorough knowledge of metallurgical processes as carried on, possessed by metal-lurgical engineers. But the idea by no means languished, and in 1899 Paul Heroult and other electro-metallurgists were active in developing a practical electric furnace for iron and steel work. The Swedish engineer, F. A. Kjellin, was also active and as the result of the efforts of these and other workers, by 1909 electric furnaces were employed, not only in the manufacture of special steels whose composition and making were attended with special care, but for rails and structural material. There were reported to be between thirty and forty electric steel plants in various countries, and the outlook for the future was distinctly bright. The application of electro- metallurgy at this time was confined to the manufacture of steel, as the smelting of iron had not emerged from the experimental stage of its development, though extensive trials on a large scale of various furnaces have been undertaken in Europe and by the Canadian government at Sault Ste. Marie, where the Heroult furnace, soon to be described, was employed. Electro-metal-lurgy of steel, as in all utilization of electrical power, depends upon obtaining electricity at a reasonable cost, and then utilizing the heat of the arc or of the current in the most practical and economical form. One of the pioneer furnaces for this purpose which has seen considerable development and practical application is the Heroult furnace, which is a tilting furnace of the crucible type, whose operation depends upon both the heat of the arc and on the heat produced by the resistance of the molten material. In the Heroult process the impurities of the molten iron are washed out by treatment with suitable slags. The furnace consists of a crucible in the form of a closed shallow iron tank, thickly lined with dolomite and mag-nazite brick, with a hearth of crushed dolomite. The electric current enters the crucible through two massive electrodes of solid carbon, 70 inches in length and 14 inches in diameter, so mounted that they can be moved either vertically or hor-izontally by the electrician in charge. These electrodes are water-jacketed to reduce the rate of consumption. The furnace contains an inlet for an air blast and openings in its covering for charging the material and for the escape of the gases. The actual process of steel-making consists of charging the crucible with steel scrap, pig iron, iron ore, and lime of the proper quality and in the right propor-tions, placing this material on the hearth of the furnace. Combined arc and resist-ance heating is applied to raise the charge to the melting point. The current is of 120 volts or the same as that used in an ordinary incandescent lighting circuit, but is alternating and of 4,000 amperes. This is for a three-ton furnace. As the material melts the lime and silicates form a slag which fuses rapidly and covers the iron and steel in the crucible, so that the molten bath is protected from the action of the gases which are liberated and the oxygen in the atmosphere. The next step in the process is to lower the electrodes until they just touch beneath the surface of the molten slag so that subsequent heating is due not to the effect of the arc but to the resistance which the bath offers to the passage of the current.

Air from an air blast is introduced into the crucible to oxidize the impurities of the metal, particularly the sulphur and the phosphorus which are carried into the slag and this is removed by the tilting of the furnace. Fresh quantities of lime, etc., are added, and the operation is repeated until a comparatively pure metal remains, when an alloy high in carbon is added and whatever other constituents are desired for the finished steel. The charge is then tipped into the casting ladle and the part of the electric furnace is finished. For three tons of steel eight to ten hours are required in the Heroult crucible furnace.

Furnaces of an altogether different type are those employing an alternating current, such as the Kjellin and Rochling furnaces, where the metal to be heated really forms the secondary circuit of a large and novel form of transformer which in principle is analogous to the familiar transformer seen to step down the potential of alternating current as for house lighting. For such a transformer the primary coil is formed of heavy wire and the secondary circuit is the molten metal which is contained in an annular channel. The current obtained in the metal is of considerable intensity, but at lower potential than that in the primary coil, and roughly is equal to that of the primary multiplied by the number of turns in the coil. The condition is similar to that in the ordinary induction coil where the current from a battery at low potential flows around a coil of a few turns and is surrounded by a second coil with a large number of turns of fine wire in which current of small intensity but of high potential is generated. In the induction furnace the reverse takes place and the current flowing in the metal derived from that of the heavy coil in the primary is of great intensity. For this type of furnace molten metal is required and the furnace is never entirely emptied, so that its process is continuous. The temperature attained is not as high as in the arc furnace, so that the raw materials used have to be of a high degree of purity, and this has proved a restriction of the field of usefulness of this type of furnace in many cases. It, however, has been improved recently and two rings of molten metal employed instead of one so that a wide centre trough is obtained in which the metal is subjected to ordinary resistance heat by direct or alternating currents. This furnace permits of various metallurgical operations and the elimination of impurities as in the Heroult type.

A third type of furnace that is meeting with some extensive use is the Giroud, which, like the Heroult furnace, is based on the arc and resistance in principle, but in its construction has a number of different features. As the current passes horizontally from the upper electrodes through the slag and molten metal in the furnace chamber to the base electrodes of the furnace, it permits of the easy regulation of the arcs and the use of lower electromotive force, while there is only one arc in the path of the current instead of two as in the Heroult type.

Sufficient quantities of steel have been made in electric furnaces to permit of the determination of the quality of the product as well as the economy of the process. It has been found in Germany that rail steel made in the induction furnace has a much higher bending and breaking limit than ordinary Bessemer or Thomas rail steel, and in Germany in 1908 rails so made commanded a considerably higher price per ton than those of ordinary rail steel. After trial orders had proved satisfactory, in 1908 5,000 tons of rails were ordered for the Italian and Swiss governments at a German works, where furnaces of eight tons capacity had been installed. In the United States only a few electric steel furnaces are in operation, and these, for the most part, for purposes of demonstration and experiment. But in Europe the industry is well established, and while at present small, is constantly growing and possesses an assured future.

In addition to the manufacture of steel, the application of the electric furnace for producing what are known as ferro-alloys, or alloys of iron, silicon, chromium, manganese, tungsten and vanadium, is now a large and important industry. Special steels have their uses in different mechanical applications and the advantage of alloying them with the rarer metals has been demonstrated for several important purposes, as for example, the use of chrome steel for armor plate, and steel containing vanadium for parts of motor cars. These industries for the most part contain electric arc furnaces and have, as their object, the manufacture of ferro-alloys, which are introduced into the steel, it having been found advantageous to use the rare metals in this form rather than in their crude state.

There is one electro-metallurgical process that has made possible the production in commercial form and for ordinary use of a metal that once was little more than a chemical curiosity. In 1885 there were produced 3.12 tons of aluminum, and its value was roughly estimated at about $12 a pound. By 1908 America alone produced over 9,000 tons valued at over $500,000,000, while European manufacturers were also large producers. In 1888 the electrolytic manufacture of aluminum was commenced in America and in the following year it was begun in Switzerland. Aluminum is formed by the electrolysis of the aluminum oxide in a fused bath of cryolite and fluorspar. The aluminum may be obtained in the form of bauxite, and is produced in large rectangular iron pots with a thick carbon lining. The pot itself is the cathode, while large graphite rods suspended in the bath serve as the anodes. After the arc is formed and the heat of the bath rises to a sufficient degree the material is decomposed and the metal is separated out so that it can be removed by ladling or with a siphon. The application of heat to obtain this metal previous to the invention of the electric furnace could only be considered a laboratory problem and the expense involved did not permit of commercial application. Now, however, aluminum is universally available and with the expiration of certain patents, the material has sold as low as 25 cents a pound.

Electrolytic methods serve also for the refining of nickel and for the production of lead, and as in other fields of metallurgy, these processes are attracting the attention of chemists and of engineers. While tin as yet has not yielded to electrolytic or electro-thermal methods with any success, the removal of tin from tin scraps and cuttings has been carried on with considerable success. With zinc the electrolytic and electro-thermal processes have not been able yet to compete with the older metallurgical method of distillation, but an important industry is electro- galvanizing, where a solution of zinc sulphate is deposited on iron and gives a protective coating. Experimental methods with the use of electricity in extracting zinc from its ores are being tested at various European plants, but the matter has not yet reached a commercial scale.

One of the earliest notable uses of the electric furnace in a large electro-chemical industry was for the production of carborundum, a carbide of silicon, which is remarkably useful as an abrasive, being available in the manufacture of grinding stones and other like purposes to replace emery and corundum. It is produced by the use of a simple electric furnace of the resistance type, where coke, sand, and sawdust are heated to a temperature of between 2000 degrees and 3000 degrees C. The chemical reaction involves the production of carbon monoxide, and gives a carbide of silicon, a crystalline solid which has the excellent abrasive properties mentioned. The manufacture was first started by its inventor, E. G. Acheson, about 1891 on a small scale, and in the following year 1,000 pounds of the material were produced at the Niagara Falls works. Within fifteen years its output had increased to well over six million pounds.

The electric furnaces at Niagara Falls have supplied many interesting electro-chemical processes. After making a carbide in the electric furnace it was found possible to decompose it by further increasing the heat to a point where the second element is volatilized and the pure carbon in the form of artificial graphite remains. In more recent work the carbide containing the silicon has been done away with and ordinary anthracite coal used as a charge from which the pure graphite is obtained. This graphite has been found especially useful in electrical work as for electrodes, while a more recent process enables a soft variety of graphite to be obtained which becomes a competitor of the natural material.

One of the most interesting of the many electro-chemical processes is the heating of lime and coke in the electric furnace so as to obtain a product in the form of calcium carbide, which, on solution in water, forms acetylene gas, a useful and valuable illuminant. This process dates from 1893 when T. L. Willson in the United States first started its manufacture on a large scale, and the great electro-chemist, Henri Moissin, about the same time independently invented a similar process as a result of his notable work with the electric furnace. The process involves merely a transformation at a high temperature, a portion of the carbon in the form of coke, uniting with pulverized lime to give the calcium carbide or $CaC2$. Now this material, when water is added to it, decomposes, and acetylene or $C2H2$ is formed, which is a gas of high illuminating value as the carbon separates and glows brightly after being heated to incandescence in the flame.

The electric furnace at Niagara Falls has been able to produce still another combination in the form of siloxicon by heating carbon and silicon to a temperature slightly below that required to produce carborundum. This product is a highly refractory material and is valuable for the manufacture of crucibles, muffles, bricks, etc., for work where extreme temperatures are employed. The electric furnace enables various elements to be isolated, such. as silicon, sodium, and phosphorus, and when obtained in their pure state they find wide application.

The most important electro-chemical work of the future is to devise some means of obtaining nitrogen from the air. It is stated by scientists that the nitrogen of the soil is being exhausted and that at some future time the Earth may not be able to bear crops sufficient for the sustenance of man, unless some artificial means be found to replenish the nitrogen. Unlimited supplies of nitrogen exist in the air, but to fix it with other materials in such form that it will be useful as a fertilizer has been one of the problems to which the electro-chemists have recently devoted much attention. By the use of the electric arc and passing air through a furnace, various substances have been tried to take up the nitrogen of the air. Thus when calcium carbide is heated and brought into contact with nitrogen one atom of carbon is given up and two atoms of nitrogen take its place, resulting in the production of cyanamide.

Other important electro-chemical processes are involved in the electrolysis of the various alkaline salts to obtain metallic sodium and such products as chlorates. Thus by the electrolysis of sodium chloride metallic sodium and chlorine is obtained. From the metallic sodium solid caustic soda is then derived by a secondary reaction, while the chlorine is combined with lime to form chloride of lime or bleaching powder. In some processes the electrolysis affords directly an alkaline hypochlorite or a chlorate, the former being of wide commercial use as a bleaching agent in textile works and in the paper industry. The same process employed in the electrolysis of sodium salts is used in the case of magnesium and calcium.

Electrolysis is also made use of in the manufacture of chloroform and iodoform, as the chlorine or iodine which is produced in the electrolytic cell is allowed to act upon the alcohol or acetone under such conditions that chloroform or iodoform is produced.

Electro-chemistry plays an important part in many other industries whose omission from our description must not be considered as indicating any lack of their importance. New processes constantly are being discovered which may range all the way from the production of artificial gems to the wholesale production of the most common chemicals used in the arts. In many branches of chemical industry manufacturing processes have been completely changed, and from the research laboratories, which all large progressive manufacturers now maintain, as well as from workers in universities and scientific schools, new methods and discoveries are constantly forthcoming.

CHAPTER XII.

ELECTRIC RAILWAYS.

The electric railway of Dr. Werner von Siemens constructed at Berlin in 1879 was the forerunner of a number of systems which have had the effect of changing materially the problems of transportation in all parts of the world. The electric railway not only was found suitable as a substitute for the tramway with its horse-drawn car, but far more economical than the cable cars, which were installed to meet the transportation problems of large cities with heavy traffic, or, as in the case of certain cities on the Pacific slope, where heavy grades made transportation a serious problem. Furthermore, the electric railway was found serviceable for rural lines where small steam engines or "dummies" were operated with limited success, and then only under exceptional conditions. As a result, practically every country of the world where the density of population and the state of civilization has warranted, is traversed by a network of electric railways, securing the most complete intercommunication between the various localities and handling local transportation in a manner impossible for a railway line employing steam loco-motives.

The great advance in electric transportation, aside from its meeting an economic need, has been due to the development of systems of generating and transmitting power economically over long distances. If water power is available, turbines and electric generators can be installed and power produced and transmitted over long distances, as, for example, from Niagara Falls to Buffalo, or even to much greater distances as in the case of power plants on the Pacific coast where mountain streams and lakes are employed for this purpose with considerable efficiency. A high tension alternating current thus can be transmitted over considerable distances and then transformed into direct current which flows along the trolley wires and is utilized in the motors. This transformation is usually accomplished by means of a rotary converter, that is, an alternating current motor which carries with it the essential elements of a direct current dynamo and receiving the alternating current of high potential turns it out in the form of direct current at a, lower and standard potential. The alternating current at high potential can be transmitted over long distances with a minimum of loss, while the direct current at lower potential is more suitable for the motor and can be used with greater advantage, yet its potential or pressure decreases rapidly over long lengths of line, so that it is more economical to use sub-stations to convert the alternating current from the power plant. It must not be inferred, however, that all electric railways employ direct current machinery. In Europe alternating current has been used with great success and also in the United States where a number of lines have been equipped with this form of power. But the greater number of installations employ the direct current at about 500-600 volts and this is now the usual practice. Whether it will continue so in the future or not is perhaps an open question.

The electric car, as we have seen, employs a motor which is geared to the axle of the driving trucks, and the current is derived from the trolley wire by the familiar pole and wheel and after flowing through the controller to the motor returns by the rail. The speed of the car is regulated by the amount of current which the motorman allows to pass through the motor and the circuits through which it flows in order to produce different effects in the magnetic attraction of the magnet and the armature. In the ordinary electric car for urban or suburban uses there has been a constant increase in the power of the motor and size of the cars, as it has been found that even large cars can be handled with the required facility necessary in crowded streets and that they are correspondingly more economical to maintain and operate.

The success of electric traction in large cities had been demonstrated but a few years when it was appreciated that the overhead wires of the trolley were unsightly and dangerous, especially in the case of fire or the breaking of the wires or supports. Accordingly a system was developed where the current was obtained from conductors laid in a conduit on insulated supports through a slot in the centre of the track between the rails. A plow suspended from the bottom of the car was in contact with the conductors which were steel rails mounted on insulated supports, and through them the current passed by suitable conductors to the controller and motors. This system found an immediate vogue in American cities, and though more costly to install than the overhead trolley, was far more satisfactory in its results and appearance. In certain cities, Washington, D. C., for example, the conduit is used in the built-up portion of the town and when the suburbs are reached the plow is removed and the motors are connected with the trolley wire by the usual pole and wheel.

Perhaps the most important feature of the electric railway in the United States has been the development and increase of its efficiency. Wherever possible traffic conditions warranted, it was comparatively easy to secure the right of way along country highways with little, if any, expense, and the construction of track and poles for such work was not a particularly heavy outlay. It was found, as we have seen, that the current could be transmitted over considerable distances so that the opportunity was afforded to supply transportation between two towns at some small distance where the local business at the time of the construction of the road would not warrant the outlay. This led to the systems of interurban lines, small at first, but as their success was demonstrated, gradually extending and uniting so that not only two important towns were connected, but eventually a large territory was supplied with adequate transportation facilities and even mail, express, and light freight could be handled.

Again the success of such enterprises made it feasible for the electric railways to forsake the public highway and to secure a right of way of their own, and gradually to develop express and through service, often in direct competition with the local service of the steam railways in the same territory. Here larger cars were required and power stations of the most modern and efficient type in order to secure proper economy of operation. The general character of machinery, both generators and motors, was preserved even for these long distance lines, and their operation became simply an engineering problem to secure the maximum efficiency with a minimum expenditure.

With the success of electric railways in cities and for suburban and interurban service naturally arose the question, why electric power whose availability and economy had been shown in so many circumstances could not be used for the great trunk lines where steam locomotives have been developed and employed for so many years? The question is not entirely one of engineering unless as part of the engineering problem we consider the various economic elements that enter into the question, and their investigation is the important task of the twentieth century engineer. For he must answer the question not only is a method possible mechanically, but is it profitable from a practical and economic standpoint? And it is here that the question of the electrification of trunk lines now rests. The steam locomotive has been developed to a point perhaps of almost maximum efficiency where the greatest speed and power have been secured that are possible on machines limited by the standard gauge of the track, 4 feet 8 1/2 inches, and the curves which present railway lines and conditions of construction demand. Now, withal, the steam locomotive mechanically considered is inefficient, as it must take with it a large weight of fuel and water which must be transformed into steam under fixed conditions. If for example, we have one train a day working over a certain line, there would be no question of the economy of a steam locomotive, but with a number, we are simply maintaining isolated units for the production of power which could be developed to far greater advantage in a central plant. Just as the factory is more economical than a number of workers engaged at their homes, and the large establishment of the trust still more economical in production than a number of factories, so the central power station producing electricity which can be transmitted along a line and used as required is obviously more advantageous than separate units producing power on the spot with various losses inherent in small machines.

But even if the central station is theoretically superior and more economical it does not imply that it is either good policy or economy to electrify at once all the trunk lines of a country such as the United States and to send to the scrap heap thousands of good locomotives at the sacrifice of millions of dollars and the outlay of millions more for electrical equipment. In other words, unless the financial returns will warrant it, there is no good and positive reason for the electrification of our great trans- continental lines and even shorter railroads. That is the situation to-day, but to-morrow is another question, and the far- seeing railroad man must be ready with his answer and with his preparations. To-day terminal services in large cities can better be performed by electricity, and not only is there economy in their operation, but the absence of dirt, smoke and noise is in accord with public sentiment if not positively demanded by statute or ordinance. Suburban service can be worked much more economically and effectively by trains of motor cars, and time table and schedule are not limited by the number of available locomotives on a line so equipped. On mountain grades, where auxiliary power or engines of extreme capacity are required, electricity generated by water power from melting snow or mountain lakes or streams in the vicinity may be availed of. Under such conditions powerful motors can be used on mountain divisions, not only with economy, but with increased comfort to passengers, especially where there are long tunnels. All this and more the railway man of to-day realizes, and electrification to this extent has been accomplished or is in course of construction. For each one of the services mentioned typical installations can be given as examples, and to accomplish the various ends, there is not only one system but several systems of electrical working, which have been devised by electrical engineers to meet the difficulties.

To summarize then, electric working of a trunk line results in increased economy over steam locomotives by concentration of the power and especially by the use of water power where possible. Thus economy is secured to the greatest extent by a complete electrical service and not by a mixed service of electric and steam locomotives. Electrification gives an increase in capacity both in the haulage by a locomotive, an electric locomotive being capable of more work than a steam locomotive, and in schedule and rate of speed, as motor car trains and electric terminal facilities make possible augmented traffic, and an increased use of dead parts of the system such as track and roadbed. There is a great gain in time of acceleration and for stopping, and for the Boston terminal it was estimated that with electricity 50 per cent, more traffic could be handled, as the headway could be reduced from three to two minutes. The modern tendency of electrification deals either with special conditions or where the traffic is comparatively dense. From such a beginning it is inevitable that electric working should be extended and that is the tendency in all modern installations, as for example, at the New York terminal of the New York Central and Hudson River Railroad where the electric zone, first installed within little more than station limits, is gradually being extended. As examples of density of traffic suitable for electrification, yet at the same time possessing problems of their own, are the great terminals such as the Grand Central Station of the New York Central and Hudson River Railroad in New York City, the new Pennsylvania Station in the same city, and that of the Illinois Central Station in the city of Chicago. Not only is there density here but the varied character of the service rendered, such as express, local, suburban, and freight, involves the prompt and efficient handling of trains and cars. Now, with suburban trains made up of motor cars, a certain number of locomotives otherwise employed are released; for these cars can be operated or shifted by their own power. Such terminal stations are often combined with tunnel sections, as in the case of the great Pennsylvania terminal, where the tunnel begins at Bergen, New Jersey, and extends under the Hudson River, beneath Manhattan Island and under the East River to Long Island City. It is here that electric working is essential for the comfort of passengers as well as for efficient operation. But there are tunnel sections not connected with such vast terminals, as in the case of the St. Clair tunnel under the Detroit River.

While the field and future direction of electrification is fairly well outlined and its future is assured, yet this future will be one of steady progress rather than one of sudden upheaval for the economic reasons before stated. To-day there are no final standards either of systems or of motors and the field is open for the final evolution of the most efficient methods. Notwithstanding the extraordinary progress that has been made many further developments are not only possible now but will be demanded with the progress of the art.

The great problem of the electric railway is the transmission of energy, and while power may be economically generated at the central station, yet, as Mr. Frank J.

Sprague, one of the pioneers and foremost workers in the electrical engineering of railways has so aptly said, it is still at that central station and it will suffer a certain diminution in being carried to the point of utilization as well as in being transformed into power to move locomotives, so that these two considerations lie at the bottom of the electric railway and on them depend the choice of the system and the design and construction of the motor. The two fundamental systems for electric railways, as in other power problems, are the direct current and the alternating current. In the former we have the familiar trolley wire, fed perhaps by auxiliary conductors carried on the supporting poles or the underground trolley in the conduit, or the third rail laid at the side of the track. All of these have become standard practice and are operated at the usual voltage of from 500 to 600 volts. The current on lines of any considerable length is alternating current, supplied from large central generating stations and transformed to direct as occasion may demand at suitable sub-stations. Recently there has been a tendency to employ high voltage direct current systems where the advantages of the use of direct current motors are combined with the economies of high voltage transmission, chief of which are the avoiding of power losses in transmission and the economy in the first cost of copper. These high voltage direct current lines were first used in Europe, and during the year 1907 experimental lines on the Vienna railway were tested. IN Germany and Switzerland tests were made of direct current system of 2,000 and 3,000 volts and in 1908 there was completed the first section of a 1,200-volt direct current line between Indianapolis and Louisville, which marked the first use of high tension direct current in the United States, and this was followed by other successful installations.

With alternating current there can be used the various forms of single phase or polyphase current familiar in power work, but the latter is now preferred, and in Europe and in the United States in the latter part of 1908 the number of single phase lines was estimated at 27 and 28 respectively, with a total mileage of 782 and 967 miles. A trolley wire or suspended conductor is used. To employ a single phase current, motors of either the repulsion type or of the series type are used and are of heavier weight than the direct current motors, as they must combine the functions of a transformer and a motor. It is for this reason that we often see two electric locomotives at the head of a single train on lines where the single phase system is employed, while on neighboring lines using direct current, one locomotive of hardly larger size suffices. With the polyphase current a motor with a rotating field is used, and they have considerable efficiency as regards weight when compared with the single phase and with the direct current motor. The polyphase motor, however, is open to the objection that it does not lend itself to regulations as well as the direct current form, and with ingenious devices involving the arrangement of the magnetic field and the combination of motors, various running speeds can be had. The usual voltage for these motors is 3,000 volts, but in the polyphase plant designed for the Cascade Tunnel 6,000 volts are to be used. They possess many advantages, especially their ability to run at overload, and consequently a locomotive with polyphase motor will run up grade without serious loss of speed. The single phase system has been carried on on Swiss and Italian railroads, notably on the Simplon Tunnel and the Baltelina lines with great success, and the distribution problems are reduced to a minimum. In the United States a notable installation has been on the New York, New Haven & Hartford Railroad, where the section between Stamford and New York has been worked by electricity exclusively since July 1, 1908. Here the single phase motors use direct current while running over the tracks of the New York Central from Woodlawn to the Grand Central Terminal. On both the New York, New Haven & Hartford and the New York Central locomotives the armature is formed directly on the axle of the driving wheels, so consequently much interest attaches to the new design adopted for the Pennsylvania tunnels, where the armatures of the direct current motors are connected with the driving wheels by connecting rods somewhat after the fashion of the steam locomotive, and following in this respect some successful European practice.

APPENDIX

UNITS OF MEASUREMENT.

(From Munro and Jamieson's Pocket-book of Electrical Rules and Tables).

I. FUNDAMENTAL UNITS.—The electrical units are derived from the following mechanical units:—

The Centimetre as a unit of length;
The Gramme as a unit of mass;
The Second as a unit of time.

The Centimetre is equal to 0.3937 inch in length, and nominally represents one thousand-millionth part, or 1/1,000,000,000 of a quadrant of the earth. The Gramme is equal to 15.432 grains, and represents the mass of a cubic centimetre of water at 4 degrees C. Mass is the quantity of matter in a body.

The Second is the time of one swing of a pendulum making 86,164.09 swings in a sidereal day, or 1/86,400 part of a mean solar day.

II. DERIVED MECHANICAL UNITS.-

Area.-The unit of area is the square centimetre.

Volume.—The unit of volume is the CUBIC CENTIMETRE.

VELOCITY is rate of change of position. It involves the idea of direction as well as that of magnitude. VELOCITY is UNIFORM when equal spaces are traversed in equal intervals of time The unit of velocity is the velocity of a body which moves through unit distance in unit time, or the VELOCITY OF ONE CENTIMETRE PER SECOND.

MOMENTUM is the quantity of motion in a body, and is measured by mass x velocity.

ACCELERATION is the rate of change of velocity, whether that change take place in the direction of motion or not. The unit of acceleration is the acceleration of a body which undergoes unit change of velocity in unit time, or an acceleration of one centimetre-per-second per second The acceleration due to gravity is considerably greater than this, for the velocity imparted by gravity to falling bodies in one second is about 981 centimetres per second (or about 32.2 feet per second). The value differs slightly in different latitudes. At Greenwich the value of the acceleration due to gravity is g=981.17; at the Equator g=978.1; at the North Pole g=983.1.

FORCE is that which tends to alter a body's natural state of rest or of uniform motion in a straight line.

FORCE is measured by the acceleration which it imparts to mass—i. e., mass x acceleration.

THE UNIT OF FORCE, or DYNE, is that force which, acting for one second on a mass of one gramme, gives to it a velocity of one centimetre per second. The force with which the earth attracts any mass is usually called the "weight" of that mass, and its value obviously differs at different points of the earth's surface The force with which a body gravitates—i e, its weight (in dynes), is found by multiplying its mass (in grammes) by the value of g at the particular place where the force is exerted.

Work is the product of a force and a distance through which it acts. The unit of work is the work done in overcoming unit force through unit distance—i e, in pushing a body through a distance of one centimetre against a forch of one dyne. It is called the Erg. Since the "weight" of one gramme is 1 X 981 or 981 dynes, the work of raising one gramme through the height of one centimetre against the force of gravity is 981 ergs or g ergs. One kilogramme-metre = 100,000 (g) ergs = 9 8 1 X 10^7 ergs. One foot- pound = 13,825 (g) ergs, = 1 356 X 10^7 ergs.

Energy is that property which, possessed by a body, gives it the capability of doing work. Kinetic energy is the work a body can do in virtue of its motion. Potential energy is the work a body can do in virtue of its position. The unit of energy is the Erg.

Power or Activity is the rate of work; the practical unit is called the Watt—10^7 ergs per second.

A Horse-power = 33,000 ft—lbs per minute = 550 ft—lbs per second, but as seen above under Work, 1 ft—lb = 1 356 X 10^7 ergs, and under Power, 1 Watt = 10^7 ergs per sec a Horsepower = 550 X 1 356 X 10^7 ergs = 746 Watts; or, $=EC/746=C^2R/746=E^2/(746\ R)=HP$ where E = volts, C = amperes, and R = ohms.

The French "force de cheval" = 75 kilogramme metres per sec = 736 Watts = 542 48 ft—lbs. per sec. = .9863 H.P.; or one H.P. = 1.01385 "force de cheval."

DERIVED ELECTRICAL UNITS.—There are two systems of electrical units derived from the fundamental "C.G.S." units, one set being based upon the force exerted between two quantities of electricity, and the other upon the force exerted between two magnetic poles. The former set are termed electro-static units, the latter electro-magnetic units.

III. ELECTROSTATIC UNITS.—

UNIT QUANTITY of electricity is that which repels an equal and similar quantity at unit distance with unit force in air.

UNIT CURRENT is that which conveys unit quantity of electricity along a conductor in a second.

UNIT ELECTROMOTIVE FORCE, or unit DIFFERENCE OF POTENTIAL exists between two points when the unit quantity of electricity in passing from one to the other will do the unit amount of work.

UNIT RESISTANCE is that of a conductor through which unit electromotive force between its ends can send a unit current.

UNIT CAPACITY is that of a condenser which contains unit quantity when charged to unit difference of potential.

IV. MAGNETIC UNITS.—

UNIT MAGNETIC POLE is that which repels an equal and similar pole at unit distance with unit force in air.

STRENGTH OF MAGNETIC FIELD at any point is measured by the force which would act on a unit magnetic pole placed at that point.

UNIT INTENSITY OF FIELD is that intensity of field which acts on a unit pole with unit force.

MOMENT OF A MAGNET is the strength of either pole multiplied by the distance between the poles.

INTENSITY OF MAGNETISATION is the magnetic moment of a magnet divided by its volume.

MAGNETIC POTENTIAL.—The potential at a point due to a magnet is the work that must be done in removing a unit pole from that point to an infinite distance against the magnetic attraction, or in bringing up a unit pole from an infinite distance to that point against the magnetic repulsion.

UNIT DIFFERENCE OF MAGNETIC POTENTIAL.—Unit difference of magnetic potential exists between two points when it requires the expenditure of one erg of work to bring an (N. or S.) unit magnetic pole from one point to the other against the magnetic forces.

V. ELECTRO-MAGNETIC UNITS.—

UNIT CURRENT is that which in a wire of unit length, bent so as to form an arc of a circle of unit radius, would act upon a unit pole at the centre of the circle with unit force.

UNIT QUANTITY of electricity is that which a unit current conveys in unit time. UNIT ELECTRO-MOTIVE FORCE or DIFFERENCE OF POTENTIAL is that which is produced in a conductor moving through a magnetic field at such a rate as to cut one unit line per second.

UNIT RESISTANCE is that of a conductor in which unit current is produced by unit electro-motive force between its ends.

UNIT CAPACITY is that of a condenser which will be at unit difference of potential when charged with unit quantity.

Electric and magnetic force varies inversely as the square of the distance.

PRACTICAL UNITS OF ELECTRICITY.

RESISTANCE-R.—The Ohm is the resistance of a column of mercury 106.3 centimetres long, 1 square millimetre in cross-section, weighing 14.4521 grammes, and at a temperature of 0 degrees centigrade. Standards of wire are used for practical purposes. The ohm is equal to a thousand million, 10^9, electro-magnetic or Centimetre-Gramme-Second ("C. G. S.") units of resistance.

The megohm is one million ohms.

The microhm is one millionth of an ohm.

ELECTROMOTIVE FORCE—E.—The Volt is that electromotive force which maintains a current of one ampere in a conductor having a resistance of one ohm. The electromotive force of a Clark standard cell at a temperature of 15 degrees centigrade is 1.434 volts. The volt is equal to a hundred million, 10^8, C. G. S. units of electromotive force.

CURRENT—C.—The Ampere is that current which will decompose 0.09324 milligramme of water (H_2O) per second or deposit 1.118 milligrammes of silver per second. It is equal to one-tenth of a C. G. S. unit of current.

The milliampere is one thousandth of an ampere.

QUANTITY—Q.—The Coulomb is the quantity of electricity conveyed by an ampere in a second. It is equal to one-tenth of a C. G. S. unit of quantity.

The micro-coulomb is one millionth of a coulomb.

CAPACITY—K.—The farad is that capacity of a body, say a Leyden jar or condenser, which a coulomb of electricity will charge to the potential of a volt. It is equal to one thousand-millionth of a C. G. S. unit of capacity.

The micro-farad is one millionth of a Farad.

By Ohm's Law, Current = Electromotive Force/ Resistance,

or C = E/R

Ampere = Volt/Ohm

Hence when we know any two of these quantities, we can find the third. For example, if we know the electromotive force or difference of potential in volts and the resistance in ohms of an electric circuit, we can easily find the current in amperes.

POWER—P.—The Watt is the power conveyed by a current of one ampere through a conductor whose ends differ in potential by one volt, or, in other words, the rate of doing work when an ampere passes through an ohm. It is equal to ten million, 10^7, C. G. S. units of power or ergs per second, that is to say, to a Joule per second, or 1/746 of a horse-power.

A Watt = volt X ampere, and a Horse-power = Watts/746.

HEAT OR WORK—W.—The Joule is the work done or heat generated by a Watt in a second, that is, the work done or heat generated in a second by an ampere flowing through the resistance of an ohm. It is equal to ten million, 10^7, C. G. S. units of work or ergs. Assuming "Joule's equivalent" of heat and mechanical energy to be 41,600,000, it is the heat required to raise .24 gramme of water 1 degrees centigrade. A Joule = Volt x ampere x second. Since 1 horse-power = 550 foot pounds of work per second,

W = 550/746 E. Q. = .7373 E. Q. foot pounds.

HEAT UNITS.

The British Unit is the amount of heat required to raise one pound of water from 60 degrees to 61 degrees Fahrenheit. It is 251.9 times greater than the metric unit, therm or calorie, which is the amount of heat required to raise one gramme of water from 4 degrees to 5 degrees centigrade.

Joule's Equivalent—J.—is the amount of energy equivalent to a therm or calorie, the metric unit of heat. It is equal to 41,600,000 ergs.

The heat in therms generated in a wire by a current = Volt X ampere X time in seconds X 0.24.

LIGHT UNITS

The British Unit is the light of a spermaceti candle 7/8-inch in diameter, burning 120 grains per hour (six candles to the pound). They sometimes vary as much as 10 per cent, from the standard. Mr. Vernon Harcourt's standard flame is equal to an average standard candle.

The French Unit is the light of a Carcel lamp, and is equivalent to 9 T/Z British units.

Printed in the United Kingdom
by Lightning Source UK Ltd.
9453900001B

The Mighty Bean

THE COUNTRYMAN PRESS
A Division of W. W. Norton & Company
Independent Publishers Since 1923

The Mighty Bean

JUDITH CHOATE

100 Easy Recipes That Are
Good for Your Health,
the World, and Your Budget

PHOTOGRAPHS BY STEVE POOL

COUNTRYMAN KNOW HOW

CONTENTS

Introduction

I grew up eating beans and rice, just as my grandchildren have.
For me, pinto beans and long-grain rice was the ultimate comfort
food. For my grandchildren, their menu looks even more eclectic
given today's diversified market. They enjoy a variety of beans,
from refried or highly seasoned black beans to Italian-scented
cannellini, borlotti beans, or other legumes, each paired with a rice
of unique color, size, and flavor.

I have been delighted to discover and enjoy these new varieties of beans and other legumes alongside my grandchildren. Because we have one granddaughter who is a vegan and one who is a pescatarian, I've also come to know new products focused on the use of protein-rich legumes as their base or primary ingredient, such as lentil or chickpea pasta or other bean-based chips and snacks. Almost thirty years ago I wrote *The Rediscovered Bean,* one of my favorite cookbooks. Though the title labeled beans *rediscovered,* I had never forgotten this most basic of the world's nutritional, inexpensive foods, and

in recent years it seems we've all begun to find joy in legumes.

Legumes, also known as pulses, are the edible seeds of a pod-bearing plant. We describe these seeds with common names like beans, peas, lentils, and peanuts. Legumes are among nature's most balanced foods. They are consumed daily all over the world; are a basic component of plant-based or meat-free diets; and are exceedingly low in fat, and what fat they do contain is unsaturated. They are cholesterol-free, yet they help manage blood cholesterol and glucose as well as remain high in vegetable protein, fiber, vitamins, and minerals. For instance, a serving of cooked dried chickpeas offers more folate than a serving of kale as well as three times as much iron as a 3-ounce chicken breast. And legumes have one of the lowest carbon footprints in agriculture because they recycle nutrients from the atmosphere back into the soil, drastically reducing the use of chemical fertilizers. Most importantly in today's economy, they are cheap: a generous serving of lentils costs from ten to fifteen cents, and other legumes are not much more. An even more important fact is that they are easy to cook and lend themselves to a myriad of cuisines and flavors.

Recently, a team of scientists from Oregon State University, Bard College, and Loma Linda University doing a study on climate change and food made an extraordinary proclamation. They estimated that if everyone in America was willing and able to make just one dietary change—substitute beans for their annual consumption of beef (cattle are responsible for almost half of the greenhouse gas emissions that come from livestock)—the United States could come close to meeting the greenhouse gas emission goals for 2020 set in 2009 by President Barack Obama. This means that if nothing at all was concurrently being done about changing transportation systems, energy infrastructure, or other impacting climate issues, "beans for beef" could possibly bring greenhouse gas reductions to somewhere between 46 and 74 percent to meet that 2020 target. At the same time, we could continue to eat other meats and proteins.

In addition, as more research has focused on plant-based diets, it has been shown that eating meat increases the risk of cardiac diseases as well as some cancers. It has also been found that all processed meats show signs of contamination by fecal matter, which is then ingested when the product is cooked and eaten. The use of antibiotics to ensure the health of livestock and poultry has also increased human resistance to them. And companies continue to try to mimic the taste of meat in plant- or science-based meat substitutes. Together, these points only further demonstrate the healthfulness of a meal built on legumes.

It is easy to state that legumes are versatile, packed with nutrition, gluten-free, easy on the budget, long-storing, and agriculturally enriching. To the point, they are one of the world's most valuable food sources and, fortunately, there are now so many more of them to enjoy. This diversity is the main reason that I decided to revisit the subject, as I have made the exciting discovery of "rediscovered" beans and other legumes of the international kitchen and today's growers. Legumes are true health harbingers for the planet as well as for humanity, and it has been an exciting and tasty adventure to learn more about the deliciousness of these health-rewarding foods.

NAME THAT LEGUME: BEAN, LENTIL, PEA, OR PEANUT?

Beans

Cultivated since ancient times, beans have, throughout centuries, been used as an excellent source of protein. Although they come in a variety of shapes, colors, and tastes, the flavor of each one is usually rich and deeply satisfying. They are high in protein, complex carbohydrates, iron, fiber, and folate. Beans also offer about 16 grams of fiber per 1 cup, which—together with their other healthy attributes—can help lower blood cholesterol.

Adzuki: One of the most basic beans of East Asia and the Himalayas. Small, reddish-brown in color and extremely versatile. Available fresh, sprouted, dried, or ground into a fine flour. **AKA Red mung bean**

Alubia: Native to the Americas. Can be categorized by growth, for example: bush beans (or dwarf beans), climbing beans (or pole beans). **AKA Common bean**

Amethyst: Native to South America. The pods resemble string beans but are thinner with a stunning purple color.

Anasazi: Native to South America. This bean was cultivated by the Anasazi Indians. It is a beautiful kidney-shaped bean with splashes of purple and ivory. Related to the pinto bean, it is commonly used in Latin, Mexican, and Southwestern cuisines including refried beans, chilis, and robust stews.

Appaloosa: Named after the famous Appaloosa ponies of the Nez Percé tribe, this bean is ivory colored on one end and a splashy combination of purple and mocha on the other. Used in chili, refried beans, casseroles, soups, and stews.

Ayocote Blanco: The Ayocote family of fat, dense beans is originally from Oaxaca, Mexico. The Blanco is a rich and creamy midsized bean that holds its shape during cooking. It has a slightly starchy, almost potato-like taste when cooked, making it perfect for use in salads, casseroles, soups, pot beans, and cassoulet.

Ayocote Morado: Like its sister Ayocote Blanco, the Ayocote Morado is also big, rich, and creamy. Raw, the bean is a pretty lilac shade but the color fades during cooking as it goes from starchy to creamy. It is delicious in soups, chilis, and casseroles.

Ayocote Negro: Again, as expected, the Ayocote Negro is a large, hearty bean. Thick-skinned, it creates a lovely inky bean broth and is popularly used in bean soups or paired with smoky guajillo chile or chiles in adobo.

Black Calypso: Native to the Americas, the Calypso bean is a kidney bean hybrid. Half white and half black, it is a striking bean that doubles in size when cooked. **AKA Yin-yang bean (due to its striking coloration)**

Black-Eyed Peas: Identified with the cuisine of the southern United States. Medium-sized, pale creamy yellow with a black heel (or dot). Thin-skinned and quick cooking. Available fresh, frozen, or dried. **AKA Black-eyed beans, cowpeas**

Black Turtle: Native to South America. Small, with a shiny black exterior, often with a tiny white dot. Very rich flavor. Used to fill burritos and as a component of the Brazilian dish, feijoada. Available dried or canned and as black bean flour. **AKA Black beans, *frijoles negros***

Black Valentine: Introduced in 1897, this versatile heirloom bean is small and shiny black. It has tasty pods and can be used fresh as a snap bean or, as it ages, a dried bean for soups and stews.

Bolita: Native to Mexico and the American Southwest, this small pinkish bean cooks up quickly and sweetly. It is perfect for burritos and refried beans.

Borlotti: See **Cranberry.**

Butter Beans: See **Lima.**

Butterscotch: This heirloom bean dates back to the 17th century and is considered to be the original Boston baked bean. A plump ivory bean with butterscotch coloring around the eye of the bean, this is a great baking bean that keeps its shape after cooking. It has a mild flavor and a firm texture. A versatile bean, it can be used in soups, stews, and salads, besides being famously baked. It is traditionally used in the South in Hoppin' John (page 202). **AKA Steuben Yellow Eye**

Caballero: Recently arrived from Peru, this mid-sized white bean has a big, fleshy, super-creamy taste. It works in everything from rich Southwestern chilis to lemony Italian bean salads.

Cannellini: Large, kidney-shaped bean from Italy. When cooked, it has a delightful fluffy texture while maintaining its shape. A versatile bean, it works in soups, dips, salads, wraps, and even fritters. **AKA White kidney beans**

Chickpeas: Used extensively throughout the Mediterranean, India, and the Middle East in a variety of traditional dishes. Round, medium-sized, pale beige when dried, and pale green when fresh. Extremely versatile. Available as flour or dried, canned, and, occasionally, fresh. **AKA Garbanzo, *ceci, chana dal,* Bengal gram, Egyptian pea**

Christmas Lima: Native to Peru, this lima bean has a rich and nutty flavor similar to chestnuts. Big and bold, it is a beautiful speckled burgundy and white bean. It is robust and stands up well in soups, salads, casseroles, chilis, and even curries. **AKA** *Fagioli del Papa* **(Pope's beans), chestnut lima, calico bean**

Corona: Native to Europe, this very large, white heirloom bean has been called poor man's meat. Twice the size of a regular lima bean, the corona has a surprisingly creamy interior when cooked and is considered a versatile giant in the world of bean cuisine. **AKA Sweet white runner**

Cranberry: Used most frequently in Italian cooking in soups, stews, and with pasta. Medium-sized, pale pink with beige to brown mottling. May be used interchangeably with other pink beans or with medium, flavorful white beans. Available dried, frozen, and fresh. **AKA Borlotti or Roman(o) beans, horticulture**

Crowder Peas: See **Field Peas.**

Dapple Greys: Native to Arizona, this pretty gray heirloom bean is about the same size as a pinto but has a deeper flavor. It is creamy and filling and can be used in everything from soups to chilis to pesto.

Domingo Rojo: A small, mild yet dense heirloom bean from Mexico, the Domingo Rojo is a classic red bean that is used extensively in Mexican and Caribbean cooking. It holds its shape when cooked

and produces an incomparable bean broth, making it the bean of choice in the New Orleans classic: Red Beans and Rice (page 168).

Dragon Tongue: Originating in Holland, this heirloom bean can be used as a fresh snap bean when young, or as a shelled bean when fully mature. **AKA Dragon Langerie,** *Merveille de Piemonte*

European Soldier: A lovely cream-colored bean with a small splash of dark red. This bean keeps its shape when cooked and is great as a baking or a soup bean. It can substitute for almost any white bean in recipes. **AKA Red eye bean,** *Haricot St-Esprit* à *Oeil Rouge*

Eye of the Goat: Because of its thin skin, this bean releases a massive amount of flavor into its broth yet still manages to keep its shape during cooking. It is slightly kidney shaped with a tan-colored background and curved brown swirls. It is excellent in pot beans, soups, chilis, dips, and casseroles. **AKA** *Ojo de Cabra*

Fava: Native to Europe and used throughout the Mediterranean. Large, delicate pale green when fresh; beige to light brown and crenulated when dried. Very young, fresh pods are also edible. Fresh beans may be eaten raw or cooked. Available as fresh, dried, or flour. Some specialty markets may have them frozen and/or canned. **AKA Horse bean, broad bean**

Feijao: The most popular bean in Brazil, this black bean is not to be confused with small Asian black beans. The feijao is similar to a kidney bean and is used in feijoada and *caldinho de feijao*. **AKA *Feijao preto***

Field Peas: A variety of different beans, known familiarly as cowpeas because they were grown in fields as a rotational crop rather than in gardens. They are an intricate part of the cuisine of the American South. Black-eyed peas are the most well-known field pea, although there are many different sizes, shapes, and flavors. Grown in the southern United States. Available fresh, frozen, or dried. Crowder, Washday, Purple Hull, Zipper, Lady, Whippoorwill, and Red Ripper are some of the types. **AKA Cowpeas**

Flageolet: Originally from Oaxaca, Mexico, the French-sounding flageolet is now extensively grown in California. Known as the caviar of beans, the flageolet has an inedible green pod about 3 inches long and small kidney-shaped seeds that range from cream to pale green. It is picked before full maturity to take advantage of its delicate flavor.

Flor de Mayo: Native to the southwestern United States, the Flor de Mayo can be used as both a fresh shell bean or fully mature for a dried bean. It has a beautiful pink color, a plump oval shape, and an almost smoky taste. Their rich smooth texture makes these beans particularly suited to chilis.

Flor de Mayo beans

French Navy: This is a small round white bean. One of the best-known beans in the family, they are great all-rounders and are commonly used in baked beans, soups, stews, and salads. **AKA White pea bean**

Garbanzo: See **Chickpeas.**

Gigandes: Native to the Mediterranean region, this giant white runner bean is extensively used particularly in Greek cuisine. While they may look similar to lima beans and butter beans, gigandes are creamier and hold their shape better when cooked. **AKA *Gigantes, yigandes, hija***

Good Mother Stallard: This heirloom bean is dense and meaty-flavored. The mature pod is creamy white with five or six plump speckled maroon and white beans inside each pod. Fantastic in soups and chilis, the bean keeps its shape well and its deep rich nutty flavor makes a superb broth.

Great Northern: Great Northern beans are a medium-sized white bean, larger than the navy bean but smaller than the cannellini. Used extensively in French cassoulets and baked beans. It has a mild nutty flavor and is often paired with ham or bacon in casseroles. **AKA Large white**

Green Beans: Young, fresh green pods of haricot beans. Also available as yellow wax beans or tiny haricots verts with little taste variation between them. Available fresh, frozen, or canned. **AKA String beans, haricots, snap beans**

Haricot: These are the many varieties of the seeds of a strain of legumes. The mature seeds come in assorted sizes and may be either creamy white and slightly kidney-shaped (Great Northern, navy, small white kidney, cannellini, Yankee beans) or pink to red to reddish-brown kidney-shaped (kidney, red, pink, pinto, and others). The immature seeds are known as flageolets and are the caviar of the bean world. They are removed from the pod when very young and tender, just as they begin to mature. Available dried; some are canned, with the exception of flageolets, which can sometimes be purchased frozen and/or canned.

Hija: See **Gigandes.**

Horticulture: See **Cranberry.**

Jacob's Cattle: A native New England heirloom, this sweet-tasting bean is related to the kidney bean. A plump white kidney-shape with mottled burgundy splashes. Long a staple for baking and soups. **AKA Trout beans, jakes, forellen**

Kidney: Highly popular, kidney beans are so called because of their shape. They can come in many colors from ivory to bloodred, even black. With a sweet flavor and light texture, kidney beans hold their shape well during cooking.

Lady Cream: Common in Southern cooking, the Lady Cream pea is pale, small, sweet-tasting, and creamy. It is similar to black-eyed peas. **AKA Cowpea**

Lila: Native to Mexico, this pretty, medium-sized lavender-colored heritage bean is flavorful and creamy. Good in soups and refried beans. **AKA** *Frijol apetito*

Lima: Native to Central and South America, with several varieties now available, such as Fordhook and baby. Fresh limas are a flat, pale, fuzzy green pod that holds either very small pale green seeds (baby) or large, almost white seeds. The larger seeds can be very dry with a flat flavor and are best used in soups, stews, and purees. Available fresh, dried, frozen, and canned. **AKA Butter beans**

Lupini: Popular throughout the Mediterranean, where they were first described over 4,000 years ago, lupini beans are often served as an antipasto alongside olives or as a pickled snack. Allergic reactions to lupin may cause anaphylaxis in sensitive individuals. **AKA Lupin beans,** *altramuces, tremoços, turmus*

Marcella: Named for the beloved Italian cookbook writer Marcella Hazan, this is a small, thin-skinned white cannellini bean. **AKA** *Sorana*

Marrow: Popular in Italian cuisine, this is a plump, round white bean that cooks up creamy with meaty flavors reminiscent of smoked bacon. **AKA Marrowfat**

Mayocoba: Native to Peru, this is a medium-sized, oval-shaped, pale yellow bean. These beans have a mild flavor and a soft creamy texture. Good for soups, creamy refried beans, dips, and pot beans. **AKA Peruvian, canary, Mexico yellow**

Midnight Black: A small black turtle bean, its thin skin allows its flavor to create rich delicious broths.

Moro: Native to Mexico. This is a small bean with a beautiful dark speckled appearance. Like black beans, the Moro creates a dense rich-flavored broth and is ideal for pot beans, soups, salads, casseroles, dips, and refried beans.

Mortgage Lifter: Originally cultivated in the American Southwest, this is a gigantic white bean with a delicious meaty flavor. **AKA White bordal, pueblo, white Aztec, potato bean,** *poraro*

Mung: Native to India. A tiny round bean with a green or drab green exterior and a yellow interior. Their primary use is as sprouts in Asian cooking, but the bean itself is cooked in Indian cuisine. May also be eaten whole. Available dried, sprouted, or as flour. **AKA** *Moong, mug,* **or green gram**

Navy: Native to the Americas, this small white bean has a slightly oval and flat appearance. It develops a creamy texture when cooked and is ideal for baking, hearty soups, and salads. **AKA Pea, white pea bean, Boston navy bean, haricot bean, pearl haricot**

Orca: See **Black Calypso Bean.**

Pea: See **Navy.**

Pebble: These beans are multicolored with rich intricate markings. They have a dense texture and a meaty flavor and make excellent soups and chilis.

Peruviana: A pretty, midsized, pastel-colored bean that grows in a slender yellow pod.

Petite French: See **Navy.**

Pigeon Peas: Native to India, these dried, round beige beans are used throughout the Caribbean,

Africa, Asia, the Middle East, and the American South, most particularly in dishes called peas and rice. Available dried, canned, and, occasionally, fresh. **AKA Congo beans,** *gandules, arhar dal, tuvar dal*

Pink Pearl: The seed pods are strikingly pink and hold inside beautiful pink-spotted beans that cook up soft and creamy with a slightly nutty taste. **AKA Borlotti, cranberry, Roman**

Pinto: Native to Mexico, this pretty (*pinto* is Spanish for "painted") orange-pink bean has an earthy flavor and smooth texture that makes it ideal for chilis, refried beans, and stews.

Poquito: Native to California, this is a small pink bean used to make Santa Maria–style barbecue beans, a robust bean, beef, and garlic chili. **AKA Santa Maria pinquito**

Pueblo: Cultivated by the ancient Pueblo peoples of the American Southwest, this full-bodied bean is meaty in texture with a nutty flavor and a good aftertaste. It is prized in bean and rice casseroles, vegetable stews, and bean dips.

Raquel: An heirloom from the southwestern United States, this bean is a striking white and tan color. Its thin skin produces a rich nutty broth. It is especially good in soups and baked beans. **AKA Prairie Appaloosa**

Rattlesnake: Named for the way its bean pods twist and snake around climbing poles and frames, this pinto bean hybrid has a dark red appearance with dark brown and black splashes. Great in chilis, refried beans, soups, or casseroles.

Rebosera: An heirloom grown for generations in Hidalgo, Mexico, this small and rather compact bean has lacy lilac markings reminiscent of a local rebozo, or shawl. It produces a rich flavorful broth and is perfect in place of any traditional bean, especially in Mexican cooking.

Red Calypso: See **Black Calypso.** This is the red variety.

Red Pearl: This heirloom bean has a vibrant red skin and a smooth white interior. Its delicious flavor lies between a red kidney bean and a black turtle bean. Often used in New Orleans–style bean stews.

Red Silk: Central to Central American cuisine, this small, sweet, smooth, and vibrant red and pink bean arrives in a stunning red seedpod. Used extensively in rice and bean dishes, it is also perfect in robust soups and stews. **AKA** *Frijol rojo de seda*

Rice: Grown in temperate climates, rice is popular in India and Southeast Asia where it is often used in stews or soups.

Rio Zape: Native to southwestern America, this stunning midsized purple bean with dramatic black swirls cooks up into a rich dense texture with flavors reminiscent of coffee and chocolate. It is ideal for soups and stews. **AKA Hopi string bean**

Romano: See **Cranberry.**

Royal Corona: Native to Europe, this is a large, fat white bean, similar to gigandes. They have a luscious, rich, and creamy texture and are perfect in soups and lemony salads, tomato sauce, and stews.

Santa Maria Pinquito: See **Poquito.**

Scarlet Emperor: See **Scarlet Runner.**

Scarlet Runner: My husband first had these beans in Oaxaca, Mexico, and I remember their name from my childhood in eastern Colorado. Native to Central America, they are large, fat beans with an intense deep red coloration. They have thick skin and always require soaking. They are very creamy after a long cooking period and are terrific in stews, soups, chilis, and baked dishes. Available dried or, occasionally, fresh. **AKA Scarlet Emperor, multiflora, runner bean, Oregon lima bean**

Sea Island Red Peas/Beans: Grown in the southern United States, this is a small, ruddy pea. It is an heirloom that cooks to a sweet creamy richness and is the hallmark of South Carolina from the cuisine of the Carolina Gullah to dishes like Hoppin' John (page 202). **AKA Cowpea**

Snowcap: This heirloom is related to the cranberry bean. It is named for the white "cap of snow" that covers half of the ½-inch-long reddish speckled body. When cooked, it has a velvety consistency and retains its beautiful coloring. Its striking coloring, size, and smooth taste makes it ideal for salads.

Soybeans: Native to China, soybeans are small, round, cream-colored beans when dried and pale green with bright green pods when fresh. They are also called the miracle bean. They are used as the primary ingredient in a wide variety of products, ranging from fuels to all manner of food stuffs. In Asia,

Romano beans, AKA cranberry beans

soybeans are the number one bean used in sauces, tofu, miso, tempeh, flour, and "milk." In recent years, soy milk has risen in popularity throughout the world. Fresh, steamed soybeans in the pod, known as edamame, formerly only found in Japanese restaurants and homes, are often found as hors d'oeuvres at cocktail time throughout the United States. Available fresh, frozen, dried, as flour, and in a variety of food products.

Spanish Tolosana: Similar in size and shape to red kidney beans, this bean has a lovely mocha- and burgundy-specked appearance. It is especially good in seafood dishes. **AKA Tolosana, prince**

Split Green Mung: Small and green. **AKA Mungo bean, mung pea, green gram**

Steuben Yellow Eye: See **Butterscotch.**

Swedish Brown: A midsized oblong bean with squat ends. This bean has a butterscotch color and a lightly sweet flavor. It is closely associated with Swedish sweet and sour bean stew but is also useful in salads and other stews.

Sweet White Runner: See **Corona.**

Tarbais: Grown for generations in Tarbes, France, this large, white, and super creamy bean is essential to traditional French cassoulet. It is perfect in casseroles, soups, baked beans, and dips.

Tepary (Brown and White): Native to the American Southwest, this small bean ranges in color from pale mocha to dark coffee. It is good in refried beans and chilis.

Tiger Eye: A midsized, golden-colored heirloom bean with lovely purple swirls. Its thin skin dissolves while cooking, and the bean produces a thick, creamy consistency. A great choice for refried beans, dips, and casseroles. **AKA** *Pepa de zapallo*

Tongues of Fire: Ivory with burgundy swirls, this highly popular bean is a close relative of the cranberry bean. Despite its name, it is not hot tasting. Commonly used in minestrone and *pasta e fagioli*.

Trout: See **Jacob's Cattle.**

Vaquero: A cousin to the Anasazi bean, this is a beautiful bean with striking black and white splashes. Vaqueros are prized for their creamy and tasty broth. As they maintain their shape during cooking, they are ideal in chilis, casseroles, and stews.

White Aztec: See **Mortgage Lifter.**

White Emergo: Similar to scarlet runner beans. **AKA Sweet white runner bean**

White Marble: A plump white bean with a rich, creamy texture with the flavor of bacon. It was popular in the United States in the 1850s. It purees well and is ideal for dips, refried beans, and soups.

White Pea: See **Navy.**

Yellow Eye: Related to the kidney bean, this gold and yellow bean has a very creamy texture. It is versatile and works particularly well in baked beans and soups.

Yellow Indian Woman: Creamy and mild, this small golden bean is mild and dense, yet versatile. Its rich broth makes it an ideal bean for soups, pot beans, and casseroles. **AKA Buckeye**

Yin-Yang: See **Black Calypso.**

Yin-Yang beans

Zuni Gold: Native to southwestern United States, this speckled ivory and gold heirloom bean has a creamy texture and a slightly nutty flavor. It is excellent in soups and casseroles and retains its markings when cooked. **AKA Four corners gold, shalako**

Lentils

Probably the oldest cultivated legume, lentils are known as the biblical legume. Although they come in a variety of colors, the flavor of each one is quite similar. Because of their tremendous nutritional value, they have been used as a meat substitute for generations. They offer 8 grams of fiber per ½ cup. One serving contributes 9 grams of plant-based protein and delivers double the iron of a 3-ounce piece of steak. All lentils are quick-cooking and make great soups and purees. They are also known as pulses.

Black Beluga: These are very small, round, shiny black lentils that get their name from their resemblance to beluga caviar. They hold their shape when cooked and remain al dente. They have a very delicate flavor and therefore easily absorb other flavors.

Brown Whole: The most common variety of lentil, browns are small, whole brown discs that are very quick-cooking. Often sold with the seed coat on to help them hold their shape when cooked. Used primarily in soups and stews. Available dried.

Indian: Indian lentils are red lentils. In their seed coats, they are known as brown masoor; with the seed coat removed, they are called masoor dal. Used primarily in Indian cooking.

Lentilles du Puy: Small, olive-green discs that are soft and quite tender. The best variety is grown in the South of France, although they are also grown in the United States. Called the gourmet lentil because of its use in French cooking, this green variety has a slightly spicy flavor as well as a deeper, richer essence than brown lentils. **AKA Green lentil or tiny green**

Orange or Yellow Split: Used mainly in Middle Eastern and Indian cooking, these are small, soft orange or yellow discs without a seed coat. Sweeter in flavor than brown lentils, they can overcook very easily, rendering a lentil mush. Mainly used in dals, stews, and soups where their mushiness is an asset.

Red: Used mainly in Middle Eastern and Indian cooking, these are small, soft red discs similar in flavor to orange or yellow lentils with approximately the same consistency when cooked. Mainly used in dals, stews, and soups.

Spanish Pardina: Originally grown only in Spain, Pardina lentils are now grown in limited production in the United States. A bit smaller with deeper flavor than other lentils, Pardina lentils have a brownish-green or gray exterior and a yellow interior. They

tend to remain whole when cooked. Available dried. May be sprouted.

Peas

Green peas are up there with lentils as an ancient legume. For centuries, the globe-shaped seeds of a crisp pod were grown to be dried. The fresh green peas that we enjoy today were not cultivated until the 17th century, and they are known as garden or English peas. A broader base of peas, often called field peas, are grown to be used both fresh and dried. In this book they are listed under Beans (see page 14), as that is how they are generally sold and eaten.

Green Peas: For centuries green peas have been coveted for their sweet flavor. They are a signal of the arrival of spring. They are available fresh, frozen, dried, canned, and as a flour. **AKA Garden peas or English peas**

Marrowfat Peas: Mature, starchy, large green peas that are dried in the pod while still in the field. In England they are used to make mushy peas, a childhood favorite. They are also used to make the Japanese snack food, wasabi peas.

Snap Peas: A recent strain of green pea that can be eaten in its entirety or with the seeds out of the pod. A simple tug on the tip will break off the stem end and pull out the string. Available fresh or frozen. **AKA Sugar snap peas or, occasionally, mangetout**

Snow Peas: Another strain of green pea. It is similar to the snap pea, but with a thicker, flatter pod with undeveloped seeds. Used often in Chinese and South Asian cooking. Available fresh or frozen. **AKA Asian peas or mangetout**

Split Green or Yellow Peas, Dried: The dried, peeled, and split round seeds of a field pea that is grown specifically for drying. They are, like many legumes, extremely nutritious. They have a high fiber content: a serving of split pea soup offers 18 grams of plant-based protein as well as 19 grams of fiber. Green split peas are generally sweeter and less starchy than the milder yellow split peas. They are used much like lentils in soups, stews, and purees.

Peanuts

Although a legume, peanuts are generally eaten as a snack food or as the base for spreads, butters, or sauces. Peanuts are an extremely important food source throughout Africa and the tropics. Their flavor and nutritional values are similar to tree nuts. Highly prized both as a legume and as an oil source, they are an important cash crop around the world. Spreads and butters are also frequently used in des-

serts. They may also be known as goobers, groundnuts, or monkey nuts.

Runner: These are the predominant peanut grown in the United States. A high volume of this production is used to make peanut butter. This variety has a high yield and the kernels come in a range of sizes. They account for about 80 percent of the total US peanut production.

Spanish: Covered with a reddish-brown skin, these peanuts have small kernels and are used primarily as an ingredient in candies as well as for some peanut butters and roasted, salted nuts. They have a higher oil content than the other types of peanuts, which makes them an excellent source for processing into peanut oil. Spanish-type peanuts account for 4 percent of US production.

Tennessee Red: An heirloom plant with high yields. Large kernels with red skin, usually with at least five kernels per pod. A favorite of home gardeners and generally sold roasted in the pod.

Valencia: This very sweet variety generally has three or more small kernels in each pod. Most commonly, they are roasted and sold in the shell or sold fresh to make boiled peanuts (see Instant Pot Boiled Peanuts on page 214), a favorite snack in the southern United States. Valencias are usually found in "natural" peanut butter and account for less than 1 percent of US production.

Virginia: These peanuts have the largest kernels and account for most of the peanuts roasted and eaten in their shells. Because of the large kernels, this variety is also desirable for roasted, salted peanuts. Virginia-type peanuts are sold hot as ballpark peanuts at baseball stadiums and account for about 15 percent of total US production.

ABOUT LEGUMES: BUYING, STORING, AND COOKING

I first discovered new varieties of beans (at least new to me) a number of years ago at Rancho Gordo (see page 234) in the Ferry Plaza Farmers Market in San Francisco. Later, I began to see them at stalls of some of my favorite farmers at New York City green markets. And, more recently, I've found the terrific Kandarian Organic Farms' (see page 234) legumes, grains, herbs, and spices at the San Rafael farmers' market in California, as well as many, many other online growers, such as Purcell Mountain Farms (see page 234), which I frequently order from. A whole new world of legumes has opened up for me, and I truly have been on a path of discovery.

When I decided to revisit my original bean cookbook, I had to decide whether I should just talk about pulses, the dried seeds of legume plants used for food, such as beans, split peas, and lentils, or if I should include as many of the edible legumes as I could, such as fresh green beans and peanuts (I got a little carried away when I started looking at alfalfa and clovers suitable only for animal consumption). I decided to tackle the whole kit and caboodle of edible legumes if only for the diversity of recipes and their spread throughout the world. And every day I learn something new about them, whether it is the history of runner beans, which so generously provide us with the edible pod as well as both fresh and dried seeds, or whether it is hearing about extraordinary recipes incorporating pulses from cooks all over the world.

Some cuisines around the world have used beans for centuries, leaping ahead of European cooks who, for a long time, considered legumes peasant food. But thankfully pulses are now afforded an honored spot throughout the culinary world. Available in many sizes, shapes, colors, and flavors, pulses offer an almost limitless expansion of a cook's repertoire. Nearly every one of the world's cuisines embrace superb dish featuring pulses: France's cassoulet, Louisiana's red beans and rice, Mexico's refried beans: Brazil's feijoada, the Middle East's *hummus bi tahini,* Cuba's black bean soup, Japan's red bean cake, Italy's *pasta e fagioli, mujadara* of the Israeli table, and the dals of India are just a few of the diverse recipes featuring legumes.

Please keep in mind that all the recipes provided in this book are extremely versatile, such that almost any pulse can be used in place of any other. If you don't care for the flavor or texture of one type, experiment using one of your favorites. For instance, I make hummus with many legumes other than the traditional chickpeas and often even use a vegetable like cauliflower. Most of the recipes

Introduction 24 The Mighty Bean

that call for animal protein can be easily adjusted for a vegetarian diet by simply eliminating the animal protein or by replacing it with tofu, meat protein replacements, winter squashes, eggplant, or large, meaty mushrooms. You really can make every recipe your own.

The most innovative chefs the world over are continuously introducing legumes into their menus. There are now legume flours, pastas, snacks, and milks, which were probably created to meet today's rush for gluten-free products as much as for their taste. Lentil crackers taste familiar but have more protein and fiber than white flour crackers. Bean-based chips have about the same calorie content but double the protein, five times the fiber, and four times the iron of corn chips. Chickpea or bean pastas are continuously being improved upon, highlighting taste and texture. Various flours made from beans and peas can be used in combination with wheat flours to add nutritional benefits to breakfast foods and desserts. The enthusiastic interest of chefs and consumers has sparked that of farmers who are rediscovering and introducing long-lost or forgotten pulses: the snow cap, Appaloosa, Eye of the Goat, Good Mother Stallard, Tongues of Fire, and Christmas lima are but a few of these newfound bean treasures. Many home gardeners are exploring varieties other than the old-fashioned pole bean. No matter the heritage, all of them are good enough to eat and are healthy for you and the planet, too!

Buying Legumes

I have found that buying legumes from the sources that grow them is the best option, as this ensures the highest quality and freshness. Oftentimes this means buying online or from farmers' markets, but I can guarantee that the freshness will make all the difference in the world when it is time to cook them. The other alternative is to purchase from ethnic markets where product turnover is frequent; this is also usually the least expensive option. Plastic-bagged supermarket varieties are what most cooks use—and I often do also—but you have no way to tell just how old the contents are or how they have been stored. No matter the origin, most dried legumes will yield around 2 to 2½ cups cooked from 1 cup dried. Following are some of my suggestions on what to look for when purchasing legumes.

Fresh beans, peas, and sprouts should be crisp and free of any brown spots. The pods should be firm and almost crisp with few or no brown spots. The exception to this is with those pods that normally might have spotting, such as fresh fava beans. When the pods are very dry, the seeds have also started to dry and won't be as tender as they would be when just picked. When buying loose dried legumes, if you can, pick through them to eliminate dirt and pebbles and to ensure they are insect-free.

When packaged, be certain that the package is well sealed and, if possible, examine the contents by looking through any transparent part of the wrapping. Move the legumes around so you can inspect them for insects and other unwanted materials.

Frozen legumes should be purchased only when their containers are damage-free and clean.

Many canned beans are of excellent quality (although they may contain more salt than you desire). They are a great pantry item to keep on hand at all times as they can be the base for a quick and easy meal. A 15-ounce can of beans will usually yield about 1½ cups of drained beans. Some beans and peas (such as green beans, lima beans, or soybeans, and green and snap peas) can be bought either canned, fresh, or frozen.

The liquid in canned chickpeas/garbanzos, called aquafaba, can be used as a replacement for whipped egg whites. I first found a reference to the term "aquafaba" when working on a project for a vegan cookbook. I had absolutely no idea what it was. After some research and tests, I found that this viscous liquid could, in fact, be used to replicate a meringue. Since I am not vegan, I don't use it much, but our vegan granddaughter has shown me how she makes meringue cookies and lightens baked goods with this quite amazing product. To make it, you simply drain all the liquid from the can and use the beans for another dish. If you don't want to make the aquafaba immediately, you can freeze it; this does not seem to impact its whipping strengths. When whipping, a teaspoon of cream of tartar helps the foam stay firm. Sugar and flavorings may be added along with the stabilizer.

Peanuts are in a class by themselves. Although technically a legume, they are classified under nuts and seeds by the US government. They can be purchased raw, boiled, roasted, either salted or salt-free in the shell, and as "nuts" loose or in cans or jars. The "nuts" also may be sold seasoned, sweetened, or candied. Like any legume, they should be as high quality as possible, regardless if they are freshly boiled, roasted, or processed. I use them frequently in sauces and in Asian-inspired dishes.

Storing Legumes

Fresh beans, peas, and sprouts must be refrigerated until used. However, refrigerated storage for long periods of time is less than desirable, as they will begin to deteriorate and become unusable. As with all fresh vegetables, the sooner they are used after picking, the better. Frozen green beans and green peas are often preferred to fresh, as they are picked and frozen in their finest state.

Dried legumes are best stored in a cool spot in a see-through, airtight container. Do not store in damp, humid, or refrigerated conditions or they will toughen and become unusable. Dried legumes seem to keep almost indefinitely when properly stored, but older ones generally require a longer cooking period than fresher ones. Do not freeze any dried legume.

Frozen and canned products should be stored as recommended by their manufacturer.

Peanuts should always be stored, tightly covered, in a cool, dry spot. Humidity is an enemy as it turns them soggy and unappetizing.

Freezing Cooked Legumes

Bean and lentil soups and casseroles are terrific to make in advance and freeze for later use. Most bean soups are, in fact, better when they are given some extra time for the flavors to blend. When freezing, cover tightly and label with the name and date frozen. Freeze for no more than one month. Frozen green beans and green peas are often preferred to fresh, as they are picked and frozen in their finest state.

Cooking Legumes

Although a lot of restaurant chefs and cooks who use pressure cookers, multifunction cookers like the Instant Pot, and other conveniences now seem to forego the traditional presoak for beans, I generally stick to my old-fashioned ways. Beans purchased directly from farms will often cook nicely without a long soak. To soak or not has been an ongoing argument for years. I have noticed that many cooks of Mexican or Latin American heritage do not soak beans before cooking, whether by tradition or secret knowledge, I don't know. I would guess that moms just put the pot of beans on the fire and let them cook until they were done which, I would think, would have been by the end of the day. The esteemed Diana Kennedy, writer of award-winning Mexican cookbooks, advocates no soaking, but starting the bean-cooking process in hot water. I'm afraid that I have had too many beans served a bit more than al dente in restaurants to give up presoaking.

To soak dried beans, place them in 10 times as much water as beans, changing the water at least once over a 6-hour period. If you feel like changing it more, it won't hurt, but I haven't seen that it helps, either. (To tell you the truth, I often don't change it at all!) You can also soak them overnight, and then they should only take about an hour to cook through—something that can be done while you get the family (and yourself) ready for the day. If you choose a long soak, just make sure that they are in a cool spot, otherwise they will begin to ferment. There also is an ongoing argument about salting the soaking water. I never have added salt to the soaking water, but I'm told it doesn't seem to hurt or help in the cooking process. Discard the soaking liquid and then place the soaked beans in cold water or whatever cooking liquid you will be using. The soaking is supposed to reduce the possibility of flatulence often associated with cooked beans and lentils.

The nom de guerre "musical fruit" keeps many home cooks from preparing beans. It shouldn't. This unpleasant reputation is really not a valid one, as beans really don't produce any more flatulence than that caused by strongly flavored vegetables, nuts, or raisins. Cultures with a preponderance of beans and other legumes in their diets do not seem to have a problem at all. Flatulence is caused by the human body's inability to digest the bean's complex sugars, called oligosaccharides. Because they are not absorbed, these compounds are passed into the large intestine, where they become gaseous. On the positive side, the gas formed by beans is more easily controlled than that produced by other foods. In my experience, presoaking eliminates some of the production of gases, although the US Department of Agriculture disputes this. A healthy digestive system—one that gets plenty of fiber, leafy green vegetables, fruits, and legume protein—will have only a minimal problem absorbing oligosaccharides.

With the exception of lentils, split peas, and some split beans and black-eyed peas, I soak all dried beans before cooking to restore some moisture and to reduce the power of the oligosaccharides. Before soaking as described above, beans and peas should be picked clean of debris and well rinsed.

Soaked dried beans usually cook in a little over an hour, depending upon the thickness of the bean. I have cooked them on top of the stove, in the oven, and in an Italian glass container that sits over very low heat and takes many hours to create tender beans. The last method yields beans with a rich, thick broth, but it also raises the possibility of a broken vessel spilling beans all over the top of the stove. This device has, as you might guess, been taken off the market, but I still have mine and use it often. The only difference that I have found in beans cooked in the oven versus on top of the stove is that the oven-baked beans usually have a thicker, richer gravy. Legumes

do seem to cook quicker and create a thicker gravy when they are covered while being cooked.

Lentils, split peas, and black-eyed peas generally do not require any soaking. If you do choose to soak them, lentils and split peas will cook in a matter of minutes. For firm cooked red lentils, soak them in hot water for about 30 minutes and then place them in boiling water for about 3 minutes. Drain well. Red lentils cook very quickly under almost any circumstances, but they also rapidly lose their intense color. By following the instructions for firm cooked red lentils, the lentils will retain their color and shape for use in sauces or as a garnish.

Split peas and black-eyed peas usually cook in about 30 minutes in covered, gently simmering liquid. Fresh beans, such as cranberry, fava, and cannellini, are usually cooked, covered, in gently simmering liquid for about 20 minutes. Fresh green beans and peas are steamed or cooked in simmering salted water until tender and brightly colored. As a rule, they usually don't take more than a few minutes to be cooked through. However, they should be closely watched as they can overcook quickly, losing their flavor and bright color. Overcooked green peas will be starchy and tough.

When time does not allow a long soak for dried beans, you can place the rinsed, dried beans in a deep saucepan, cover with at least 3 inches of cold water, cover the pan, and place over high heat. Bring to a boil and boil for five minutes. Remove the pan from the heat and allow the beans to sit in the liquid for at least one hour, but no more than two hours.

Drain and rinse well before proceeding with your recipe. The beans will never get as tender as pre-soaked beans, but they will be more than edible.

After soaking, dried beans and/or peas should be placed in a deep, heavy-lidded saucepan and covered with at least 2 inches of liquid. Bring to a boil over high heat. Immediately lower the heat to a gentle simmer. Simmer for about an hour or until very tender, but not mushy, adding liquid as needed. You can add aromatics, such as onion or garlic, herbs and spices, and vegetables as the beans cook. I have found that adding salt and/or acidic ingredients like tomatoes early in the cooking cycle (when the beans begin to soften) does not seem to negatively affect the end result, as I had been taught it would.

All legumes, dried or fresh, may be cooked in a pressure cooker, slow cooker, or multifunction cooker like an Instant Pot, according to manufacturer's directions. Microwave ovens are not suitable for cooking dried legumes.

Peanuts are usually processed before buying, although throughout the southern United States it is possible to buy raw peanuts in the shell, which can then be boiled. Boiled peanuts are identified with the South and very rarely found in other parts of the country.

Methods of Cooking Legumes

Standard Stove Top: Presoaked beans are cooked, covered, in a deep pot. At least 2 to 3 inches of unsalted liquid should cover the beans. I add seasonings and acids after the beans begin to soften. There is some debate about this, as some cooks season and add aromatics at the beginning of the cooking process. Stove-top cooking can take anywhere from one to three hours, depending upon the bean, to fully cook.

Other legumes that are not soaked, such as black-eyed peas, lentils, and split peas, may be seasoned at the beginning of cooking and can take from a few minutes to about an hour to thoroughly cook.

Instant Pot: Beans cooked in this multifunction cooker can be either soaked or not. Either way,

---

COOKED EQUIVALENTS FOR DRIED BEANS AND LENTILS

Dried bean yield: 1 pound dried beans will equal from 4½ to 6 cups cooked. The yield depends upon the size of the bean and the length of cooking time. I generally count on a yield of 5 cups.

Dried lentil yield: 1 pound lentils will equal about 5 cups cooked. This, too, depends on the lentil size and length of cooking time.

Fresh bean yield: 1 pound of fresh shell beans or English peas will usually yield only about 1 cup fresh beans or peas.

they take far less time to cook than the stove-top method, but when soaked they will take even less time. If this is your method of choice, follow your manufacturer's instructions for cooking a specific legume. Generally, dried beans will cook in an Instant Pot in about 25 minutes, although some recipes require much less. They should be covered by at least 2 inches of water with any seasonings added at the beginning of the cooking process. I find beans cooked in this fashion to be firmer and much less creamy than those cooked traditionally, but that may reflect my own bias. You may also find that you will need a couple of trial runs before the legumes are cooked to the consistency you desire. Dried peas and lentils cook in very little time. Again, it is best to follow the manufacturer's instructions for cook times. Because the Instant Pot replaces so many kitchen appliances, such as a slow cooker, pressure cooker, rice cooker, steamer, and yogurt maker—it also serves to sauté, sear, and warm—many cooks rely on it as their only device. I am, however, not one of them!

Slow Cooker: This is, as the name suggests, a cooking device that cooks at a much lower temperature and longer time than other cooking methods. It does, however, produce creamy beans and luscious gravy. It allows the cook to leave the electrical device unattended as it stews, boils, or simmers the evening's meal. It has been mainly replaced by the Instant Pot. It is also known as a Crock-Pot.

Standard Pressure Cooker: As the name indicates, items are quickly cooked under pressure. Soaked or unsoaked legumes are placed in the pressure cooker. They are covered with liquid that should come up to 2 inches above the beans, or no more than the maximum fill line suggested by the manufacturer of the cooker. A tablespoon of oil should be added to keep the foam that will form from clogging the vent. Legumes are cooked on high pressure for anywhere from 5 minutes to 40 minutes depending upon the type being cooked. It is best to follow the manufacturer's directions.

Baking: Similar to the stove-top method, soaked beans are placed in a deep ovenproof pan along with aromatics and liquid to cover by 2 to 3 inches. The pan is covered and the beans are baked from one to three hours. This method is often used when cooking beans with sausages or other meats where a thicker gravy is desired.

INTRODUCTION TO THE RECIPES

Although almost all the recipes that follow will give a specific bean as the primary ingredient, don't refrain from trying a particular recipe if you don't have that specific bean on hand. This is because, with few exceptions, beans are interchangeable. For instance, even though the traditional New Orleans recipe for Red Beans and Rice (page 168) calls for

OLD WIVES' TALES

Don't salt dried beans until the end of the cooking process. The rumor is that salting beans before they finish cooking will toughen them, but this does not seem to be true. By habit, I still salt at the end, but many great cooks, as well as food scientists like Harold McGee, say it doesn't matter.

Add baking soda when either soaking or cooking dried beans. Some cooks think this helps soften, and some cooks disagree. However, the addition of baking soda does slightly reduce the nutrients as well as make the cooked beans taste somewhat soapy or even salty. It may even change the texture, making the cooked beans mushy. It does not, as the old wives' tale says, reduce the possibility of flatulence. I never use baking soda in my soaks.

Don't add any acidic ingredients until the beans have begun to soften. Some cooks say that you can add acidic ingredients, such as tomatoes, at any point in the cooking process. I, perhaps out of habit, always wait until the beans are beginning to soften before I add tomatoes or acidic liquids, such as wine or vinegar. I have put tomatoes in earlier in the cooking process and have always found that the cooked beans were a little tougher than I like.

Do not boil dried legumes. Some people believe this method results in unfavorable texture. I like to bring my beans to a boil but then cook them at a slow, gentle simmer. I believe this method results in a soft, easily digestible texture.

red beans, it will be just as tasty with white, black, or pink beans. You might not want to use something like gigante beans or large lima beans simply because their size will overwhelm the much smaller rice grains, but otherwise the flavor will be very familiar no matter the bean.

On the other hand, recipes calling for a specific type of lentil or pea generally require that specific type to be used, as the cooking properties of each one is somewhat different. This is particularly true if the recipe requires that the lentil hold its shape after cooking, as some types do that better than others. Field peas can be used interchangeably as can the different-colored dried split peas.

The important thing to note about all of this is that you can enjoy experimenting and getting to know the vast numbers of legumes available to add economy and good health to your diet.

Texas Caviar

CHAPTER ONE

Appetizers

Bean-based appetizers offer everyone a bite to eat at any gathering: meat-eaters, vegetarians, gluten-free—all appetites can be met. They are particularly welcome at cocktail parties, where beans can be made into dips, spreads, salsas, or even—in the case of Fava Beans with Parmigiano (page 40)—just simply placed in a basket so guests can create their own snack.

Texas Caviar

Makes about 5 cups

A version of this "caviar" was first introduced at a Texas country club in the 1940s. It is also sometimes called Cowboy Caviar or Poor Man's Caviar. Obviously tongue in cheek, as nothing could be further away from the highfalutin fish roe than black-eyed peas. As seen on page 32, serve with tortilla chips for dipping, as a side dish, or as a salad.

INSTRUCTIONS

1. Place the peas in a medium mixing bowl. Add the chile, onion, bell pepper, and cilantro, and toss to blend.

2. Add the oil, vinegar, and lime juice. Season with salt and pepper and stir to blend well.

3. Cover and refrigerate for at least 4 hours or up to 5 days before serving. The longer it marinates, the better it will be.

INGREDIENTS

3 cups cooked black-eyed peas or two 15.5-ounce cans, well drained

1 jalapeño chile, trimmed, seeded, and minced

1 cup finely diced onion

1 cup finely diced red or yellow bell pepper

¼ cup chopped cilantro

½ cup canola oil

¼ cup apple cider vinegar

¼ cup fresh lime juice

Salt and pepper

Edamame

Serves 4 to 6

This is about the easiest dish for cocktail time you can put together. Once reserved for the occasional dine-out at a Japanese restaurant or sushi bar, frozen edamame in the pod can now be purchased by the bag at almost all supermarkets and big box stores. A quick boil, some crunchy salt, and you've got a fun snack to have while enjoying a chilled refreshment.

INGREDIENTS

One 1-pound bag frozen edamame in the pod
Coarse sea salt for sprinkling

INSTRUCTIONS

1. Bring a large pot of highly salted water to boil over high heat. Add the frozen edamame and cook according to the package directions—usually between 5 and 10 minutes.

2. Remove from the heat, drain well, and pat dry.

3. Place the edamame in a serving bowl. Add a generous sprinkle of sea salt and serve. Just make sure you have another bowl handy to hold all the empty pods!

Black Bean Nachos

Serves 4 to 6

When I first started making nachos, I made the chips as well as all the components. Nowadays, of course, you can buy the chips ready-made, along with preseasoned refried or whole beans and many, many different types of salsas. However, I still think that this version is one of the best. It uses fresh tomatillo salsa and well-seasoned black beans. You could also use pinto or refried beans in place of the black beans.

INGREDIENTS

3 tomatillos, cored and finely chopped (see Note)

2 garlic cloves, peeled and minced

1 medium tomato, cored and finely chopped

1 small onion, peeled and finely chopped

1 small hot green chile, stemmed, seeded, and finely chopped

¼ cup chopped cilantro

1 tablespoon fresh lime juice

Salt

One 12-ounce bag tortilla chips, preferably unsalted

1 tablespoon bacon fat or vegetable oil

2 cups cooked black beans

¼ cup finely diced sweet onion

Hot sauce

1½ cups shredded Monterey Jack cheese

Sliced pickled jalapeño chiles, optional

Sour cream for serving, optional

INSTRUCTIONS

1. Place the tomatillos in a medium mixing bowl. Add half of the garlic along with the tomato, onion, and chile, and stir to blend. Add the cilantro and lime juice and season with salt. Set aside to marinate while you prepare the nachos.

2. Preheat the oven to 450°F.

3. Mound the chips on a baking sheet with sides. Place the bacon fat or vegetable oil in a medium frying pan over medium heat. Add the beans along with the sweet onion and remaining garlic. Season with hot sauce and salt and cook, stirring frequently, for about 5 minutes or until very hot and flavorful.

4. Spoon the beans over the tortilla chips. Then spoon about half of the reserved salsa over the beans. Sprinkle the top with the cheese and, if using, the pickled jalapeños.

5. Transfer to the preheated oven and bake for about 7 minutes or until the cheese has melted and the nachos are hot.

6. Remove from the oven and serve with the remaining salsa and sour cream, if desired.

Cannellini Bean Bruschetta

Makes enough to top a sliced baguette

This recipe is where the pantry comes in handy. Unexpected guests pop in for "happy hour," and all you have to do is drain a can of cannellini beans—or black, navy, Great Northern, or any other canned bean you might have—and stir in whatever savory Italian-seasoned condiments you have on hand. Add some fresh herbs, spoon the mix onto some toasted baguette slices, and voilà! This is a tasty accompaniment to that glass of wine or cocktail.

INGREDIENTS

One 15-ounce can cannellini or white kidney beans, well drained

¼ cup chopped sun-dried tomatoes packed in oil

1 tablespoon chopped capers

1 teaspoon minced garlic (or Roasted Garlic, page 53)

3 tablespoons extra virgin olive oil

1 tablespoon finely chopped basil, rosemary, or flat-leaf parsley

Salt and pepper, optional

1 baguette, cut crosswise into thin slices and toasted

Aged balsamic vinegar for drizzle, optional

INSTRUCTIONS

1. Combine the beans, sun-dried tomatoes, capers, and garlic in a small mixing bowl. Add the olive oil and chopped herb, season with salt and pepper, if needed, and stir to combine well.

2. Place a heaping spoonful of the bean mixture onto each slice of toast. Drizzle with a bit of balsamic vinegar, if desired, and serve.

Fava Beans with Parmigiano

Serves as many as you would like

This isn't really a recipe, but it is one of my two favorite ways to enjoy fresh fava beans. Make sure to leave time for prep, as you have to carefully pull off the outer skin of the fava beans once you've shelled them. It does keep you occupied and slows down your consumption of a chilled libation, as you open the pods and peel the beans. Along with ramps, fava beans are one of the blessed signs of spring.

INGREDIENTS

As many fresh fava beans in their pods as you would like
Chilled beverages for the pickers, optional
One ½-pound block Parmigiano-Reggiano cheese

INSTRUCTIONS

1. Begin the ritual by giving everyone a big handful of the beans in their pod. Then pour something chilled for each picker and begin popping the beans from their pods. You can either open the pod, remove the beans, and peel off the skin one bean at a time *or* you can hoard all the beans you've removed and peel them as you eat. I tend to be a hoarder!

2. If you have a cheese slicer, it is the best utensil to shave off a piece of the cheese. If not, cut off a small chunk, and as you pop a couple of beans into your mouth, take a bite of the cheese to excite the flavor. This is a fun way to enjoy the cocktail hour with little work for the host—everybody prepares their own hors d'oeuvres.

Note: *If not eating them raw, as above, you still need to remove the outer skin from the bean. First, blanch the raw shelled beans for a few seconds in boiling water to loosen the outer skin. Chill immediately in ice water and then carefully peel off the skin before proceeding to use them in recipes calling for raw fava beans. If you've never cooked with them, don't let spring go by without trying fresh favas. They really are worth the work—you'll be rewarded with a slightly sweet, slightly acidic, bright green taste that will liven up almost any dish.*

My other favorite way of eating fresh favas is to season them with lemon, extra virgin olive oil, sea salt, and pepper and toss them into a cast-iron skillet on the grill for just a couple of minutes to warm them slightly. We pile them on a cracker or a small toast and top with a shaving of Parmigiano or ricotta salata cheese. This is particularly delicious, especially when sitting outside with a cool glass of rosé or other chilled summer drink.

Cured Ham and Peas

Serves 4

This combo makes a lovely hors d'oeuvre at cocktail time or an equally wonderful predinner appetizer. If you are not a pork eater, use smoked poultry or game; or you can make the peas without the ham and toss the warm mix with smoked trout. All delicious!

INGREDIENTS

1 baguette, sliced and toasted

¼ cup extra virgin olive oil, plus more for brushing the toasts

1 large garlic clove, peeled

3½ ounces fine-quality cured ham, such as prosciutto or Iberico ham, cut into small sticks or pieces

2 garlic cloves, peeled and slivered

2 cups fresh peas or frozen peas, thawed and patted dry

½ cup low-sodium chicken broth

3 tablespoons chopped fresh mint

Salt and pepper

INSTRUCTIONS

1. Using a pastry brush, lightly coat one side of each piece of toast with some of the olive oil. Holding the whole garlic clove in your fingers, rub it back and forth over the oil-coated side of the toasts. You just want to give a light hint of garlic to the toasts. When all the toasts are seasoned, set them aside.

2. Place the remaining ¼ cup of olive oil in a medium frying pan over medium heat. Add half of the ham and fry for about a minute or just long enough to add some ham flavor to the oil. Add the slivered garlic and continue to fry, stirring frequently, for about 3 minutes or until the garlic is beginning to turn golden.

3. Add the peas along with the broth and cook for about 4 minutes if the peas are fresh or about 2 minutes if frozen. You want the broth to thicken slightly.

4. Remove from the heat and stir in the remaining ham along with the mint. Season with salt and pepper.

5. Mound equal amounts of the ham mixture on each toast or, alternately, place the ham and peas and toasts separately in a serving dish and allow people to serve themselves.

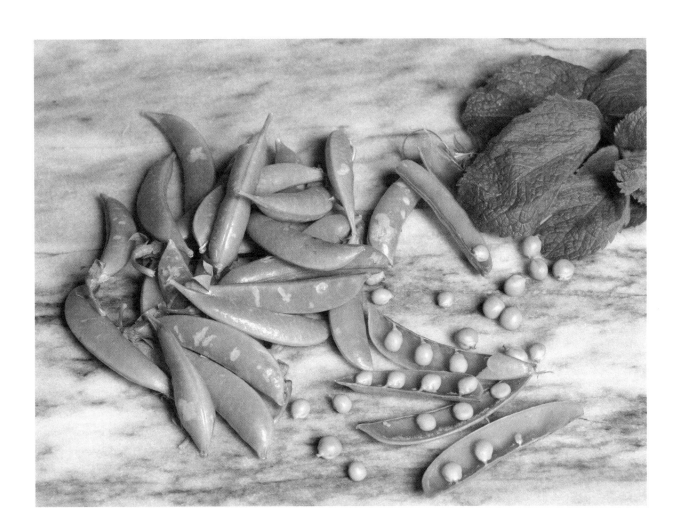

Hummus

Makes about 4 cups

Since my teenage years, I have continuously made some version of hummus, and even now I almost always have at least one version in the fridge. I use it for sandwich fillings, as a dip, thinned down as a sauce for grilled vegetables, or as a salad dressing. My husband dips straight into the container as an afternoon filler-upper.

This version, which makes a substantial amount intended for gift giving or sharing, remains my standard. The quantity of the ingredients can be easily cut to make a smaller amount, but I always make more than I need so that I have plenty to share with friends and neighbors. Canned chickpeas (garbanzos) or other white beans work very well in this recipe.

If you want an elegant touch, sprinkle the top with fresh pomegranate seeds or with a mix of black and toasted sesame seeds when serving.

INGREDIENTS

1 pound chickpeas, cooked, or three 1-pound cans chickpeas, well drained with juice reserved

8 garlic cloves, or to taste (see Note)

¾ cup tahini (sesame seed paste)

2 teaspoons ground cumin

Juice of 5 lemons, or to taste—I like mine to be very lemony

Extra virgin olive oil to taste, optional

Salt

Hot sauce, optional

INSTRUCTIONS

1. Combine the chickpeas, garlic, tahini, and cumin in the bowl of a food processor fitted with the metal blade. Begin processing and, with the motor running, add the lemon juice a bit at a time until you get the amount of acidity that you like. I like to add some extra virgin olive oil to smooth out the paste and add a bit of fruitiness to the mix. However, it isn't at all traditional or necessary. Season with salt and, if you like a little hint of heat, hot sauce and process to incorporate.

2. Scrape into a nonreactive container, cover, and refrigerate for up to 1 week.

3. Serve at room temperature with crisp chips or raw vegetables.

Note: *Fresh garlic can be sweet, pungent, or tasteless—it all depends upon how fresh it is and the particular bulb you have. I think that really fresh garlic is usually sweeter and much less pungent than the older bulbs. If you are uneasy about the strength, go easy; you can always add more.*

Spicy Bean Dip

Makes about 8 cups

For as long as I can remember, this dip has been a staple in our house. When my mom made it, the cooking fat of choice was bacon or lard and the beans were mashed with butter. No matter the mix-ins, this is the go-to dip (with homemade tortilla or pita chips) for television watching, cards or game playing, or even for a late-night, easy-to-put-together burrito, taco, or tostada. My mom had a wonderful electric bean crock that she served the dip in to keep it warm and cheesy.

INGREDIENTS

1 pound dried pink beans, such as pinquito or pinto, soaked and picked clean of any debris (see page 27)

1 jalapeño or other hot chile, seeded and minced, or to taste

1 cup chopped onion

1 tablespoon minced garlic

2½ tablespoons chili powder

2 teaspoons ground cumin, or to taste

½ cup olive oil, vegetable oil, bacon fat, or lard

¾ cup Cheddar

⅓ cup sour cream

Hot sauce to taste

Salt

INSTRUCTIONS

1. If cooking via the presoak method as I do here, place the beans in cold water to cover by 1 inch and set aside to soak for 8 hours or overnight. If using a slow cooker or multifunction pot, follow the directions for cooking on page 30 or as directed by the pot's manufacturer.

2. Drain the beans and transfer to a large, heavy-bottomed saucepan. Add water to cover by 2 inches along with the jalapeño, onion, and garlic. Stir in the chili powder and cumin. Place over medium-high heat, stir in the olive oil, and bring to a boil. Lower the heat and simmer, stirring frequently and adding additional boiling water as needed to keep the beans moist, for about 2 hours or until the beans are very, very soft and almost all the liquid has been absorbed. If very liquidy, drain off some of the liquid; the beans should be almost liquid-free. Remove from the heat and stir in the cheese, sour cream, hot sauce, and salt to taste.

3. Transfer the mixture to the bowl of a heavy-duty mixer with the paddle attachment and beat until the cheese has melted into the beans and the mixture is almost smooth. Taste and, if necessary, season with additional hot sauce and salt.

4. Scrape into a bowl and serve with chips or as a filling for burritos or enchiladas. Or set aside to cool.

5. When cool, transfer to a container with a tight-fitting lid and refrigerate for up to 5 days or freeze for up to 6 months. If frozen, thaw and reheat before using.

Hot and Spicy Black-Eyed Pea Dip

Serves 6 to 8

You could use any field pea or any fresh or cooked dried bean to make this dip. I personally prefer black-eyed peas for their strong, earthy flavor. You do want to keep the final mixture chunky so that it has some texture to hold on to the toasts. It is rather reminiscent of hot dips that were popular at cocktail parties in the 1950s. This dip makes a terrific cocktail tidbit served with toasts or crackers.

INGREDIENTS

¾ cup grated Parmesan cheese

¼ cup fine bread crumbs

3 cups cooked black-eyed peas, well drained

1 medium sweet onion, peeled and finely chopped

1 garlic clove, peeled and minced

1½ cups frozen chopped kale, thawed and well drained

¼ cup chopped chives

1 teaspoon minced hot green or red chile

Salt

2 cups shredded mozzarella cheese

One 8-ounce package cream cheese, at room temperature

½ cup mayonnaise

1 tablespoon Dijon mustard

½ teaspoon cayenne pepper

INSTRUCTIONS

1. Preheat the oven to 350°F.

2. Generously butter a 1½-quart baking dish. Set aside.

3. Combine the Parmesan cheese and bread crumbs in a small mixing bowl. Set aside.

4. Place the peas in a large mixing bowl. Add the onion, garlic, kale, chives, and chile, and stir to blend completely. Season with salt, noting that the cheeses will add salt to the mix.

5. Combine the mozzarella, cream cheese, mayonnaise, mustard, and cayenne in a medium mixing bowl. Using a wooden spoon, mix until completely blended. Add the reserved pea mixture and beat until thoroughly incorporated without breaking up the peas too much.

6. Scrape the mixture into the buttered baking dish. Smooth the top with a rubber spatula. Sprinkle the reserved Parmesan mixture over the top and transfer to the preheated oven.

7. Bake for about 35 minutes or until golden brown and bubbling.

8. Remove from the oven and place on a wire rack to settle for about 15 minutes before serving hot.

White Bean Puree with Olives

Serves 4 to 6

This is a lively mixture that works for cocktail time, as the center of a salad plate, as a light lunch—or even as a sandwich filling. Using canned beans makes it easy to put together. Serve with toasts or crackers on a plate of bitter greens.

INGREDIENTS

2 cups cooked or canned white beans

1 small onion, peeled and finely diced

1 garlic clove, peeled and minced

2 tablespoons extra virgin olive oil, plus more if needed

1 tablespoon sherry wine

1 cup water

Salt and pepper

Juice of ½ lemon

½ cup crumbled goat cheese

¼ cup finely chopped Kalamata olives

INSTRUCTIONS

1. Combine the beans with the onion and garlic in a medium frying pan over medium heat. Add the olive oil and wine along with the water. Season with salt and pepper and cook, stirring occasionally, for about 10 minutes or until the onion and garlic are soft. Remove from the heat.

2. Scrape the bean mixture into a fine mesh sieve and allow any excess moisture to drip off. Then transfer the beans to a food processor fitted with the metal blade. Add the lemon juice and goat cheese and process to a smooth puree. Taste and, if necessary, season with additional olive oil and salt and pepper, noting that the olives are going to add more salt.

3. Scrape the mixture from the bowl into a medium mixing bowl. Add the olives and gently fold them into the beans.

White Bean Flatbread Pizza

Makes 6

Although I use white beans for this pizza, you could use pink, fava, lima, or other creamy beans.

I just like the look of the luscious white bean mix. This recipe looks long and daunting, I know, but it really is well worth making the flatbreads from scratch. The topping is easy to do, but if you don't have the time or the inclination to make the bread, you can use premade flatbreads or even pita breads, making it easy-peasy to bring to the table.

INGREDIENTS

1½ cups cooked white beans, well drained

3 tablespoons chopped sun-dried tomatoes

1 tablespoon Roasted Garlic (recipe follows)

Approximately ⅓ cup extra virgin olive oil

Salt

Red pepper flakes

1½ cups all-purpose flour, plus more if needed

1 teaspoon baking powder

1 teaspoon Italian seasoning

½ cup very cold water, plus more if needed

Olive oil for cooking

¾ cup sliced black olives

1¼ cups shredded mozzarella cheese

1 cup arugula leaves

continued

INSTRUCTIONS

1. Place the beans in the bowl of a food processor fitted with the metal blade. Add the tomatoes and garlic puree and process to blend. With the motor running, slowly add about ¼ cup of the extra virgin olive oil. You want a smooth, thick puree, but not a runny mix, so you may not need all the oil. Season with salt and red pepper flakes and process to blend.

2. Remove from the processor bowl and set aside.

3. Combine the flour, baking powder, Italian seasoning, and salt to taste in a medium mixing bowl. Make a well in the middle and add 1 tablespoon plus 1 teaspoon of the remaining extra virgin olive oil along with ½ cup very cold water. Use your fingers to work the liquid into the flour. If the dough is too sticky, add more flour a tablespoonful at a time. If too dry, add cold water a few drips at a time. It should be damp to the touch but not sticky. Form into a ball, wrap in plastic film, and set aside to rest for 15 minutes.

4. Preheat the oven to 400°F.

5. When ready to cook, heat about a tablespoon of olive oil in a medium heavy-bottomed frying pan (such as cast iron) over medium-high heat.

6. Unwrap the dough and divide it into 6 equal pieces. Lightly flour a clean, flat surface and, working with one piece at a time, roll into a circle a bit less than a ¼-inch thick.

7. When the oil is glistening, add the flatbreads, one at a time, and cook, turning once, for about 6 minutes or until slightly puffed and charred in spots.

8. Remove from the pan and set aside to keep warm while making the remaining breads.

9. When all the breads are cooked, lay them out in a single layer. Spoon an equal portion of the bean puree over the top of each one. Sprinkle an equal portion of the olives and mozzarella over the top of each one.

10. Place the finished "pizzas" on a cookie sheet. Transfer to the preheated oven and bake for about 5 minutes or until heated through and the cheese has melted.

11. Remove from the oven and sprinkle some arugula over the top. Serve hot.

Note: *You can easily double the recipe for the flatbreads. They are terrific for dipping, open-face sandwiches, and as an accompaniment to soups and salads.*

Roasted Garlic

Makes as much as you would like

INGREDIENTS

Whole heads garlic, as many as you like

Olive oil for coating

INSTRUCTIONS

1. Preheat oven to 400°F.

2. Using a sharp knife, slice off the top of each head of garlic, exposing as many cloves as possible. Lightly coat each head with olive oil.

3. Place the garlic heads, cut side up, on a double sheet of aluminum foil large enough to enclose them. Pull the foil up and around the garlic, scrunching it together to tightly seal.

4. Place in the preheated oven and roast for about 1 hour or until the garlic cloves are very, very soft.

5. Remove from the oven, unwrap, and let stand until cool enough to handle. Then, pushing from the bottom up, force the garlic pulp out of the skin into a clean container. If any cloves remain in their skin, carefully peel the skin away and scrape out the pulp.

6. Store, covered and refrigerated, for up to 2 weeks. May also be frozen for up to 3 months.

White Bean Pâté

Makes one 8-inch loaf

This recipe takes some time to make, but it is an elegant vegetarian appetizer or hors d'oeuvre. It can also be served warm as the first course at a dinner party with garlic toasts and a handful of bitter greens. However you serve it, it must be weighted first or it will not hold together. Serve with toasts, crackers, or raw vegetables.

INGREDIENTS

1½ cups bread crumbs

2 tablespoons olive oil

3 garlic cloves, peeled and chopped

½ cup chopped shallots

1 cup vegetable or low-sodium chicken broth

¼ cup grated carrots

1½ teaspoons minced fresh thyme

1 teaspoon minced fresh basil

¼ teaspoon ground cloves

2½ cups cooked white beans, well drained

2 large eggs

2 tablespoons dark beer

1 teaspoon fresh lime juice

¼ teaspoon hot sauce, plus more if needed

Salt

1½ cups cooked black beans, well drained

1 tablespoon melted unsalted butter

1 teaspoon chopped cilantro

½ teaspoon ground cumin

INSTRUCTIONS

1. Preheat the oven to 375°F.

2. Lightly coat the interior of an 8-by-4-inch loaf pan with butter. Then coat with ½ cup of the bread crumbs. Set aside.

3. Heat the oil in a large frying pan over medium heat. Add the garlic and shallots and cook, stirring frequently, for about 4 minutes or until softening without color. Add the broth and carrots along with ½ teaspoon of the thyme and the basil and cloves. Cook, stirring frequently, for about 8 minutes or

until the carrots have softened and some of the broth has evaporated. Remove from the heat and set aside.

4. Place the white beans in the bowl of a food processor fitted with the metal blade. Add the carrot mixture and process to a smooth puree. Add the eggs and the beer and continue to process until smooth and thick. Add the lime juice and hot sauce. Season with salt and process to just incorporate.

5. Scrape the mixture from the processor bowl into a mixing bowl. Add the remaining 1 cup of bread crumbs and fold it into the bean puree, taking care that it is well blended into the mix. Taste and, if necessary, season with additional salt and hot sauce. Set aside.

6. Place the black beans in a medium mixing bowl. Add the remaining 1 teaspoon thyme along with the melted butter, cilantro, and cumin. Stir to combine.

7. Pour one-third of the black bean mixture into the bottom of the prepared loaf pan, spreading it out to an even layer. Pour half of the white bean puree over the layer of black beans, smoothing out to an even layer. Cover the white bean puree with another third of the black bean mixture; again

smoothing out. Top with the remaining half of white bean puree, smoothing the top with a spatula. Sprinkle the final layer of black beans over the top, lightly pressing the black beans down into the puree.

8. Tightly seal the entire loaf pan with aluminum foil. Then place it into a pan large enough to hold it and water to come halfway up its sides. Transfer to the preheated oven and pour enough cold water into the outer pan to come halfway up the sides of the loaf pan.

9. Bake for 45 minutes or until a small knife inserted into the center of the loaf comes out clean.

10. Remove from the oven and place the loaf pan on a wire rack. Place a weight on top of the loaf to press it down into the pan. Let stand, weighted, for at least 2 hours.

11. Remove the weight and transfer the still-covered loaf pan to the refrigerator for at least 4 hours or until very well chilled.

12. Remove from the refrigerator. Unwrap and dip the pan into hot water to loosen the pâté. Carefully turn the pan upside down onto a serving platter and gently tap the pâté out.

Adzuki Bean Cakes with Crème Fraîche

Serves 4 or 6

This is a fancied-up version of a very simple bean cake. You can easily serve them as is, tucked into a flatbread, or on top of a green salad. You can serve three small patties per person when serving four, or you can stretch the mix to make two slightly larger patties per person to serve six. As always, you can use any type of bean to create the cakes.

I have given you the recipe to make crème fraîche, but premade versions are available at many supermarkets. You could also replace it with fine-quality Greek yogurt.

INGREDIENTS

3 cups cooked adzuki beans
3 garlic cloves
¼ cup chopped scallion
1 tablespoon chopped cilantro
½ teaspoon ground cumin
½ teaspoon ground coriander
1 large egg yolk
1 teaspoon baking powder
Salt and pepper
1 cup all-purpose flour
3 tablespoons olive oil
Approximately ½ cup Crème Fraîche (recipe follows)
Approximately ¼ cup golden whitefish caviar, optional

INSTRUCTIONS

1. Place the beans in the bowl of a food processor fitted with the metal blade. Add the garlic, scallion, cilantro, cumin, and coriander. Process, using quick on and off turns, for just a minute or until the mixture is coarsely chopped.

2. Scrape the mixture from the processor bowl into a medium mixing bowl. Add the egg yolk and baking powder and season with salt and pepper. Stir to blend completely.

3. Cover and place in the refrigerator for 1 hour to firm.

4. When chilled and firm, remove from the refrigerator. Using your hands, form the mixture into 12 patties of equal size.

5. Place the flour in a shallow soup bowl. Carefully roll and dredge each patty in the flour.

6. Heat the oil in a large frying pan over medium heat. When hot but not smoking, add the patties. Do not crowd the pan. Fry, turning once, for about 6 minutes or until golden brown on both sides.

7. Using a slotted spatula, transfer to a double layer of paper towel to drain.

8. Place two to three patties (depending upon how many you are serving) in the center of each of four or six luncheon plates. Place a dollop of crème fraîche on top of each one and spoon a bit of caviar on top, if using.

9. Serve immediately.

Crème Fraîche

Makes 2 cups

INGREDIENTS

2 cups heavy cream
¼ cup buttermilk

INSTRUCTIONS

1. Combine the heavy cream and buttermilk in a glass jar with a lid. Cover and allow to rest for 24 hours at room temperature to thicken.

2. When thick, transfer to the refrigerator to rest for 12 hours before using.

3. The crème fraîche will keep, refrigerated, for about 2 weeks.

Chickpea Tempura Fritters

Serves 4 to 6

This is a great way to get anyone to eat their daily vegetables. The crisp tempura-like coating and the slightly spicy mayonnaise are such a tempting match. This is a wonderful gluten-free recipe, which uses chickpea flour. You can make it a legume bonanza by using the batter on green beans, snap peas, or snow peas.

INGREDIENTS

1 cup chickpea flour (see Note)

½ teaspoon baking powder

½ teaspoon curry powder

¼ teaspoon ground cumin

⅛ teaspoon cayenne pepper

Salt

¾ cup warm water

Vegetable oil for deep frying

Approximately 4 cups bite-sized mixed raw vegetable pieces, such as carrots, cauliflower or broccoli florets, onion rings, bell pepper, sweet potatoes, green beans, or snap peas

Curry Mayonnaise (recipe follows)

INSTRUCTIONS

1. Sift the chickpea flour with the baking powder, curry powder, cumin, cayenne, and salt into a medium mixing bowl. Whisk in ¾ cup warm water to make a loose batter. Set aside to rest for 1 hour.

2. When ready to cook, place at least 3 inches of oil in a deep-fat fryer. Place over medium-high heat and bring to 350°F on an instant-read thermometer.

3. Whisk the reserved batter to loosen it. Working with one piece at a time, dip the vegetables into the batter. They should be well coated, but not dripping.

4. Place the coated vegetables into the hot oil without crowding the pan. Fry, turning frequently, for about 2 minutes or until hot and golden brown.

5. Using a slotted spoon or spatula, transfer the vegetables to a double layer of paper towel to drain.

6. Continue frying until all the vegetables are done.

7. Serve warm with Curry Mayonnaise for dipping.

Curry Mayonnaise

Makes about 1½ cups

INGREDIENTS

1½ cups mayonnaise

1 tablespoon honey

1 tablespoon chopped cilantro

1 tablespoon chopped scallion

2 teaspoons hot curry powder

1 teaspoon minced hot green chile

1 teaspoon fresh lime juice

½ teaspoon ground cumin

INSTRUCTIONS

1. Combine the mayonnaise with the honey, cilantro, scallion, curry powder, chile, lime juice, and cumin in a small mixing bowl. Whisk vigorously to blend completely.

2. Taste and, if desired, add any one or more of the components to your liking.

3. Refrigerate until ready to serve.

Note: *Chickpea flour, also known as garbanzo flour or Bengal gram flour, is available at many supermarkets, online, and at South Asian markets.*

Black Gram Bean Fritters

Makes about 60

These are a very typical Indian street or snack food. You do need a chutney to dip them into—the chutney can be homemade or store-bought. The traditional method uses curry leaves, which are just too difficult to find, so I use cilantro to add a little touch of green.

Urad dal is available from Indian markets or online. If you've never tried cooking with them, now is the time!

INGREDIENTS

¾ cup urad dal (split and husked black gram beans)

2 tablespoons uncooked rice

¼ cup of water

1 medium onion, peeled and chopped

1 hot green chile, trimmed, seeded, and chopped

1 tablespoon chopped fresh ginger

½ teaspoon ground cumin

¼ teaspoon baking soda

1 tablespoon minced cilantro

Salt

Vegetable oil for frying

Mango- or tomato-based chutney for serving

INSTRUCTIONS

1. Combine the urad dal and rice in a small bowl. Add water to cover by at least 1 inch. Cover and set aside to soak for 8 hours or overnight.

2. Drain well, then rinse and drain again.

3. Transfer the mixture to the bowl of a food processor fitted with the metal blade. Add ¼ cup of water and process on high for about 2 minutes or until

the mixture is almost smooth. It will not get completely smooth.

4. Add the onion, chile, ginger, cumin, and baking soda to the mixture and process, using quick on and off turns, just until the aromatics are minced.

5. Scrape the mixture from the processor bowl into a clean medium mixing bowl. Add the cilantro and season with salt.

6. Heat about 2 inches of oil in a large, deep frying pan over medium-high heat. When the temperature reaches 360°F on an instant-read thermometer, begin frying the fritters.

7. Using a teaspoon and working with one fritter at a time, carefully slip a rounded teaspoonful of the batter into the hot oil. Fry for about 2 minutes or until golden brown and cooked through.

8. Using a slotted spoon or spatula, transfer the fritters as they are done to a double layer of paper towel to drain.

9. Serve warm with chutney for dipping.

Tuscan Soup

CHAPTER TWO

Soups

Bean soups can be elegant or earthy. Because of their nutritional value and ability to appease the deepest hunger, they can also be served as a very satisfying main course. There is nothing better on a cold winter's night than a hearty bowl of thick bean soup with a hunk of peasant bread. Nor is there any dish more welcome than a beautiful light and creamy bean soup at a lovely summer lunch. Dinner, lunch, late-night snack: a bowl of bean soup will be your go-to at any time.

Fresh Pea Soup

Serves 6

I developed this soup after I had made a quick version using leftover potato soup as the base. This uses either frozen peas or whole snap peas, which means it can be made all year long. It is yummy hot, but it's also delicious served cold on a hot summer day.

INGREDIENTS

2 tablespoons unsalted butter

1 medium white onion, peeled and diced

1 large Idaho potato, peeled and diced

2 cups chopped leeks, white part only

1 teaspoon fresh thyme

4 cups vegetable stock or low-sodium, fat-free vegetable broth (see Note)

Two 10-ounce packages frozen peas (or 6 cups fresh peas) or 12 ounces fresh snap peas, tips and strings removed

Salt and pepper

Crème fraîche, sour cream, or plain yogurt for garnish, optional

Pea shoots for garnish, optional

INSTRUCTIONS

1. Place the butter in a large saucepan over medium-low heat. Add the onion, potato, leeks, and thyme and cook, stirring frequently, for about 12 minutes or until the potato begins to soften.

2. Add the broth along with 1 cup water, raise the heat, and bring to a boil. Lower the heat and simmer for 15 minutes or until the vegetables are very tender.

3. Add the peas and season with salt and pepper. If using frozen peas, cook for about 2 minutes or just until hot. If using fresh peas, cook for about 4 minutes or until just slightly softened. (If using snap peas, place them in a high-speed blender or food processor fitted with the metal blade, add 1 cup water, and process until thick and chunky. Add the chunky peas to the soup and cook for about 5 minutes.) Whether using frozen or fresh or snap peas, do not allow them to overcook, or they will lose their bright green color

4. Remove the soup from the heat and, using an immersion blender or a food processor fitted with the metal blade, process until still slightly lumpy or, if you choose, until a smooth puree.

5. You can either whisk the crème fraîche into the soup before serving or use it as a garnish. Serve hot, garnished with pea shoots if desired.

Note: *Many canned broths are deeply colored, which affects the finished color of the soup, so if possible use a broth that is lightly colored.*

Lima Bean Chowder

Serves 6

This soup is exceptional when made in the height of summer, when all the vegetables are to perfection. The combination of the fresh, earthy limas and sweet corn creates a rich, colorful dish that sings of the season. Try using baby lima beans if you can find them because they are a bit sweeter and less starchy than the large beans. The soup is still pretty darn tasty when made with frozen beans and corn.

INGREDIENTS

2 tablespoons unsalted butter

1 cup chopped leeks, white part only

1 teaspoon minced garlic

One 16-ounce package frozen lima beans, thawed

2 tablespoons chopped cilantro, plus more for garnish if desired

6 cups vegetable broth

Salt and pepper

2 cups cooked baby lima beans

2 cups white corn kernels

1 cup finely diced red bell pepper

¼ cup finely diced onion

2 teaspoons fresh lime juice

Hot sauce, optional

INSTRUCTIONS

1. Place the butter in a medium saucepan over medium heat. When melted, add the leeks and garlic and cook, stirring frequently, for about 4 minutes or just until beginning to soften.

2. Add the thawed lima beans and cilantro, stirring to combine. Add the broth, season with salt and pepper, and bring to a boil. Immediately lower the heat and continue to cook for about 30 minutes or until the beans are very tender.

3. Transfer the mixture to a blender or the bowl of a food processor fitted with the metal blade. Process to a smooth puree. If too thick, thin with either additional broth, water, milk, or heavy cream.

4. Transfer the puree to a clean saucepan. Add the baby lima beans, corn, bell pepper, and onion and place over medium heat. Bring to a simmer and cook, stirring occasionally, for about 7 minutes or until very hot and the vegetables are still crisp-tender.

5. Remove from the heat and stir in the lime juice and hot sauce, if using. Taste and, if necessary, add salt and pepper.

6. Serve hot with a sprinkle of cilantro, if desired.

Barley and Dried Pea Soup

Serves 6 to 8

This is a hearty wintertime soup that has its origins in Eastern Russia. Although I list the sour cream as a garnish, it really can be an integral part of the soup *if* you add a heaping scoop of it to each serving of hot soup and allow it to melt in. A quite different taste, but very delicious.

INGREDIENTS

1 cup yellow split peas, well rinsed

½ cup pearl barley, well rinsed

6 cups homemade vegetable stock or canned vegetable broth

2 tablespoons extra virgin olive oil

4 ounces slab bacon cut into small cubes (see Note)

2 large garlic cloves, peeled and minced

1 large onion, peeled and diced

1 large carrot, peeled, trimmed, and diced

1 large parsnip, peeled, trimmed, and diced

1 teaspoon dried oregano

1 teaspoon dried thyme

Salt and pepper

¼ cup chopped flat-leaf parsley

Sour cream for garnish, optional

INSTRUCTIONS

1. Combine the peas and barley in a large soup pot. Add the stock along with 4 cups water and place over high heat. Bring to a boil and immediately lower the heat to a simmer.

2. While the peas and barley begin to cook, place the olive oil in a frying pan over medium-high heat. Add the bacon and fry, stirring frequently, for about 10 minutes or until very crispy. Using a slotted spoon, transfer the bacon to a double layer of paper towel to drain. Leave the fat in the pan.

3. With the frying pan on medium heat, add the garlic and onion and fry, stirring frequently, for about 5 minutes or until just beginning to soften. Add the carrot and parsnip and cook for another 7 minutes or until the onion has begun to color and the vegetables have begun to soften.

4. Add the bacon and vegetable mixture along with the oregano and thyme to the cooking peas and barley. Season with salt and pepper and continue to cook for an additional 30 minutes or until the mixture is soupy, the vegetables are cooked, and the mixture is very flavorful.

5. Remove from the heat and stir in the fresh parsley. Serve in individual shallow soup bowls or in a soup tureen, garnished with scoops of sour cream.

6. Serve piping hot.

Note: *The bacon may be eliminated entirely or replaced with any flavorful meat substitute. This will change the flavor slightly, but the soup will still be delicious.*

Old-Fashioned Split Pea Soup

Serves 6

This is a wonderful, deeply satisfying soup for a cold winter's day.

It is easy to make, with or without the addition of a ham bone, and—to boot—is one of the most economical meals I can think of. I'll bet many cooks of a certain age have their favorite family recipe—this is mine.

INGREDIENTS

1 pound dried split peas, washed and drained

2 medium carrots, peeled and chopped

1 large onion stuck with 3 whole cloves

1 celery stalk, chopped

2 tablespoons plus 2 teaspoons chopped fresh dill

1 ham bone

6 cups low-sodium chicken broth or water, plus more if needed

Salt and pepper

1 teaspoon fresh lemon juice

Hot sauce to taste

1 cup rye bread croutons, optional

INSTRUCTIONS

1. Combine the peas with the carrots, onion, celery, and 2 tablespoons of the dill in a large soup pot. Add the ham bone along with the broth. The liquid should cover the mixture by at least 2 inches.

2. Place the pot over medium-high heat and bring to a boil. Immediately lower the heat, stir, and cover loosely. Cook, stirring occasionally, for about 1 hour or until the peas have disintegrated and the vegetables are soft. Check from time to time to ensure that the mixture has not thickened too much and begun to stick to the pot. Add salt and pepper to season and broth or water as needed to keep the soup fluid but not runny.

3. Remove and discard the ham bone and the onion. Add the lemon juice and hot sauce and stir to blend well. Taste and, if necessary, season with additional salt and pepper.

4. You can serve the soup either as it is or pureed with a handheld immersion blender or in a food processor fitted with the metal blade.

5. Serve hot, garnished with the remaining 2 teaspoons of chopped dill and, if desired, the croutons.

Note: *There are many easy variations to this soup:*

1. *Add any herb or spice—other than or in combination with dill—that you like. Two teaspoons hot curry powder is a wonderful addition to the dill.*

2. *Eliminate the ham bone and use vegetable broth for the liquid. Puree and then stir in 1 cup of sour cream and 1 tablespoon of chopped fresh mint.*

3. *To make a hearty meal, just before serving add 1 pound of chopped cooked sausage, diced ham, or any other smoked meat or poultry.*

Potage Mongol

Nobody seems to know the origin of this soup. It always seemed to me to be a poor man's soup made fancy. And perhaps that is exactly what it is. It is worth trying, as it takes two great simple soups—split pea and tomato—and turns them into one delicious mix.

Potage Mongol is traditionally served garnished with blanched julienned vegetables, such as carrot, celery, or bell peppers, which turns the soup into a very elegant first course. Cooked wild rice and finely julienned chicken breast are sometimes also mixed into the soup just before serving.

INGREDIENTS

3 tablespoons unsalted butter

½ cup finely chopped onion

½ cup finely chopped shallot

1 tablespoon curry powder

½ teaspoon ground coriander

Cayenne pepper to taste

4 cups low-sodium chicken broth

½ pound green split peas, cooked

1½ cups tomato puree

Salt

1 cup heavy cream

2 teaspoons fresh lemon juice

½ cup diced seedless tomato, optional

2 tablespoons minced flat-leaf parsley, optional

INSTRUCTIONS

1. Place the butter in a large heavy-bottomed saucepan over medium heat. Add the onion and shallot and cook, stirring frequently, for about 5 minutes or until the aromatics have softened. Stir in the curry powder, coriander, and cayenne and, when blended, add the broth, split peas, and tomato puree. Season with salt. Cook, stirring occasionally, for about 30 minutes or until quite thick and flavorful. If the mixture gets too thick, add a bit of broth or water.

2. Transfer the mixture to a blender or to the bowl of a food processor fitted with the metal blade. (The latter will probably need to be done in batches.) Process to a very smooth puree.

3. Pour the puree through a fine mesh sieve into a clean saucepan. Add the cream and place over medium heat, stirring to blend. Add the lemon juice, taste, and, if necessary, add salt. Cook, stirring constantly, until very hot.

4. Pour into shallow soup bowls and serve garnished with diced tomatoes and parsley, if desired.

West African Peanut Stew

Serves 6 to 8

This is as near authentic as I've come to making this traditional African stew. It is often called groundnut stew because peanuts are called groundnuts in West Africa. Recipes always call for a hot chile, but if you don't like heat, just eliminate it. If you want it to be more soup-like, add homemade chicken stock or canned low-sodium broth. Serve as is or with a mound of rice or other grain in the center.

INGREDIENTS

One 3-pound chicken, cut into serving pieces

3 very ripe large tomatoes

3 large garlic cloves, peeled

1 large onion, peeled and halved

1 hot green chile, cored and seeded

Salt and pepper

One 1-inch knob fresh ginger, peeled and chopped

2 cups sliced okra, carrots, winter squash, or any vegetable, optional

⅓ cup smooth peanut butter

INSTRUCTIONS

1. Place the chicken pieces in a large pot. Add the tomatoes, garlic, onion, and chile along with enough water to cover by at least 1 inch. Place over high heat and bring to a boil. Season with salt and pepper, cover, and lower the heat to a gentle simmer. Simmer for about 20 minutes or until the vegetables are very soft.

2. Using a slotted spoon, transfer the tomatoes, garlic, onions, and chile to the bowl of a food processor fitted with the metal blade. Add the ginger and process to a smooth puree.

3. Pour the puree back into the pot with the chicken. At this point you can add the okra or any vegetable that appeals to you. Stir in the peanut butter and continue to cook for another 45 minutes or until the chicken is very tender and the vegetables, if using, are cooked.

Creamy White Bean Soup

Like most bean soups, this is very filling, and the addition of the smoked meat and cream also makes it quite rich. The cream can be eliminated, but the soup will not be quite as rich and delicious.

INGREDIENTS

1 pound white beans, such as cannellini or navy, soaked (see page 27)

1 smoked ham bone or smoked turkey leg

1½ cups diced potatoes

1 cup diced carrots

1 cup diced onion

½ cup diced celery

2 tablespoons chopped flat-leaf parsley

1 teaspoon chopped garlic

1 teaspoon chopped fresh thyme

1 bay leaf

2 cups low-sodium vegetable or chicken broth

½ cup tomato puree

Salt and pepper

1 cup heavy cream

INSTRUCTIONS

1. Place the beans in a large soup pot with the ham bone, potatoes, carrots, onion, celery, parsley, garlic, thyme, and bay leaf. Add the broth, along with enough water to cover by 2 inches.

continued

2. Place over high heat and bring to a boil. Then lower the heat and cook, stirring occasionally, adding water or broth as needed, for about 2 hours or until the beans are quite soft.

3. Stir in the tomato puree and season with salt and pepper. Be sure to taste before adding the salt, as the smoked meat will have added a good bit of salt to the mix.

4. Cook for an additional 30 minutes.

5. Remove the ham bone and the bay leaf. You can either reserve the meat for another use or shred it into pieces and add to the soup once you have pureed it.

6. Transfer the soup to a blender. Process until smooth and creamy.

7. Pour the puree into a clean saucepan. Add the cream. Taste and, if necessary, add salt and pepper. Place over medium heat and bring to a simmer.

8. Remove from the heat and serve, garnished with the reserved meat, if desired.

Herbed Chickpea Soup

The combination of dried and fresh herbs makes this soup wonderfully fragrant when served.

You could replace the chickpeas with any white bean, or you could use a combination of beans and chickpeas if you want to experiment. If you can't find fresh rosemary and sage, just use a combination of whatever fresh herbs you can find—even mint works well.

INGREDIENTS

1 pound dried chickpeas, soaked (see page 27)

2 bay leaves

1 large sweet onion, peeled and finely diced

1 tablespoon minced garlic

1 teaspoon dried sage

1 teaspoon dried rosemary

Salt and pepper

Chopped fresh rosemary, sage, and parsley for serving, optional

Cracked black pepper for serving

INSTRUCTIONS

1. Place the chickpeas in a large soup pot with water to cover by 2 inches. Place over high heat and bring to a boil. Immediately lower the heat and cook at a gentle simmer.

2. Add the bay leaves, onion, garlic, sage, and rosemary to the pot. Loosely cover and cook for 1 hour. Season with salt and pepper and continue to cook for an additional 2 hours or until the chickpeas are very tender. You may need to add more water.

3. Remove from the heat and ladle into serving bowls. Sprinkle the top of each serving with a good hit of the mixed chopped fresh herbs, if using, and cracked black pepper.

Tuscan Soup

Serves 6

The aroma of the fragrant rosemary will take you to the Italian countryside—along with the wonderful flavors of the beans and greens. This combination, as you can see on page 62, creates a very typical Italian dish. You can use any green that you have on hand. If you don't have red onions, use white—it will still be delicious!

INGREDIENTS

¼ cup olive oil

1½ cups diced red onion

1 cup diced canned Italian plum tomatoes or whole canned cherry tomatoes, well drained

2 tablespoons chopped flat-leaf parsley

2 teaspoons chopped fresh rosemary

Red pepper flakes

1½ pounds Swiss chard, escarole, or cabbage, well washed, dried, and shredded

4 cups cooked white, lima, fava, or pink beans

5 cups vegetable broth or water

Salt and pepper

Extra virgin olive oil for serving, optional

Grated Parmesan cheese for serving, optional

INSTRUCTIONS

1. Place the oil in a large saucepan over medium heat. Add the onion and cook, stirring frequently, for about 12 minutes or just until the onion begin to brown slightly. Add the tomatoes, parsley,

rosemary, and pepper flakes, and continue to cook, stirring occasionally, for another 10 minutes.

2. Add the Swiss chard and beans along with the vegetable broth. Season with salt and pepper and cook, stirring occasionally, for about 30 minutes or until the soup is nicely flavored.

3. Remove from the heat and serve with a drizzle of extra virgin olive oil and a sprinkle of Parmesan cheese, if desired.

Summer Minestrone

Serves 6

This recipe takes quite a bit of prep work as you neatly dice all the vegetables, but the end result is well worth the effort. You also get to combine fresh peas, green beans, and cooked dried beans in one mix. If you have a rind of Parmesan cheese on hand, throw it in the pot. It will add a lovely richness to the broth.

INGREDIENTS

¼ cup unsalted butter

2 tablespoons olive oil

1 cup diced onion

1 cup diced leek

2 tablespoons minced flat-leaf parsley

1 cup diced potato

1 cup diced carrot

1 cup diced celery

1 cup diced zucchini or yellow summer squash

1 cup diced green beans or yellow wax beans

1 cup fresh peas

1 cup chopped savoy cabbage

2 cups diced Italian plum tomatoes with their juice

6 cups low-sodium vegetable broth

Salt and pepper

2 cups cooked cannellini beans

Freshly grated Parmesan cheese for serving, optional

Extra virgin olive oil for serving, optional

INSTRUCTIONS

1. Combine the butter and oil in a large soup pot over medium heat. When hot, add the onion, leek, and parsley. Lower the heat and cook, stirring frequently, for about 5 minutes or just until the aromatics begin to soften.

2. Begin adding all the vegetables except the tomatoes, one at a time, and cook each one for 3 minutes before adding the next one. They should be added as they are listed in the ingredient list, as this allows for the proper cooking time for each one.

3. When all the vegetables have been added, stir in the tomatoes and vegetable broth. Season with salt and pepper, raise the heat, and bring to a boil.

4. Immediately lower the heat to a bare simmer. Simmer for about 30 minutes or until the soup is very thick.

5. Stir in the cannellini beans and cook for an additional 15 minutes.

6. Remove from the heat and serve with a sprinkle of grated Parmesan cheese and a drizzle of extra virgin olive oil, if desired.

Sherried Black Bean Soup

Serves 8

Years ago, a soup similar to this one was a specialty of the Coach House, a venerated New York restaurant that was *the* place to go when you wanted to celebrate. The Coach House closed in the early 1990s, but serious diners of a certain age will always mention Coach House Black Bean Soup whenever Manhattan's culinary history comes up.

If making this a vegetarian soup, eliminate the ham bone and pancetta; the flavor will still be intoxicating.

INGREDIENTS

1½ cups dried black beans, soaked (see page 27)

2 medium carrots, peeled and chopped

Peel of 1 orange (preferably organic)

1 cup chopped winter squash or pumpkin

1 cup chopped onion

1 cup chopped celery, leaves included

2 tablespoons chopped fresh flat-leaf parsley

2 teaspoons minced garlic

1 small smoked ham bone or smoked turkey leg, optional

½ pound pancetta, optional

1 tablespoon fresh lemon juice

1 tablespoon ground cumin

½ teaspoon fresh thyme leaves

Salt and pepper to taste

½ cup dry sherry wine

⅓ cup finely chopped or sieved hard-boiled egg whites, optional

Lemon slices, chopped chives, crème fraîche, plain yogurt, or whatever garnish you like

INSTRUCTIONS

1. Place the beans in a large, heavy-bottomed saucepan. Add water to cover by 3 inches along with the carrots, orange peel, squash, onion, celery, parsley, and garlic. Place over medium-high heat, stirring to blend. If using, add the ham bone and bring to a boil. Lower the heat and cook at a gentle simmer for 2 hours or until the beans are very soft. If necessary, add additional water to keep the mixture from drying out. Alternately, cook as directed in a slow cooker or Instant Pot (see pages 29–30).

2. If using the pancetta, about 30 minutes or so before the beans are done, place the cubed meat in a cold frying pan over medium-low heat. Fry, turning frequently, for about 12 minutes or until the fat has rendered out and the meat is nicely browned. Using a slotted spoon, transfer the meat to a double layer of paper towel to drain until ready to use.

3. When the beans are very soft, remove and discard the orange peel and, if used, the ham bone. Stir in the lemon juice, cumin, and thyme. Taste and season with salt and pepper. Return to medium heat and simmer for another 30 minutes.

4. Remove from the heat. Process to a smooth puree using a handheld immersion blender or transfer to a standing blender—in batches, if necessary—or food processor fitted with the metal blade and process to a smooth puree.

5. Return the puree to a clean saucepan. Stir in the sherry and place over medium heat. Cook just until heated through.

6. Remove from the heat and, if used, stir in the pancetta. Taste and, if necessary, adjust the seasoning with salt and pepper.

7. Ladle into hot shallow soup bowls. If desired, garnish the top with the egg white and a lemon slice or whatever you have on hand that will look spectacular against the lovely soft black soup.

Red Bean Soup

Serves 6

This is a rich, delicious, creamy soup. To add another dimension to the final flavor, you can garnish it with cooked diced ham, bacon, or pancetta, chopped hard-boiled egg, or minced fresh herbs. It can also be served chilled or at room temperature, but, in that case, all the beans should be added when the mixture is pureed.

INGREDIENTS

1 pound dried small red beans, cooked (see page 27) and liquid reserved

1 tablespoon olive oil

1 cup chopped onion

½ cup chopped carrot

¼ cup chopped celery

2 tablespoons chopped flat-leaf parsley, plus more for garnish if desired

3 cups vegetable or chicken broth

1 cup chopped roasted red bell pepper

½ teaspoon minced fresh marjoram

½ teaspoon minced fresh dill

Salt and pepper

1½ cups heavy cream

INSTRUCTIONS

1. Drain the cooked beans, reserving the cooking liquid. Divide the beans in half and set both halves aside.

2. Heat the oil in a large saucepan over medium heat. Add the onion, carrot, celery, and parsley. Cook, stirring occasionally, for about 10 minutes or until the vegetables are soft but have not taken on any color.

3. Add the broth, roasted pepper, marjoram, and dill. Season with salt and pepper and bring to a simmer. Simmer for about 15 minutes or until the liquid has reduced by about half.

4. Transfer to a blender or the bowl of a food processor fitted with the metal blade. Add half of the beans and process to a smooth puree. With the motor running, add the cream and process to incorporate. If the soup seems too thick, add the reserved bean cooking liquid until the proper consistency is reached.

5. Transfer the puree to a clean saucepan. Add the remaining beans. Taste and, if necessary, add salt and pepper. Place over medium heat and bring to a simmer.

6. Remove from the heat and serve hot, garnished with chopped parsley, if desired.

Lentil Soup with Cheddar Crust

Serves 6

This is a bit of a different take on the classic French onion soup. The addition of lentils turns a traditional soup into a full meal that's filled with protein. It is very rich and filling—a great main course for a chilly winter's dinner.

INGREDIENTS

2 tablespoons olive oil

2 pounds yellow onions, peeled and sliced

1 pound dried brown lentils, well rinsed

¼ cup chopped flat-leaf parsley

1 teaspoon minced garlic

5 cups low-sodium vegetable or beef broth

½ cup white wine

Salt and pepper

6 slices French or Italian bread, toasted

1½ cups grated Cheddar

INSTRUCTIONS

1. Place the oil in a large heavy-bottomed saucepan over medium heat. When hot, add the onions and cook, stirring frequently, for about 15 minutes or just until the onions are beginning to brown.

2. Stir in the lentils, parsley, and garlic. Add the broth and wine and season with salt and pepper. Bring to a boil, then lower the heat and cook at a gentle simmer for about 1 hour or until the lentils are mushy and the onions are disintegrating. Add additional broth or water if the mixture is too thick.

3. Preheat the oven to 400°F.

4. Pour an equal portion of the hot soup into each of six ovenproof soup crocks. Place a piece of toast on top of each one. Sprinkle an equal portion of the cheese on top of each toast.

5. Transfer to the preheated oven and bake for about 4 minutes or until the cheese is beginning to melt and brown. If desired, raise the oven to broil and place the soups under the broiler for a couple of minutes to char the cheese slightly.

6. Remove from the oven and serve hot with additional bread to sop up the soup.

Green Pigeon Pea Soup

Serve 6

Some type of this soup is eaten throughout Latin America and the Caribbean, where pigeon peas are almost always available fresh in the markets or from the garden.

Many islands have a traditional version, such as the Jamaican gungo peas soup and the Puerto Rican *asopao de gandules*. If you're lucky, you may be able to find fresh pigeon peas in your local market, but if you can't, canned will work just fine in this recipe.

Every cook has their own version of a sofrito. It is used to season many, many dishes throughout Latin and South America. Some cooks prefer hot chiles and some prefer sweet chiles—some prefer tomatoes, some no tomatoes. I offer you a basic sofrito recipe to follow, but you are free to devise your own to suit your family's tastes.

INGREDIENTS

5 cups fresh or frozen green pigeon peas (*gandules verdes*)

3 cups diced butternut squash

1 cup Sofrito (recipe follows)

¼ cup diced onion

1 teaspoon orange zest

6 cups low-sodium chicken broth or water

Salt and pepper

INSTRUCTIONS

1. Combine the peas, squash, sofrito, onion, and orange zest in a large heavy-bottomed saucepan. Stir in the broth and season with salt and pepper.

2. Place over medium-high heat and bring to a boil. Lower the heat and cook at a gentle simmer for about 45 minutes or until the peas and squash are thoroughly cooked and the soup is quite thick.

3. Remove from the heat and serve hot.

Sofrito

Makes about 1½ cups

INGREDIENTS

6 garlic cloves, peeled and chopped

3 Roma tomatoes, peeled, cored, seeded, and chopped

1 bunch cilantro, well washed and chopped

1 red bell pepper, cored, seeded, and chopped

1 green bell pepper, cored, seeded, and chopped

1 onion, peeled and chopped

1 hot green or red chile, cored, seeded, and chopped, or to taste

INSTRUCTIONS

1. Combine the garlic, tomatoes, cilantro, red and green bell pepper, onion, and chile in the bowl of a food processor fitted with the metal blade. Process to a fine mix—do not puree. You don't want it to be too chunky nor too runny.

2. Use as directed in a recipe or as a seasoning for soups and stews.

3. Can be stored, covered and refrigerated, for 3 days or frozen for up to 6 months.

White Bean Salad

Salads

Bean salads can stand alone or work as a very tasty base for other proteins. They can be served as side dishes, a light lunch, or the main course. A wonderful attribute of salads is that you can easily change almost any recipe by adding or subtracting seasonings and components to meet the bounty of the season or the other dishes on your menu. If you are serving a dish with Mexican, Thai, or Italian flavors, just take a basic bean salad and change the herbs and spices to fit the aromas of the main course.

Field Pea and Heirloom Tomato Salad

Serves 6

In this salad you get your legumes two ways: the fresh peas in the salad and the miso paste (made from soybeans) in the vinaigrette. You can serve the salad as is or you can pile it on some spicy greens. It is also a great base for a piece of grilled chicken or fish.

INGREDIENTS

2 cups fresh field peas, baby English peas, or frozen peas, thawed (see Note)

2 cups halved Sun Gold cherry tomatoes

1 cup chopped scallions, white and green parts

1 tablespoon chopped fresh dill

1 tablespoon chopped fresh mint

Miso Vinaigrette (recipe follows)

Salt and pepper, optional

INSTRUCTIONS

1. Place a small pot of salted water over medium-high heat. Add the field peas and bring to a boil. Lower the heat to a gentle simmer, cover, and cook fresh field peas for about 25 minutes or until tender, or fresh English peas for just about 4 minutes or until just barely cooked. Drain well and refresh under cold running water. If using frozen field peas, cook them for about 15 minutes. If using frozen baby peas, do not cook them. Pat any type dry and let come to room temperature.

2. Combine the cooled peas with the cherry tomatoes, scallions, dill, and mint, and toss to blend. Add half the vinaigrette and stir to blend. Keep adding vinaigrette until the salad is seasoned to your liking. Taste and, if necessary, add salt and pepper.

Miso Vinaigrette

Makes 1 cup

INGREDIENTS

2 tablespoons white miso paste

¾ cup rice wine vinegar

1 tablespoon soy sauce

1 teaspoon ginger juice or freshly grated ginger

¾ cup peanut oil

1 tablespoon toasted sesame oil

Salt and pepper

INSTRUCTIONS

1. Place the miso paste in a blender jar. Add the vinegar, soy sauce, and ginger juice, and process to blend. With the motor running, add the peanut and sesame oils. Process to emulsify.

2. Taste and, if necessary, add salt and pepper and process to incorporate.

3. Use as directed in a specific recipe or cover and store in the refrigerator for up to 1 week. Bring to room temperature before using.

Note: *If using frozen English peas, purchase those labeled petite peas or petit pois as they are smaller and more tender than the standard frozen peas.*

Beet and Fresh Fava Bean Salad

Serves 6

This is a perfect summer salad made with fresh young beets and fava beans. You could use red beets if you don't mind them oozing their color onto the favas and scallions. The look might be different, but the taste is still divine!

INGREDIENTS

1 pound yellow or candy cane beets, cooked and peeled

¼ cup extra virgin olive oil

1 tablespoon red wine vinegar

1 tablespoon chopped fresh tarragon

Salt and pepper

3 cups cooked and peeled young fresh fava beans
(see page 41)

1 cup bias-sliced scallions, white and green parts

INSTRUCTIONS

1. Cut the beets into bite-sized cubes. Place them in a medium mixing bowl.

2. Combine the olive oil, vinegar, and tarragon in a small mixing bowl. Season with salt and pepper and whisk to emulsify.

3. Pour about half of the dressing over the beets, tossing to coat well.

4. Add the fava beans and scallions and the remaining dressing, and toss to coat.

5. Taste and, if necessary, season with additional salt and pepper.

Eggplant, Cranberry Bean, and Herb Salad

Serves 6

This salad takes a bit of time to prepare, but it is so flavor-filled and nutritious that the time is well spent. I love making salads from herbs, rather than lettuces, for the brightness they add. Fresh cranberry beans are frequently available from late summer to early fall in farmers' markets and even many supermarkets. They are slightly sweet and very flavorful. This, to me, is a salad straight from the garden or farmers' market.

INGREDIENTS

3 Japanese eggplant, trimmed and cut lengthwise in half

2 tablespoons pomegranate molasses (see Note)

1 tablespoon freshly grated orange zest

1 teaspoon Harissa (recipe follows, also see Note)

1 teaspoon minced garlic

¼ cup extra virgin olive oil

Salt

2 cups fresh cranberry beans

Pomegranate Molasses Vinaigrette (recipe follows)

1 cup fresh basil leaves

1 cup fresh mint leaves

1 cup flat-leaf parsley leaves

Greek yogurt for serving, optional

INSTRUCTIONS

1. Preheat the oven to 375°F.

2. Place the eggplant on a rimmed baking sheet, cut side up.

continued

3. Combine the pomegranate molasses, orange zest, harissa, and garlic in a small mixing bowl. Whisk in the olive oil. Using a pastry brush, generously coat each eggplant with the molasses mixture. Season with salt and place in the preheated oven.

4. Bake for about 35 minutes or until very tender when pierced with the point of a small sharp knife.

5. While the eggplant is baking, prepare the beans: Place the cranberry beans in a medium saucepan in salted water to cover by about 2 inches. Place over high heat and bring to a boil. Immediately lower the heat and cook at a gentle simmer for about 20 minutes or until just tender.

6. Remove from the heat, drain, and pat dry.

7. Combine the beans with the vinaigrette and let marinate until the eggplant is ready.

8. When the eggplant is baked, transfer it to a large platter.

9. Combine the marinated beans with the basil, mint, and parsley leaves, tossing to blend well.

10. Mound the salad around and over the eggplant and serve with a dollop of yogurt on each eggplant, if desired.

Pomegranate Molasses Vinaigrette

Makes about ¾ cup

INGREDIENTS

¼ cup fresh lemon juice

2 tablespoons balsamic vinegar

1 tablespoon pomegranate molasses

¼ cup extra virgin olive oil

Salt and pepper

INSTRUCTIONS

1. Combine the lemon juice, vinegar, and molasses in a small mixing bowl, and whisk to combine. Add the olive oil, season with salt and pepper, and whisk to emulsify.

2. Use as directed in a specific recipe or store, covered and refrigerated, for up to 3 days. Bring to room temperature before using.

Harissa

Makes about ¾ cup

INGREDIENTS

6 dried hot red chiles, stemmed (see Note)

6 serrano or other fresh hot green chiles, stemmed (see Note)

4 garlic cloves, peeled and halved

2 scallions, trimmed and chopped

½ teaspoon ground cumin

½ teaspoon ground coriander

⅓ cup olive oil

INSTRUCTIONS

1. Place the chiles in a heatproof container and cover with boiling water. Let soak for about 1 hour or until softened.

2. Drain well and place in the bowl of a food processor fitted with the metal blade. Add the garlic, scallions, cumin, and coriander and process until finely chopped. Add the olive oil and process to a smooth puree.

3. Store, covered and refrigerated, for up to 1 month.

Note: *Pomegranate molasses is a concentrated pomegranate syrup that is sweet-tart in flavor. It is available from specialty food markets, many supermarkets, and online. There is no replacement, although a combination of dark brown sugar and lemon juice will give a hint of the flavor.*

Harissa is an extremely hot but flavorful North African chile paste. I have shared my recipe with you, but it is also available from specialty food markets, some supermarkets, and online. Although not the exact same flavor profile, it can be replaced with almost any hot sauce or chile paste.

If you want to decrease the heat of the chiles in the harissa, seed and devein them before soaking. When doing so, wear rubber gloves and avoid eye contact as they can cause serious burns.

Both of these condiments are a great addition to the kitchen.

Anchovy, Haricots Verts, and Tomato Salad

Serves 6

Despite their exotic name, haricots verts are nothing more than small, immature green beans that are more tender and sweeter than their grown-up sisters. Not too long ago they were very uncommon—now they come packaged at national markets like Trader Joe's. This is a great salad to introduce them into your diet.

INGREDIENTS

½ pound fresh haricots verts

2 cups halved cherry tomatoes

¼ cup bias-cut scallions

6 tablespoons extra virgin olive oil

2 teaspoons fresh lemon juice

Salt and pepper

10 to 12 anchovy fillets

5 ounces ricotta cheese

2 tablespoons shredded flat-leaf parsley leaves

Cracked black pepper, optional

INSTRUCTIONS

1. Bring a medium saucepan of salted water to a boil over high heat. Add the beans and blanch for about 3 minutes or until bright green and just beginning to tenderize.

2. Immediately drain and rinse under cold running water. Pat dry.

3. Place the beans in a large mixing bowl, and add the tomatoes, scallions, olive oil, and lemon juice. Season with salt and pepper, noting that the anchovies will add more salt to the finished dish. Toss to season the salad well.

4. Spoon the salad onto a serving platter. Randomly lay the anchovies over the top. Dollop the cheese around the edge of the salad and sprinkle the parsley over the top. Garnish with a bit of cracked black pepper, if desired.

Yellow Bean Salad

Serves 6

This is an old-fashioned summer salad. When I was growing up, warm bacon dressings were often used on fresh-from-the-garden lettuces, string beans, and new potatoes. I particularly love it with fresh yellow beans, simply because you only see these beans in the summertime and that takes me right back to my childhood. You can easily turn this into a main course by adding some sliced boiled potatoes and grilled German sausages to the platter.

INGREDIENTS

½ pound lean bacon

1 cup diced red onion

¼ cup white vinegar

1 teaspoon caraway seeds

¼ cup chopped sweet pickle or sweet pickle relish

1 pound yellow wax beans, trimmed

½ pound green beans, trimmed

Salt and pepper

INSTRUCTIONS

1. Place the bacon in a large frying pan over medium heat. Fry, turning occasionally, for about 12 minutes or until very crisp. Transfer to a double layer of paper towel to drain. Do not clean the pan or discard the fat.

2. Lower the heat under the frying pan. Add the onion and fry, stirring frequently, for about 5 minutes or just until the onion begins to color. Stir in the vinegar and caraway seeds and cook, stirring,

continued

for 2 minutes. Remove from the heat and stir in the sweet pickle.

3. While the vinegar–sweet pickle dressing is being prepared, bring a medium saucepan of salted water to a boil over high heat. Add both types of the beans and blanch for about 4 minutes, or until just beginning to tenderize.

4. Immediately drain and pat dry. Don't rinse as you want the beans to be warm when you add the dressing.

5. Transfer the beans to a serving bowl. Pour the hot dressing over the warm beans, tossing to coat well. Taste and, if necessary, season with salt and pepper.

6. Crumble the bacon and sprinkle it over the top of the salad. Serve immediately.

Lentil, Feta, and Mint Salad

Serves 6

This is a very pretty salad with the pale lentils accented by the bright orange carrot, yellow pepper, and bright green mint. It is a great picnic salad as well as a perfect accompaniment to grilled meats.

INGREDIENTS

1½ cups dried split red lentils, rinsed

1 bay leaf

1 sprig flat-leaf parsley

½ cup finely diced carrot

½ cup finely diced yellow bell pepper

¼ cup finely diced sweet onion

½ cup extra virgin olive oil

2 tablespoons chopped fresh mint, plus more leaves for garnish if desired

1 tablespoon fresh lemon juice

1 tablespoon white wine vinegar

Salt and pepper

4 ounces feta cheese, crumbled

INSTRUCTIONS

1. Add the lentils, bay leaf, and parsley sprig in a medium saucepan, cover with cold water, and place over medium-high heat. Bring to a boil, then immediately lower the heat and cook at a bare simmer for about 5 minutes, or just until barely tender. You want the lentils to hold their shape.

2. Remove from the heat and drain well. Discard the bay leaf and parsley sprig.

3. Transfer the lentils to a large mixing bowl. Add the carrot, bell pepper, and onion, and toss to blend. Add the olive oil, mint, lemon juice, vinegar, and toss again. Season well with salt and pepper.

4. Transfer to a serving platter. Sprinkle the feta over the top and garnish with mint leaves, if desired.

5. Set aside to marinate for at least 30 minutes before serving. Store, covered and refrigerated, for up to 3 days. Bring to room temperature before serving.

Spicy Black Bean Salad

Serves 6 to 8

You can make this salad as mild or as spicy as you like by either eliminating the chile, using just a bit of it, or replacing it with some of your favorite hot sauce. If you don't have black beans, use pinto beans, black-eyed peas, or small red beans.

INGREDIENTS

4 cups cooked black beans

1 red onion, peeled and finely diced

1 red bell pepper, cored, seeded, and finely diced

1 jalapeño chile, stemmed, seeded, and finely minced, or to taste

1 garlic clove, peeled and minced

½ green or yellow bell pepper, cored, seeded, and finely diced

¼ cup cilantro leaves

¼ cup olive oil

2 tablespoons red wine vinegar

1 teaspoon ground cumin

Salt and pepper

INSTRUCTIONS

1. Place the beans in a serving bowl. Add the onion, red bell pepper, chile, garlic, bell pepper, and cilantro, and toss to blend.

2. Combine the olive oil, vinegar, and cumin, and whisk to blend. Pour over the bean mixture and toss to coat lightly.

3. Season the salad with salt and pepper and set aside for about 30 minutes to allow flavors to blend.

4. Serve at room temperature or cover and store in the refrigerator for up to 3 days. Bring to room temperature before serving.

Cucumber-Peanut Salad

Serves 6

This is a very refreshing salad that is commonly found on the table at Thai feasts. The combination of the crisp cucumber, sweet onion, zesty dressing, and crunchy peanuts makes a perfect blend to highlight the heat of Thai cuisine. However, this does not mean that it has to be reserved for a Thai meal—it is the perfect accompaniment for barbecued meats or chicken, hot dog and burger picnics, or almost any grill or roast. This salad is best eaten fresh as soon as it is assembled, so have all the ingredients ready to go and then put the final mix together just before serving.

INGREDIENTS

¼ cup fresh lime juice

1 tablespoon fish sauce

1 tablespoon light brown sugar

1 teaspoon minced hot chile, or to taste

½ teaspoon minced garlic

2 tablespoons peanut oil

6 Persian cucumbers, trimmed and cut crosswise into ¼-inch slices

1 small sweet onion, peeled, halved, and cut crosswise into thin strips

1 cup chopped cilantro

¾ cup salted roasted peanuts, chopped

Salt

INSTRUCTIONS

1. Combine the lime juice, fish sauce, sugar, chile, and garlic in a small mixing bowl. Add the oil and whisk to blend completely.

2. Combine the cucumbers, onion, cilantro, and peanuts in a serving bowl. Add the lime dressing and toss to coat. Season with salt and serve immediately.

White Bean Salad

Serves 6

The sumac adds a Middle Eastern flavor to this salad. It goes particularly well with large white beans, which are often used in cuisines of that region. As seen in the photo on page 92, I like to use large white beans like corona or those called giant white beans, but you can really use any white bean, such as fava or large lima beans. For a quick fix, canned cannellini beans work very nicely. This salad is terrific on a picnic or buffet table along with Hummus (page 44) and a variety of Middle Eastern olives and breads.

INGREDIENTS

3 cups cooked large white beans
1 cup diced, peeled, and seeded tomato
½ cup diced red onion
½ cup diced red bell pepper
¼ cup chopped flat-leaf parsley
¼ cup chopped cilantro
1 teaspoon ground sumac (see Note)
¼ cup extra virgin olive oil
Salt and pepper

INSTRUCTIONS

1. Place the beans in a large serving bowl. Add the tomato, onion, bell pepper, parsley, and cilantro, and toss to blend.

2. Sprinkle the sumac over the top and drizzle with olive oil. Season with salt and pepper and again toss to season the salad well.

3. Set aside to marinate for 30 minutes before serving. May be stored, covered and refrigerated, for up to 3 days. Bring to room temperature before serving.

Note: *Sumac is a Middle Eastern spice that offers a bright, lemony flavor and a hint of color to dishes. It is available from Middle Eastern markets, specialty food stores, and online.*

Simple Lentil Salad

Serves 6

This is an easy-to-put-together salad that is particularly good during the summer months. It is a great picnic salad as well as a terrific accompaniment for grilled meat, poultry, or fish.

INGREDIENTS

3 cups cooked brown lentils

2 cups very ripe tomatoes, diced, peeled, and seeded

1 cup finely diced onion

¼ cup chopped flat-leaf parsley

¼ cup extra virgin olive oil

2 tablespoons balsamic vinegar

2 teaspoons grainy mustard

Salt and pepper

INSTRUCTIONS

1. Place the lentils in a medium serving bowl. Add the tomatoes, onion, and parsley, and toss lightly to mix.

2. Pour in the olive oil and vinegar. Add the mustard and again toss to blend the dressing into the salad. Season with salt and pepper.

3. Set aside to marinate for 30 minutes before serving.

4. Serve at room temperature or cover and store in the refrigerator for up to 2 days. Bring to room temperature before serving.

Chickpea, Tomato, and Bocconcini Salad

Serves 6

This salad came about on a day when I didn't feel up to doing much cooking and decided to use whatever I could find in the kitchen to make a delicious lunch. As it happened, the trio of chickpeas, tomato, and bocconcini was almost meant to be. When combined they are reminiscent of Mediterranean flavors, making them the perfect backdrop for salty olives and the fresh herby taste of basil. I recommend this system of letting your pantry and on-hand ingredients guide your cooking—you'll come up with some interesting and creative dishes. This salad would also be terrific with some lovely fresh burrata cheese.

INGREDIENTS

3 cups cooked chickpeas

1 medium sweet onion, peeled and finely diced

½ cup chopped sun-dried tomatoes

¼ cup chopped, pitted Kalamata olives

2 tablespoons chopped basil leaves

Balsamic Vinaigrette (recipe follows)

3 medium tomatoes, cored and cut crosswise into thin slices

1 pound bocconcini or cubes of mozzarella

INSTRUCTIONS

1. Place the chickpeas in a medium mixing bowl. Add the onion, sun-dried tomatoes, olives, and basil, and add just enough vinaigrette to lightly dress and toss to coat.

2. Place a mound of the salad in the center of six luncheon plates. Place an overlapping circle of tomato slices around the salad. Then add a few bocconcini to each serving. Drizzle with some of the remaining dressing and serve.

Balsamic Vinaigrette

Makes about ¾ cup

INGREDIENTS

½ cup olive oil

¼ cup balsamic vinegar

1 teaspoon Dijon mustard

Salt and pepper

INSTRUCTIONS

1. Place the olive oil in a jar with a lid. Add the vinegar and mustard. Season with salt and pepper. Cover and shake to emulsify.

2. Serve as directed in a recipe or cover and store in the refrigerator for up to 2 weeks. Bring to room temperature before using.

Ham and Pea Potato Salad

Serves 6

This is a hearty summer salad—a complete meal in one easy-to-put-together dish. Although ham is used here, you could also use smoked chicken, pork, or cooked sausages, such as bratwurst or knockwurst. Whatever your choice, it's likely to pair beautifully with the simplicity of the peas.

INGREDIENTS

2 pounds fresh peas, shelled, or one 10-ounce package frozen petite peas, thawed and patted dry

1 pound red potatoes, cooked, peeled, and diced

¾ pound smoked ham, diced

2 cups cooked black-eyed peas, well drained

1 cup diced onion

Mustard-Dill Vinaigrette (recipe follows)

Salt and pepper

INSTRUCTIONS

1. Place the fresh peas in a shallow saucepan. Add just enough salted water to barely cover. Place over medium heat and bring to a simmer. Cook, simmering, for about 2 minutes or until just tender. Remove from the heat, drain, and pat dry. Let cool to room temperature. Frozen peas do not need to be cooked.

2. Transfer the peas to a medium mixing bowl. Add the potatoes, ham, black-eyed peas, and onion, and gently toss to blend well. You don't want to mash the peas.

3. When ready to serve, pour the vinaigrette over the top and season with salt and pepper. Toss to season well.

4. Serve immediately.

Mustard-Dill Vinaigrette

Makes about 1½ cups

INGREDIENTS

¼ cup champagne or white wine vinegar

¼ cup Dijon mustard

¾ cup chopped fresh dill

¾ cup olive oil

Salt and pepper

INSTRUCTIONS

1. Combine the vinegar, mustard, and dill in a small mixing bowl. Add the oil and season with salt and pepper. Whisk vigorously to combine.

2. Use as directed in a specific recipe.

Edamame, Fennel, and Chicken Salad

Serves 6

A lovely main course salad that can easily be expanded for a crowd. It is a wonderful luncheon main course as well as a terrific component of a buffet table. If you have trouble finding the edamame, you can use fresh peas or cooked white or black beans instead.

INGREDIENTS

1½ pounds skinless boneless chicken breast

2 tablespoons olive oil

Salt and pepper

4 stalks celery, trimmed, peeled, and cut crosswise on the
  diagonal, into ¼-inch pieces

1 fennel bulb, trimmed and cut into slivers

1 orange, peeled and cut into chunks

1½ cups frozen shelled edamame, thawed and patted dry

Lemon Vinaigrette (recipe follows)

Salt and pepper, optional

Handful fresh mint leaves for garnish, optional

INSTRUCTIONS

1. Oil and preheat a grill or prepare a stove-top grill pan.

2. Lightly coat the chicken breasts with olive oil and season with salt and pepper.

3. Place the chicken on the grill (or in the grill pan) and grill, turning occasionally, for about 12 minutes or until an instant-read thermometer inserted into the thickest part reads 155°F. Remove from the grill and set aside. The chicken will continue to cook while it sits and the temperature will reach the preferred 160°F for breast meat.

4. Combine the celery, fennel, orange, and edamame in a large mixing bowl. Add just enough of the vinaigrette to gently season. Taste and, if necessary, add salt and pepper.

5. Spoon the salad onto a serving platter.

6. Using a sharp knife, cut the chicken breasts on the diagonal into thin slices. Shingle the chicken slices over the salad. Garnish the platter with mint leaves, if desired, and serve.

Lemon Vinaigrette

Makes about 1 cup

INGREDIENTS

1 large garlic clove, peeled and minced

¼ cup fresh lemon juice

1 teaspoon Dijon mustard

½ teaspoon grated lemon zest

²⁄₃ cup extra virgin olive oil

Salt and pepper

INSTRUCTIONS

1. Place the garlic in a small bowl. Add the lemon juice and using a kitchen fork or a pestle mash the garlic into the lemon juice. Stir in the mustard and lemon zest.

2. Using a whisk, beat the olive oil into the mix, whisking until well blended.

3. Taste and, if necessary, season with salt and pepper.

Salade Niçoise

Serves 6

This is a spectacular main course summer salad. Everything can be prepared in advance. The salad can even be put together early in the day, covered with a damp paper towel, and refrigerated until ready to serve. A cook's dream!

This is a perfect opportunity to use haricots verts, the traditional French green bean. They used to be difficult to find, but I now easily spot them at the supermarket in neat little packages. They are sweeter and more delicate than green string beans.

If fresh tuna is not available, you can use a fine-quality Italian or French canned tuna packed in oil.

INGREDIENTS

1½ to 2 pounds tuna steaks

2 tablespoons olive oil

Juice of ½ lemon

Salt and pepper

4 medium red potatoes, cooked and sliced

¼ pound haricots verts or green beans, trimmed and cooked

Lemon Vinaigrette (see page 117)

1 head red leaf lettuce, pulled into leaves, well washed and dried

3 very ripe tomatoes, peeled, cored, and cut into quarters

3 hard-boiled eggs, peeled and cut into quarters

½ cup pitted Niçoise or Kalamata olives

2 tablespoons capers

12 anchovy fillets

INSTRUCTIONS

1. Preheat and oil a grill or prepare a stove-top grill pan.

continued

119

2. Lightly coat the tuna steaks with olive oil and lemon juice. Season with salt and pepper.

3. Place the tuna on the grill (or in the grill pan) and grill, turning once, for about 5 minutes or until still pink in the center. Remove from the grill and set aside.

4. Place the potatoes in a medium mixing bowl and the green beans in another bowl. Drizzle just enough of the vinaigrette over each to lightly season. Toss to coat. Taste and, if necessary, add salt and pepper.

5. Line a large serving platter with the lettuce leaves. Place the potatoes at one end of the platter and the green beans at the other. Place the tomato quarters on a remaining side of the platter and the hard-boiled egg quarters on the other side.

6. Carefully cut each tuna steak crosswise into slices about ¼-inch thick. Place the tuna slices in the center of the platter.

7. Sprinkle the olives and capers over the top and randomly place anchovy fillets over all.

8. Serve with the remaining vinaigrette passed on the side.

Scallops with Pea Shoots

Serves as many as you like

Summer mornings at the green markets always inspire me. They are terrific places to buy seafood where I live, as everything is just caught, fresh from the waters off Long Island. It is all so tempting that I will often buy produce based more on how beautiful it is rather than as an ingredient of a planned dish. This recipe is a result of just that kind of shopping.

The scallops are light and tasty, and they give the sweet, earthy flavors of the pea shoots and baby peas the opportunity to shine. The edible flowers are a lively addition and an extra treat. I've always loved nasturtiums, and in this case their bite adds just enough zest to an otherwise very sweet dish.

INGREDIENTS

1 bunch fresh pea shoots for every 4 servings

1 cup fresh baby peas for every 4 servings

1 plastic clamshell of edible flowers for every 4 servings

4 sea scallops per person

½ cup Wondra flour

Salt and pepper

1 tablespoon unsalted butter

1 teaspoon corn oil

Moscato Vinaigrette (recipe follows)

INSTRUCTIONS

1. Scatter an equal portion of pea shoots and fresh peas over each of the dinner plates you will be using. Randomly scatter an equal portion of the flowers around and on top of them.

2. Pat the scallops dry and lightly dust both sides with Wondra flour and season with salt and pepper.

continued

3. Heat the butter and oil in a large skillet over high heat. When very hot but not smoking, add the seasoned scallops. Fry, turning once, for about 4 minutes or until golden brown on the outside and still slightly raw in the center.

4. Using a slotted spatula, place the scallops on a double layer of paper towel to drain. Then transfer 4 scallops to each garnished plate. Drizzle each plate with some of the vinaigrette and serve.

Moscato Vinaigrette

Makes about 1 cup

INGREDIENTS

3 tablespoons Moscato vinegar
1 small shallot, peeled and finely minced
1 teaspoon Dijon mustard
¾ cup peanut oil
Salt and pepper

INSTRUCTIONS

1. Combine the vinegar, shallot, and mustard in a jar with a lid. Add the peanut oil and season with salt and pepper. Cover and shake vigorously to emulsify.

2. May be stored, covered and refrigerated, for up to 10 days.

Chickpea Pasta with
Romano Beans and Cherry Tomatoes

CHAPTER FOUR

Main Courses

Beans are often the star of the meal when sitting at the center of the table. Sometimes they are combined with other proteins in equal partnership, but more often than not, they are the headliner. This is because they are not only extremely nutritious and filling, but they also easily absorb the flavors and seasonings of so many international cuisines. Plus, they lend themselves to one-pot dishes that make their preparation easy on the cook.

Cuban Black Beans and Rice

Serves 6

This is a very old Cuban rice and beans recipe that is tradition-ally called *Moros y Christianos*, a name that references the black beans representing the Moors and the white rice representing the Christians. Although some version of this dish is found in other areas with Spanish history, its heritage is in Spain, where for centuries the Moors and Christians battled. There are now many festivals with the name *Moros y Christianos* in all parts of the world, carrying a deep Spanish influence.

INGREDIENTS

1 pound dried black beans, rinsed

2 tablespoons olive oil

1 cup diced onion

½ cup diced red bell pepper

1 tablespoon minced garlic

1 cup peeled, cored, seeded, and diced Roma tomatoes

1 teaspoon ground cumin

¼ teaspoon cayenne pepper

Salt and pepper

2 cups long grain rice

INSTRUCTIONS

1. Soak and cook beans as directed on page 27. Drain well and reserve the cooking liquid.

2. Place the oil in a large saucepan over medium heat. Add the onion, bell pepper, and garlic, and cook, stirring frequently, for about 4 minutes or until the onion has softened and the garlic has not colored. Add the tomatoes, cumin, and cayenne, and continue to cook, stirring frequently, for another 10 minutes.

3. Add the beans along with enough of the cooking liquid to make a thick gravy. Season with salt and pepper and cook at a bare simmer, adding reserved cooking liquid or water as needed, for about 30 minutes or until very flavorful with a thick gravy.

4. While the beans are cooking, prepare the rice.

5. Place 3¾ cups of salted water in a medium saucepan over high heat. Bring to a boil. Add the rice, stir, and bring to a boil. Immediately lower the heat, cover, and cook for about 20 minutes or until the water has been absorbed by the rice and the rice is tender. Remove from the heat and let stand, covered, until ready to serve.

6. Mound the rice in the center of a large platter or shallow serving bowl. Make a well in the center and spoon the beans into the well, allowing them to spill out over the rice.

7. Serve immediately.

Ayocote Negro Chili

Serves 6 to 8

This is basically the same chili recipe that my mother made when I was a child, with the exception of the heritage beans. I discovered Ayocote Negro beans through Rancho Gordo (see page 234), a seller of specialty beans. These beans are deep smoky black in color and very large, very meaty, and, when well cooked, very creamy. They turn plain old chili into something rich, soothing, and extra filling. Of course, you can make this chili using the usual pinto bean or, in fact, almost any bean you have on hand, but I guarantee it will be better with this yummy bean.

You can turn this into chili con carne by adding 2 pounds of nicely browned, coarsely chopped pork, beef, venison, sausage, or any of the ground meat substitutes now available, to the mix at any point up to half an hour before the chili is ready to be served.

You can garnish the final dish—either in a large tureen or individual soup bowls—with sour cream, guacamole, grated cheese, chopped cilantro, chopped sweet onions or scallions, tortilla chips, or any condiment that says "chili."

INGREDIENTS

1 pound Ayocote Negro beans, soaked and rinsed (see page 27)

2 dried hot red chiles

2 tablespoons mild oil, such as peanut

2 cups chopped red onion

1 tablespoon minced garlic

2 red or green bell peppers, cored, membrane removed, seeded, and diced

1 jalapeño chile, stemmed and seeded, or to taste

¼ cup pure ground chile powder

2 tablespoons masa harina (see Note)

1 tablespoon ground cumin, or to taste

1 tablespoon cocoa powder

½ teaspoon ground epazote or oregano

¼ teaspoon ground cinnamon

4 cups diced canned tomatoes with their liquid

1 cup tomato sauce

Salt and pepper

continued

INSTRUCTIONS

1. Begin cooking the beans as directed on pages 29–30, following the suggested method for whatever type of pot you are using. Personally, I prefer the basic open pot cooking as I love the steps and the aromas filling the kitchen as you go.

2. Place the dried chiles in a small heatproof bowl with boiling water to cover by about an inch. Set aside to soften for about 15 minutes. When softened, drain well and split, removing and discarding the stem and any seeds. Set aside.

3. Heat the oil in a large heavy frying pan over medium heat. Add the onion and garlic and cook, stirring frequently, for about 5 minutes or until beginning to soften. Add the reserved softened dried chiles along with the bell and jalapeño peppers. Cook, stirring occasionally, for 5 more minutes.

4. Stir in the chile powder, masa, cumin, cocoa, epazote, and cinnamon, and cook for another minute or two. Scrape the mixture into the cooking beans, raise the heat and bring to a boil.

5. Add the tomatoes and the tomato sauce and season with salt and pepper. Lower the heat and continue to cook, stirring occasionally, for another hour or until the beans are soft and the flavors are well blended.

6. Remove from the heat and serve, hot, with any garnish you prefer.

Note: *Masa harina is ground dried nixtamalized corn used to make doughs for tortillas and other Mexican dishes. It is available at Mexican markets, specialty food stores, some supermarkets, and online.*

Cannellini Bean Pizza

Serves 6

Using prepared pizza dough and canned beans, this yummy pizza will come together 1-2-3! If you wish, you can also mix about a cup of mozzarella cubes or shreds in with the beans for a cheesier topping.

INGREDIENTS

2 tablespoons olive oil

1½ cups cooked cannellini beans

2 garlic cloves, peeled and thinly sliced

½ cup slivered sun-dried tomatoes

¼ cup slivered pitted black olives

¼ cup extra virgin olive oil

Salt

Red chile flakes

1 pound prepared pizza dough

¾ cup grated Parmesan cheese

Basil for topping, optional

INSTRUCTIONS

1. Preheat the oven to 450°F.

2. Coat an 11-by-7-by-2-inch baking sheet with the 2 tablespoons olive oil. Set aside.

3. Place the beans in a medium mixing bowl. Add the garlic, tomatoes, and olives, tossing to blend. Add the ¼ cup extra virgin olive oil and toss to coat well. Season with salt and chile flakes. Set aside.

4. Lightly flour a clean, flat work surface and, using your fingertips, stretch the pizza dough out to a rectangle to fit the prepared pan.

5. Spoon the bean mix over the top of the dough, taking care that it covers evenly. Sprinkle the cheese over the top.

6. Transfer to the preheated oven and bake for about 20 minutes or until the bottom and edges are well browned and crisp.

7. Remove from the oven, sprinkle with basil, if desired, cut into pieces, and serve.

Beef Tenderloin with Black Bean Chutney

Serves 6

This is a very elegant bean dish that's ready for gala entertainment or a very fancy dinner party. The chutney adds some unexpected zest and crunch to the luxe tenderness of the meat. It can be used as a condiment for almost any meat or poultry—particularly those that have been grilled.

INGREDIENTS

One 2½- to 3-pound beef tenderloin, trimmed and tied
2 tablespoons olive oil
Salt and pepper
Black Bean Chutney (recipe follows)

INSTRUCTIONS

1. Preheat the oven to 450°F.

2. Generously coat the beef with olive oil and season with salt and pepper.

3. Place a roasting pan in the oven for 3 minutes to get very hot. When hot, place the seasoned fillet in the center and roast for 12 minutes. Turn and roast for an additional 12 minutes for rare. Increase the cooking time by 4 to 5 minutes for medium.

4. Remove from the oven and allow to rest for 15 minutes before cutting, crosswise, into ½-inch-thick slices.

5. Arrange the slices down the center of a warm serving platter. Spoon some of the chutney along each side of the meat and serve immediately.

Black Bean Chutney

Makes about 4 cups

INGREDIENTS

1 jalapeño chile, trimmed, seeded, and minced, or to taste

2½ cups diced red onion

1 tablespoon minced garlic

1 teaspoon cumin seeds

½ teaspoon mustard seeds

¼ cup light brown sugar

¼ cup white vinegar

2½ cups cooked black beans

½ cup diced jicama

¼ cup chopped cilantro

INSTRUCTIONS

1. Combine the chile with the onion, garlic, cumin seeds, and mustard seeds in a medium saucepan. Stir in the sugar and vinegar and place over medium heat. Bring to a boil. Immediately lower the heat and cook at a gentle simmer for 15 minutes. Add the beans and continue to cook for another 15 minutes.

2. Remove from the heat and let stand for at least 1 hour before serving. May be stored, covered and refrigerated, for up to 1 week. Bring to room temperature before serving.

3. When ready to serve, stir in the jicama and cilantro.

Easy-Peasy Black Bean Burgers

Serves 6

Easy-peasy because these delicious burgers can be made with canned black beans, a piece of toast (any kind works), and no hard-to-find ingredients. They are great on a bun or a slice of grilled peasant bread with any fixin's you like. Or you can put them in the center of the plate with some salad and fries.

INGREDIENTS

2 slices bread, toasted

½ cup walnut pieces

Two 15-ounce cans (or 3 cups cooked) black beans, well drained

Juice of ½ lemon

½ cup chopped onion

1 tablespoon chopped garlic

1 teaspoon green hot sauce, or to taste

1 large egg

Salt

Oil for frying

INSTRUCTIONS

1. Break the toast into pieces. Place the pieces in the bowl of a food processor fitted with the metal blade. Add the walnuts and process until coarsely chopped.

2. Scrape the toast mixture from the processor into a medium mixing bowl. Set aside.

3. Return the bowl to the processor and again fit with the metal blade. Combine the beans, lemon juice, onion, garlic, and hot sauce in the bowl. Process, using quick on and off turns, to coarsely chop.

4. Scrape the bean mixture into the toast mixture. Add the egg, season with salt, and beat to incorporate.

5. Using your hands, form the mixture into six patties of equal size, pushing slightly to hold the mix together.

6. Place the oil in a large frying pan over medium-high heat. Add the patties and fry, turning once, for about 10 minutes or until nicely browned and slightly crisp around the edges.

7. Serve hot, as is, or on a bun with sliced avocado or tomato or sautéed onions, if desired.

Green Lentil and Chorizo Stew

Serves 6 to 8

Chorizo and lentils are perfect partners—the spiciness of the sausage excites the earthiness of the lentils to create a wonderful blend of flavors. You could easily substitute any sausage for the chorizo, although a spicy one would offer the most character to the finished dish.

If you are not a meat eater, there are a wide variety of options for swapping out meat in this recipe—choose tofu, tempeh, tempeh bacon, or seitan. And yet another alternative: instead of cutting the mushrooms, use medium button mushrooms (or other, more aromatic ones) and leave them whole. You could also use chunks of winter squash, such as acorn or delicata.

INGREDIENTS

2 tablespoons extra virgin olive oil

1 large onion, peeled and diced

2 teaspoons chopped garlic

4 medium carrots, peeled and diced

2 cups sliced or diced button mushrooms

½ teaspoon dried oregano

¼ teaspoon dried thyme

¼ to ½ teaspoon smoked paprika (pimenton), depending upon your taste

One 14.5-ounce can diced tomatoes with their juice

1 pound dried whole green lentils

8 cups low-fat, low-sodium chicken broth or vegetable broth

Salt and pepper

12 ounces fully cooked Spanish chorizo, cut into pieces

1 cup chopped scallion

½ cup chopped cilantro

Grated Pecorino Romano cheese for garnish, optional

INSTRUCTIONS

1. Heat the oil in a large heavy-bottomed saucepan over medium heat. Add the onion and garlic and cook, stirring frequently, for about 5 minutes or until the onions have sweat their juices and are quite soft.

2. Add the carrots and mushrooms along with the oregano, thyme, and smoked paprika, and continue to cook, stirring frequently, for about 10 minutes or until the carrots begin to soften. Stir in the tomatoes.

3. Add the lentils and stir to blend. Then add the broth and season with salt and pepper. Raise the heat and bring to a boil. Lower the heat and simmer for about 20 minutes or until the flavors have blended and the lentils have softened but are not mushy.

4. Add the chorizo and continue to cook for about 5 minutes or until the chorizo has added some flavor to the mix. Stir in the scallion and cilantro and remove from the heat.

5. Serve in a large serving bowl or in individual shallow soup bowls garnished with grated cheese, if desired.

Lentil Falafel

Serves 6

This falafel is a bit different from the traditional falafel made with chickpeas. It is, however, just as tasty. And because it is baked rather than fried, it's even healthier. You can make a complete meal by adding a green salad or a cucumber-tomato salad.

INGREDIENTS

¼ cup olive oil

4 cups cooked lentils, very well drained

1 large egg, at room temperature

4 ounces ricotta

1 cup bread crumbs

¼ cup chopped flat-leaf parsley

1 teaspoon lemon juice

1 teaspoon ground cumin

½ teaspoon baking soda

½ teaspoon ground coriander

¼ teaspoon cayenne pepper, or to taste

Salt and pepper

Lemon-Yogurt Sauce (recipe follows)

Warm pita bread for serving, optional

INSTRUCTIONS

1. Preheat the oven to 450°F.

2. Line a baking sheet with sides with a silicone liner, parchment paper, or aluminum foil, and set aside.

3. Place the oil in a small bowl and set aside.

4. Place the lentils in the bowl of a food processor fitted with the metal blade. Process, using quick on and off turns, until coarsely ground. You do not want a puree; it should be coarse.

5. Scrape the lentils into a medium mixing bowl. Add the egg, ricotta, bread crumbs, parsley, lemon juice, cumin, baking soda, coriander, and cayenne, and stir to blend. Do not beat or mash.

6. Scrape the mixture into a medium mixing bowl. Season with salt and pepper. Working with about ¼ cup at a time and using your hands, form the mixture into small patties.

7. Using a small pastry brush, lightly coat each side of the patties with the reserved oil. Place the oiled patties on the prepared baking sheet.

8. When all the patties have been formed, transfer the baking sheet to the preheated oven and bake for about 20 minutes, turning once, or until golden brown and crisp.

9. Remove from the oven and serve piping hot with Lemon-Yogurt Sauce and warm pita bread, if using.

Lemon-Yogurt Sauce

Makes about 1½ cups

INGREDIENTS

1 cup plain Greek yogurt

2 tablespoons tahini (sesame seed paste)

2 tablespoons fresh lemon juice

2 tablespoons finely chopped flat-leaf parsley

2 tablespoons finely chopped fresh chives

Green hot sauce to taste

Salt

INSTRUCTIONS

1. Place the yogurt in a small mixing bowl. Add the tahini, lemon juice, parsley, chives, and hot sauce, and whisk to blend well. Taste and, if necessary, season with salt.

2. Serve immediately or cover and store in the refrigerator for no more than a day.

Red Lentil Penne with Arugula Pesto

Serves 6

Red lentil pasta is available at most supermarkets, health food stores, specialty food markets, and online. In recent years it has gained popularity due to its low gluten, which makes it a nutritious swap for dishes that are usually gluten heavy. As an added bonus, the lentils and beans used to make these pastas infuse extra color and flavor into a dish. Lentil pasta was developed for the gluten-free market, but you don't have to be on a gluten-free diet to enjoy it. The slightly sharp pesto is the perfect mate for the earthiness of the pasta. Lots of Parmesan cheese is a bonus!

INGREDIENTS

1 pound red lentil penne

Arugula Pesto (recipe follows)

Grated Parmesan cheese for serving

INSTRUCTIONS

1. Prepare the penne according to the package directions for al dente pasta.

2. Drain well, reserving ½ cup of the pasta cooking water.

3. Return the penne to the cooking pot, add the pesto along with just enough of the cooking water to loosen the sauce.

4. Spoon the pasta into a serving bowl and top with Parmesan cheese.

5. Serve immediately.

Arugula Pesto

Makes about 2 cups

INGREDIENTS

2 bunches arugula, well washed, dried, and thick stems discarded

2 garlic cloves, peeled and chopped

1½ cups toasted walnuts

¾ cup grated Parmesan cheese

⅓ cup extra virgin olive oil

Salt

INSTRUCTIONS

1. Place the arugula in the bowl of a food processor fitted with the metal blade. Add the garlic and walnuts and process until very finely chopped. Add the cheese and process to just incorporate.

2. With the motor running, add the oil in a slow, steady stream and process until quite smooth.

3. Season with salt and scrape from the bowl into a container.

4. Use as directed in a specific recipe or store, tightly covered and refrigerated, for up to 2 weeks. Bring to room temperature before using.

Easy Couscous with Chickpeas

Serves 6

Years ago, when I first began making couscous, I had to search for it and, once I found it, I had to soak and steam it in the traditional manner. Now you can buy packaged quick-cooking couscous in a variety of flavors. If you enjoy cooking as much as I do, you can make your own Harissa (page 99) for this dish, but if you're looking to whip up this dish in a hurry, you can buy premade harissa at your local grocery store.

This is a quick and easy version of the classic Berber dish that usually incorporates semolina grains with meat and vegetables. Steaming vegetables on top of the couscous is the traditional method, but since we now have almost-instant couscous, the vegetables need to be cooked separately. You can use any combination of vegetables that appeals to you and your family. Whatever I use, I either roast or grill them.

INGREDIENTS

2 medium onions, peeled and cut into quarters

2 cups carrot chunks

1 cup parsnip chunks

1 cup cauliflower florets

1 cup winter squash chunks

1 cup zucchini pieces

About ½ cup olive oil

Salt and pepper

2 cups cooked chickpeas

Grated zest of 1 orange

¾ teaspoon ground cinnamon

One 10-ounce package couscous

Tomato Sauce (recipe follows)

Harissa (page 99)

INSTRUCTIONS

1. Preheat the oven to 375°F.

2. Line two baking sheets with sides with a silicone liner or use a nonstick pan.

3. Lightly coat the vegetables with some of the olive oil and season with salt and pepper. Place them by type on the prepared baking sheet. This makes it easier to remove them from the pan if one type cooks quicker than the others.

4. As cooked, remove from the oven and keep warm.

5. While the vegetables are cooking, prepare the chickpeas and couscous.

6. Place the chickpeas in a small saucepan. Add 2 teaspoons of the olive oil along with the orange zest and ¼ teaspoon of the cinnamon. Place over low heat and cook for about 4 minutes or just until hot. Remove from the heat and keep warm.

7. Prepare the couscous according to the package directions, adding the remaining ½ teaspoon of the cinnamon and 1 teaspoon of the olive oil to the cooking water.

8. When cooked, fluff the couscous with a kitchen fork. Transfer to a large serving platter. Arrange the warm vegetables and chickpeas over the top. Spoon the Tomato Sauce over the top and pass the Harissa on the side.

Tomato Sauce

Makes about 2½ cups

INGREDIENTS
4 cups diced, peeled, and seeded tomatoes
1 jalapeño chile, trimmed, seeded, and minced, or to taste
1 tablespoon sugar
Salt

INSTRUCTIONS

1. Combine the tomatoes with the chile and sugar in a medium nonreactive saucepan over medium-high heat. Season with salt and bring to a simmer.

2. Lower the heat and cook at a bare simmer for about 15 minutes or until the tomatoes are very soft and the sauce is very flavorful.

3. Remove from the heat and serve as directed in a specific recipe or cool and store, covered and refrigerated, for up to 3 days. Reheat before serving.

Shrimp with Chickpea Puree

Serves 6

This is a lovely dish for a dinner party. The chickpea puree can also be used as a dip with crackers or raw vegetables. A pound of jumbo shrimp should give you four per person if serving six, but of course you can use any size shrimp as long as you have a sufficient number for your family or guests.

INGREDIENTS

2 tablespoons olive oil

1 pound jumbo shrimp, cleaned with tails on

4 sprigs fresh rosemary, plus 1 teaspoon chopped for garnish, optional

4 sage leaves

Zest of 1 lemon

Salt and pepper

Chickpea Puree (recipe follows)

INSTRUCTIONS

1. Place the olive oil in a large sauté pan over medium-high heat. Add the shrimp, rosemary, sage, and lemon zest. Season with salt and pepper and sauté for about 6 minutes or until shrimp is just pink. Don't overcook as the shrimp will toughen. Remove and discard the herbs.

2. Spoon the puree onto a serving platter. Spoon the shrimp over the top and drizzle any of the seasoned oil from the pan over all. Garnish with chopped rosemary, if desired, and serve.

continued

Chickpea Puree

Makes about 5 cups

INGREDIENTS

¾ cup olive oil

4 sprigs fresh rosemary

4 sprigs fresh sage

3 garlic cloves, peeled

1 pound dried chickpeas, soaked (see page 27)

4 cups low-sodium chicken broth

1 tablespoon tomato paste

Salt and pepper

INSTRUCTIONS

1. Place ¼ cup of the olive oil in a large saucepan over medium heat. Add the rosemary, sage, and garlic. When very hot, add the chickpeas and cook, stirring, for 3 minutes. Add the chicken broth and tomato paste along with enough water to cover by about 2 inches. Raise the heat and bring to a boil.

2. Lower the heat and cook at a gentle simmer for about 1 hour or just until the chickpeas are tender. Remove from the heat. Remove and discard the rosemary and sage.

3. Drain the chickpeas through a fine mesh sieve, reserving any liquid.

4. Transfer the chickpeas to the bowl of a food processor fitted with the metal blade. Process to chop and, with the motor running, begin adding the reserved liquid along with about ½ cup of the remaining olive oil to make a smooth puree. Taste and, if necessary, season with salt and pepper.

5. Serve as directed in a specific recipe or store, covered and refrigerated, for up to 5 days. Reheat before serving.

Linguine with Cannellini Beans and Broccoli

Serves 4

This is a quick and easy midweek pasta, particularly if you have the cooked (or canned) beans and all the pantry items on hand. You could use any other white bean, but I wouldn't suggest using pink or red beans, only for the aesthetics of them in the mix, not the taste. You don't absolutely need the pancetta, but it does add a bit of fattiness and aroma. The broccoli can be replaced with any green—kale, escarole, spinach, chard—whatever you have on hand is just fine to make this a hearty, healthy blend.

INGREDIENTS

1 small head broccoli, well washed

3 tablespoons extra virgin olive oil

4 ounces finely diced pancetta, optional

3 large garlic cloves, peeled and thinly sliced

2 cups cooked cannellini beans with reserved broth, or one 15-ounce can

2 teaspoons tomato paste

1 teaspoon dried basil or 2 teaspoons chopped fresh

Chile flakes

Vegetable or low-sodium, fat-free chicken broth, optional

8 ounces dry linguine pasta

Sea salt

Grated Parmesan cheese, optional

INSTRUCTIONS

1. If the broccoli head still has its leaves, trim them off and cut them into thin threads. Set aside.

2. Using a vegetable peeler, peel the stalk and then cut it off near the head. Cut the stalk crosswise into

continued

thin slices. Then pull off the florets into bite-sized pieces. Separately set the stalk pieces and the florets aside.

3. Place a large saucepan of heavily salted water over high heat.

4. Heat the oil in a large sauté pan over medium-high heat. Add the pancetta and cook, stirring frequently, for about 7 minutes or until it begins to crisp.

5. Add the garlic, beans along with their broth, tomato paste, basil, and chile flakes. Cook, stirring frequently, for about 10 minutes or just until the flavors begin to meld. Add the broccoli stalk slices, lower the heat, and continue to cook while you prepare the pasta. If the sauce gets too thick, add vegetable or chicken broth, about ¼ cup at a time.

6. When the salted water comes to a boil, add the pasta. Try not to let the water slow down too much; you want to keep the boil going. Boil according to the manufacturer's suggestion—for linguine, it is usually about 10 minutes. At about 7 minutes, add the broccoli florets to the boiling water and continue to boil. You want the pasta to be al dente and the broccoli to still be a bit crisp and bright green.

7. Drain the pasta, reserving about 1 cup of the cooking water. Return the pasta to the cooking pot. Add the bean mixture and, if necessary, a bit of pasta water to lighten up the sauce. Taste and season with sea salt and more chile flakes if necessary.

8. Serve hot with grated cheese sprinkled over the top, if desired.

Chickpea Pasta with Romano Beans and Cherry Tomatoes

Serves 6

Steve, my photographer husband, does not much like green beans.

When I introduced him to what I call broad beans, but which are actually Romano or Italian beans, he took a liking to them. I now use them in familiar dishes whenever I can. I find their flavor richer than green beans, and I add them in pastas or mix them up with other vegetables—corn, onion, and broad beans being one combo I'm particularly fond of. See the photo on page 124 for this hearty chickpea pasta dish.

INGREDIENTS

¼ cup olive oil

1 small onion, peeled and diced

1 teaspoon minced garlic

½ pound fresh Romano beans, trimmed and cut crosswise on the diagonal

1 basket cherry tomatoes, stems removed

Salt and pepper

1 pound dried chickpea pasta

2 tablespoons unsalted butter

2 tablespoons slivered basil

Grated Parmesan cheese for serving

INSTRUCTIONS

1. Heat the olive oil in a large frying pan over medium heat. Add the onion and garlic and cook, stirring frequently, for about 4 minutes or just until softening. Add the beans and cherry tomatoes, season with salt and pepper, cover, and let cook for 5 minutes.

2. Uncover and remove from the heat.

3. While the sauce is cooking, prepare the pasta.

4. Bring a large pot of salted water to boil over high heat. Add the pasta and bring to a boil. Boil according to package directions for al dente.

5. Remove from the heat and drain well, reserving ½ cup of the pasta cooking water.

6. Return the pasta to the pot, add the reserved sauce along with the butter and toss to coat, adding the pasta cooking water as needed to loosen the sauce. Add the basil and toss to blend. Taste and, if necessary, season with salt and pepper.

7. Spoon into a large pasta serving bowl or into individual pasta dishes. Sprinkle with Parmesan cheese and serve.

Curried Chickpeas with Sweet Rice

Serves 6

This is a perfect vegetarian meal that will satisfy any meat eater.

The creamy curry sauce, the aromatic rice, and the hearty chickpeas make a terrific one-course dinner. You can use hot or sweet curry powder and eliminate the cayenne if you don't like heat.

INGREDIENTS

1 pound dried chickpeas, soaked (see page 27)

¼ cup fresh lemon juice

1 cinnamon stick

Salt

1 tablespoon peanut oil

1 teaspoon mustard seeds

1 teaspoon coriander seeds

1 large red bell pepper, cored, seeded, membrane removed, and diced

1 large sweet onion, peeled and diced

1 tablespoon minced garlic

1 tablespoon minced fresh ginger

One 28-ounce can crushed tomatoes

One 13.5-ounce can unsweetened coconut milk

2 tablespoons chopped cilantro

1 tablespoon curry powder

2 teaspoons ground turmeric

Cayenne pepper

Sweet Rice (recipe follows) or plain rice, cooked

INSTRUCTIONS

1. Place the chickpeas in a large saucepan. Add the lemon juice and cinnamon stick along with enough water to cover by about 2 inches. Place over high heat and bring to a boil. Lower the heat and cook at a bare simmer for about 1 hour, adding salt about halfway through the cooking time.

2. While the chickpeas are cooking, prepare the curry base.

3. Heat the oil in a large saucepan over medium heat. Add the mustard and coriander seeds and cook, stirring, for about 3 minutes or just until the mustard seeds have begun to brown. Add the bell pepper, onion, garlic, and ginger, and cook, stirring frequently, for about 4 minutes or just until the vegetables begin to soften. Stir in the tomato and coconut milk along with the cilantro, curry powder, and turmeric. Season with salt and cayenne.

4. When the chickpeas are ready, drain, reserving the cooking liquid. Add the chickpeas to the curry base. Bring to a simmer and cook at a gentle simmer for about 40 minutes or until very flavorful.

Add the reserved cooking liquid in small amounts if the curry seems too thick.

5. Serve hot with Sweet Rice.

Sweet Rice

Serves 6

INGREDIENTS

1½ cups basmati or jasmine rice
1 tablespoon unsalted butter
1 teaspoon peanut oil
½ cup slivered almonds
1 teaspoon orange zest
¼ teaspoon saffron threads
4 whole cloves
2 green cardamom seeds
1 stick cinnamon
Salt

INSTRUCTIONS

1. Rinse the rice and let it drain.

2. Combine the butter and oil in a medium saucepan over medium heat. When melted, add the almonds, orange zest, and saffron, and stir to blend. Cook, stirring, for 3 minutes. Stir in the rice along with the cloves, cardamom, and cinnamon. Add 3 cups water, season with salt, and bring to a boil. Cover, lower the heat, and cook for about 18 minutes or until the water has been absorbed and the rice is about tender.

3. Remove from the heat and let stand, covered, for about 5 minutes to steam a bit.

4. Serve immediately.

Grilled Tuna with Herbed White Beans

Serves 6

Although I use tuna in this recipe, you could easily use almost any protein as a topper for these delicious herby beans. This is a terrific summer dish, as the beans can be made ahead and the tuna (or other protein) can be done on the grill.

To make the mix more salad-like, you can add more fresh herbs and chopped bitter greens to the beans when you're ready to serve.

INGREDIENTS

Six 7-ounce tuna steaks

1 tablespoon olive oil

Salt and pepper

Herbed White Beans (recipe follows)

¼ cup basil leaf slivers, optional

INSTRUCTIONS

1. Heat and oil a grill or preheat a stove-top grill pan.

2. Generously coat both sides of the tuna with the olive oil. Season with salt and pepper.

3. Place the tuna on the prepared grill and grill, turning once, for about 6 minutes or until just barely cooked. You want it to remain pink in the center.

4. Spoon equal portions of the beans in the center of each of six large shallow soup bowls. Lay a piece of tuna on top and garnish with slivers of basil, if desired.

5. Serve immediately.

Herbed White Beans

Serves 6

INGREDIENTS

1 pound dried cannellini or other white beans, soaked (see page 27)

2 cups low-sodium chicken broth

8 whole cloves

1 large onion

One 3-inch piece orange peel

1 bay leaf

1 cup dry white wine

1 tablespoon Roasted Garlic (see page 53)

1 teaspoon minced fresh thyme

1 teaspoon minced fresh chervil

¼ teaspoon red chile flakes

¼ cup minced flat-leaf parsley

1 tablespoon minced basil

Salt and pepper

INSTRUCTIONS

1. Place the beans in a large saucepan. Add the chicken broth and enough cold water to cover by 2 inches and place over high heat.

2. Stick the cloves into the onion and add it to the beans. Bring to a boil; immediately lower the heat and cook at a gentle simmer for 30 minutes.

3. Add the orange peel and bay leaf along with the wine, garlic, thyme, chervil, and chile flakes. Raise the heat and again bring to a boil. Lower the heat and cook at a gentle simmer for another hour or so or until the beans are tender but not mushy.

4. Remove from the heat and discard the onion, orange peel, and bay leaf.

5. Add the parsley and basil and season with salt and pepper. Set aside to cool and allow flavors to blend.

6. Use as directed in a specific recipe or cover and store in the refrigerator until ready to use or for no more than a week.

7. Bring to room temperature before serving.

White Bean Gnocchi with Bacon and Cream

Serves 6

Gnocchi are traditionally made with potatoes or cheese or semolina flour, but here beans are the base. Although gnocchi are delicious, it takes a bit of finessing to create those light, soft pillows that we all know and love. Work slowly and carefully when adding the flour to the base. The trick is to incorporate it without making the dough sticky or floury. It should feel quite light to the touch.

INGREDIENTS

3 cups cooked cannellini or other large white beans
1 pound slab bacon
1 large egg, at room temperature
Approximately 1 cup all-purpose flour
½ teaspoon salt plus more for seasoning
1½ cups warm heavy cream
1 cup grated Parmesan cheese
Pepper

INSTRUCTIONS

1. Place the beans in a heavy-bottomed saucepan over low heat. Cook, stirring frequently and shaking the pan, for about 3 minutes or until the beans are almost dry. Do not allow them to brown. Remove from the heat and set aside to cool.

2. Cut the bacon into bite-sized pieces. Place in a medium frying pan over low heat and fry, stirring frequently, for about 10 minutes or until all the fat has been rendered out and the bacon is crisp.

3. Transfer to a double layer of paper towel to drain. Place the beans in the bowl of a food processor fitted with the metal blade. Process, using quick on and off turns, until completely mashed.

4. Scrape the bean mash into a medium mixing bowl. Add the egg and about ¾ cup of the flour. Add ½ teaspoon of salt and, using your hands, work the mix into a soft dough, adding flour as needed. This is the tricky part—if the dough is too soft, the gnocchi won't hold together when boiled; if too dense, the gnocchi will be tough.

5. Sprinkle a clean, flat work surface with flour.

6. Working with about a handful of the dough at a time and using your hands, roll out the dough into a long, finger-sized rope. Using a kitchen knife, cut the rope crosswise into 1-inch pieces. Set the pieces aside as you continue making ropes and cutting them into pieces.

7. Bring a large pot of salted water to a boil over high heat. Drop the gnocchi into the rapidly boiling water and cook for about 3 minutes or until the dough rises to the surface. Using a slotted spoon, remove the cooked gnocchi from the water and place in a warm serving bowl.

8. When all the gnocchi are cooked, add the cream and cheese along with the reserved bacon to the serving bowl, tossing lightly to coat. Season with salt and pepper.

9. Serve immediately.

Black-Eyed Peas and Meatballs

Serves 6

This is a great dish to put together on a weekend for cooking later in the week. It can be made and stored—unbaked, cooked, and refrigerated—for three days, or it can be frozen for up to one month. It will need to bake for at least an hour when cold.

INGREDIENTS

1 pound black-eyed peas, rinsed

1 pound ground beef

½ pound ground pork

1 cup chopped spinach

½ cup minced onion

½ cup chopped flat-leaf parsley

1 large egg

½ cup bread crumbs

Salt and pepper

2 cups Tomato Sauce (recipe follows) or your favorite commercial seasoned tomato sauce

1 cup grated sharp Cheddar or other sharp cheese

6 strips uncooked bacon

INSTRUCTIONS

1. Soak and cook the black-eyed peas according to directions on page 27.

2. While the peas are cooking, prepare the meatballs.

3. Preheat the oven to 375°F. Generously grease a 3-quart casserole.

4. Place the ground beef and pork in a large mixing bowl. Add the spinach, onion, parsley, and egg and, using your hands, mash the mixture together to blend well. Add the bread crumbs, season with salt and pepper, and, again, mash the mixture together until very well blended. You don't want to see clumps of unseasoned meat or spinach.

5. Using your hands, roll the mixture into 1-inch balls. As formed, place on a baking sheet with sides in the preheated oven and bake, turning occasionally, for about 25 minutes or until nicely browned on all sides. Do not turn off the oven.

6. Remove from the oven and, using a slotted spoon, transfer the meatballs to a double layer of paper towel to drain.

7. When the peas are done, stir in the tomato sauce.

8. Spoon a layer of the peas over the bottom of the greased casserole. Top with a layer of meatballs and continue laying peas and meatballs until all are used, ending with a layer of meatballs.

9. Cover the top with the cheese and crisscross the bacon strips over the cheese.

10. Place in the preheated oven and bake for about 35 minutes or until the casserole is bubbly, the cheese has melted, and the bacon has cooked.

11. Remove from the heat and let rest for 10 minutes before serving.

Tomato Sauce

Makes about 3 cups

INGREDIENTS

2 tablespoons olive oil

¼ cup minced onion

1 teaspoon minced garlic

3 cups peeled, cored, seeded, and chopped Roma tomatoes

Pinch sugar

Salt and pepper

INSTRUCTIONS

1. Heat the oil in a heavy saucepan over medium heat. Add the onion and garlic and cook, stirring occasionally, for about 4 minutes or until just softening.

2. Add the tomatoes and sugar. Season with salt and pepper and bring to a simmer. Lower the heat and simmer for about 20 minutes or just until nicely flavored but still bright red.

3. Remove from the heat and use as directed in a specific recipe or as a sauce for pasta or grains or spooned over grilled meats or fish.

Pea and Ricotta Fritters with Baba Ganoush

Serves 6

The most important ingredient in this recipe is the chia seeds, as they expand and help hold the fritters together. They are, like legumes, very good for you, too. The peas add the necessary lightness and sweetness to the mix. Although the eggplant mix makes a great addition, you could also garnish with some Greek yogurt.

The baba ganoush is delicious on its own, served with crackers, chips, or raw vegetables for dipping.

INGREDIENTS

2 bunches Swiss chard, tough stems removed

2 cups frozen petite peas, thawed and patted dry

1½ cups ricotta cheese

6 tablespoons chia seeds

2 tablespoons finely chopped fresh basil

1 tablespoon freshly grated orange zest

4 large eggs, at room temperature

Salt and pepper

3 tablespoons olive oil

Baba Ganoush (recipe follows)

INSTRUCTIONS

1. Working with a bit at a time, place the chard and peas in the bowl of a food processor fitted with the metal blade and process until coarsely chopped. Scrape the chopped vegetables into a large mixing bowl as they are done and continue chopping until all the vegetables have been processed.

2. Add the ricotta, chia seeds, basil, and orange zest to the mix, stirring to blend well. Add the eggs,

season with salt and pepper, and mix to blend completely.

3. Cover the bowl and set aside to rest for 30 minutes.

4. Using your hands, form the mixture into six large patties.

5. Heat the oil in a large frying pan over medium heat. Add the patties and fry, turning once, for about 7 minutes or until golden brown and cooked through.

6. Remove from the heat and serve with the Baba Ganoush on the side.

Baba Ganoush

Makes about 2 cups

INGREDIENTS

3 garlic cloves in their skin
1 medium eggplant
2 tablespoons tahini (sesame paste)
2 tablespoons fresh lemon juice
½ teaspoon smoked paprika
Salt and pepper
¼ cup finely chopped fresh flat-leaf parsley

INSTRUCTIONS

1. Preheat the oven to 450°F.

2. Wrap the garlic cloves in aluminum foil. Set aside.

3. Using a kitchen fork, randomly prick the eggplant on all sides. Place the eggplant in a roasting pan along with the wrapped garlic. Transfer to the preheated oven and bake for about 30 minutes or until the eggplant is very soft when pierced with the point of a small sharp knife and the garlic cloves are soft.

4. Remove from the heat and let rest for 10 minutes. Then cut the eggplant in half lengthwise. Scoop out the flesh into a fine mesh sieve and let drain for about 15 minutes to allow excess moisture to drip off.

5. Transfer the eggplant to the bowl of a food processor fitted with the metal blade. Unwrap the garlic cloves and squeeze the flesh into the eggplant. Add the tahini, lemon juice, and smoked paprika. Season with salt and pepper and process, using quick on and off turns, until the mixture is creamy but not runny. Add the parsley and do one quick turn to incorporate.

6. Scrape the mixture from the food processor into a container. Serve as directed in a specific recipe or store, covered and refrigerated, for up to 1 week. Bring to room temperature before serving.

Pasta with Fresh Peas and Prosciutto

Serves 6

You can use any pasta you like for this dish—something as simple as spaghetti or as extravagant as cheese tortellini. This dish is very rich, but the fresh peas add vibrancy and a lovely color, so make sure you keep them bright green.

INGREDIENTS

¼ pound prosciutto, cut into slivers

2 cups fresh peas or frozen petite peas, thawed and patted dry

1 pound dried pasta of choice

2 cups heavy cream

½ cup grated Parmesan cheese plus more for garnish

Salt and pepper

INSTRUCTIONS

1. Place the prosciutto in a medium frying pan over medium-low heat. Fry, tossing and turning occasionally, for about 5 minutes or until crisp. Transfer to a double layer of paper towel to drain off any excess fat.

2. If using fresh peas, bring a medium saucepan of salted water to boil over high heat. Add the peas and cook for about 2 minutes or just until barely cooked and bright green. Immediately remove from the heat, pour into a fine mesh sieve, and place under cold running water. When cool, set aside to allow the water to drip off.

3. Cook the pasta according to the package directions for al dente.

4. While the pasta is cooking, place the cream in a heavy saucepan over medium-high heat and bring to a simmer. Lower the heat and continue to cook at a gentle simmer for 5 minutes or until slightly reduced.

5. Drain the pasta and return it to the pan. Add the cream, peas, and prosciutto, stirring to blend. Add the ½ cup of cheese, season with salt and pepper, and toss to combine.

6. Transfer to a serving bowl or to individual pasta bowls and serve with additional cheese sprinkled over the top.

Rice Bean Stew

Serves 6

Until I began my deep research into beans, I had never seen or heard about rice beans. Although not the size of a grain of rice, they are much smaller than other beans I have eaten. They are unique in their size, but their flavor is quite similar to other small white beans. I have also discovered black rice beans, which have a similar taste.

INGREDIENTS

¼ pound pancetta, diced

1 onion, peeled and diced

3 garlic cloves, peeled and minced

1 pound rice beans or other small white bean, cooked and drained

¾ cup sun-dried tomatoes

½ cup Classic Pesto (recipe follows)

2 cups chopped broccolini

4 cups low-sodium chicken broth or water

Salt and pepper

Grated Parmesan cheese for serving, optional

INSTRUCTIONS

1. Place the pancetta in a large frying pan over medium-low heat. Fry, stirring occasionally, for about 7 minutes or until the pancetta begins to crisp. Add the onion and garlic and continue to fry for about 5 more minutes or just until the onion begins to soften and the garlic begins to color.

2. Add the cooked beans along with the sun-dried tomatoes and pesto, stirring to blend. Add the broccolini along with 3 cups of the broth. Season with salt and pepper, raise the heat, and bring to a simmer. Lower the heat and cook, stirring occasionally and adding broth as needed to create a stew-like consistency, for about 30 minutes or until the greens have cooked and the stew is well flavored.

3. Remove from the heat and serve garnished with Parmesan cheese, if desired.

continued

Classic Pesto

Makes about 2 cups

INGREDIENTS

3 to 4 peeled garlic cloves

½ cup pine nuts, toasted if you have the time

3 cups firmly packed fresh basil leaves

1 cup extra virgin olive oil

¾ cup grated Parmigiano-Reggiano cheese

Salt

INSTRUCTIONS

1. Combine the garlic and pine nuts in the bowl of a food processor fitted with the metal blade and process, using quick on and off turns, until coarsely chopped. Add half the basil and, again using quick on and off turns, process to coarsely chop. Add the remaining basil and, with the motor running, begin adding the oil, processing until a thick green sauce forms.

2. Add the cheese, season with salt, and give a quick couple of turns to incorporate. If the pesto is too thick for your taste, add more oil. If too thin, add more basil and perhaps a bit more cheese. The flavor is yours to decide.

3. If not using immediately, scrape the sauce into a nonreactive container. Smooth the top and cover it with extra virgin olive oil to prevent discoloration. Cover and refrigerate for up to 2 weeks or freeze for up to 3 months.

Red Beans and Rice

Serves 6

There is nothing quite like a big heaping dish of red beans and rice in Creole Louisiana. Traditionally, it was made on Monday or Tuesday using the leftover bits of meat from the weekend meals. My version has no meat, but you can add smoked ham, pork bones, tasso ham, andouille, or other sausage. It is meant to be hot and spicy, but you can mellow it out to suit your taste. It is generally made with small red beans; however, red kidney beans or other larger red beans also work just fine.

INGREDIENTS

1 pound dried small red or red kidney beans, soaked (see page 27)

3 tablespoons peanut oil

1½ cups chopped onion

1 cup chopped green bell pepper

1 cup chopped celery

2 tablespoons minced garlic

1 cup canned diced tomatoes with their juice

3 bay leaves

1 teaspoon dried oregano

1 teaspoon dried thyme

1 teaspoon paprika

½ teaspoon cayenne pepper

½ teaspoon ground cumin

¼ cup apple cider vinegar plus more for serving

Salt and pepper

1 teaspoon hot sauce, or to taste plus more for serving

Red chile flakes

6 cups cooked rice

INSTRUCTIONS

1. Place the beans in a large pot with cold water to cover by about 2 inches. Place over high heat and bring to a boil. Lower the heat and cook at a gentle simmer for 1 hour.

2. While the beans are cooking, prepare the remaining ingredients.

3. Heat the oil in a large frying pan over medium heat. Add the onion, bell pepper, celery, and garlic and cook, stirring frequently, for about 7 minutes or until the vegetables are beginning to soften. Add the tomatoes along with the bay leaves, oregano, thyme, paprika, cayenne, and cumin, stirring to incorporate. Add the vinegar and season with salt and pepper.

4. Scrape the mixture into the simmering beans. Add the hot sauce and chile flakes and continue to cook, stirring occasionally, for about 1 hour or until the beans are tender and the mix is very flavorful.

5. While the beans are cooking, place 4 cups of salted water in a large saucepan over high heat. Bring to a boil, then add the rice, cover, and lower the heat to a bare simmer. Cook for about 18 minutes or just until barely tender and almost all the water has evaporated.

6. Remove from the heat and let rest, covered, for 10 minutes.

7. When ready to serve, spoon the rice into the center of a large shallow serving bowl. Spoon the beans over the top and serve with hot sauce and vinegar on the side.

Thai Green Curry with Chicken and Peanuts

Serves 6

The flavors of Thai cooking are often highlighted by the addition of salty, crisp peanuts, that familiar legume that is called a nut. This list might look like a lot of ingredients, but the dish comes together quickly and is a delicious introduction to dishes with Thai influences. It can be served over rice, rice noodles, or any thin pasta.

INGREDIENTS

$^1/_3$ cup plus 1 tablespoon peanut oil

1 cup roasted, salted peanuts

1 cup finely diced shallot

1 teaspoon minced garlic

1 teaspoon minced hot green chile

1 pound boneless, skinless chicken breast, cut into small cubes

One 15-ounce can unsweetened coconut milk

¾ cup low-sodium vegetable broth

¼ cup Thai green curry paste (see Note)

1 teaspoon curry powder

½ teaspoon ground turmeric

1 tablespoon light brown sugar

4 stalks celery, trimmed and cut crosswise into ½-inch diagonal pieces

$^1/_3$ cup chopped cilantro

INSTRUCTIONS

1. Place the ⅓ cup of peanut oil in a medium saucepan over medium heat. When very hot, add the peanuts and cook, stirring frequently, for about 5 minutes or until the peanuts are golden and slightly crisp.

2. Using a slotted spoon, transfer the peanuts to a double layer of paper towel to drain.

3. Heat the remaining tablespoon of oil in a wok or large frying pan. Add the shallot, garlic, and chile and cook, stirring frequently, for about 5 minutes or just until softening. Add the chicken and continue to cook, stirring frequently, for about 5 minutes or just until the chicken is beginning to color.

4. Stir in the coconut milk and broth and stir to combine. Add the curry paste, curry powder, turmeric, and brown sugar, stirring to incorporate. Add the celery and cook for about 7 minutes or just until the sauce has thickened slightly and is very flavorful.

5. Stir in the cilantro along with the reserved peanuts and remove from the heat.

Note: *Thai green curry paste is available at Asian markets, many supermarkets, and online.*

Miso Salmon with Edamame and Cucumber

Serves 6

Although I use salmon here, you could also use halibut or cod steaks. The edamame-cucumber combination works so well under the rich salmon: the cucumbers add crunch and the edamame adds sweetness and an extra dose of protein. This is another great summer dish, as the fish can be grilled and the vegetables require no cooking.

INGREDIENTS

3 tablespoons low-sodium soy sauce

1½ tablespoons honey

1½ tablespoons white miso paste

1½ tablespoons minced ginger

1 teaspoon toasted sesame oil

Six 6-ounce skinless salmon fillets

4 Persian cucumbers, trimmed and cut into thin slices on the diagonal

3 cups frozen shelled edamame, rinsed under hot water and patted dry

1 cup slivered scallion, white and green parts

Miso Vinaigrette (see page 95)

2 teaspoons black sesame seeds, optional

INSTRUCTIONS

1. Preheat the oven to 400°F.

2. Combine the soy sauce, honey, miso paste, ginger, and sesame oil.

3. Place the salmon in a nonstick baking pan and pour the soy sauce mixture over the top. Set aside to marinate for 15 minutes, turning occasionally to ensure that all sides are flavored.

4. Transfer the salmon to the preheated oven and roast for about 12 minutes or just until cooked through. While the salmon is roasting, combine the cucumbers, edamame, and scallion with just enough of the vinaigrette to moisten.

5. Place the cucumber mixture on a large serving platter. Place the salmon on top and drizzle the vinaigrette over all. Sprinkle with sesame seeds, if using, and serve.

Gado-Gado

Serves 6

This star of Indonesian cooking combines four legumes—the soybean in the tofu, the green beans and bean sprouts in the mix, and the peanuts in the sauce and as a garnish. It is a very, very bountiful dish—a beautiful bowl filled to the brim with fresh and tasty foods. *Gado* translates to "mix" in Indonesian, so this is a mix-mix, which means you really can use any vegetable you wish when making it—there are no rules!

INGREDIENTS

2 tablespoons peanut oil

1 pound firm tofu, cut into ½-inch cubes

1 cup finely cut carrots

1 cup diagonal-cut green beans

1 cup shredded red cabbage

1 cup shredded green cabbage

1 cup shredded spinach leaves

2 cups sliced cooked potatoes

1 cup thinly sliced hothouse cucumber

1 cup bean sprouts

2 ripe tomatoes, peeled, cored, and cut crosswise into thin slices

3 hard-boiled eggs, peeled and cut crosswise into thin slices

Peanut Sauce, warmed (recipe follows)

1 cup chopped salted peanuts for garnish

INSTRUCTIONS

1. Heat the oil in a medium frying pan over medium-high heat. Add the tofu cubes and fry, gently tossing and turning, for about 7 minutes or until the tofu has browned on all sides. Using a slotted spoon, transfer the tofu to a double layer of paper towel to drain.

2. Place a bowl of ice water near the stove.

3. Bring a small pot of salted water to a boil over high heat. Working with one type of vegetable at a time, quickly blanch the carrots and green beans in the boiling water. Using a slotted spoon, immediately transfer each vegetable to the ice water to stop the cooking. Quickly drain and pat dry.

4. Combine the cabbages with the spinach in a large mixing bowl. When well combined, scatter the mix over the bottom of a large shallow serving platter. Make a layer of green beans followed by a layer of potatoes, then cucumbers, then carrots, and finally bean sprouts. Alternate tomato and egg slices around the edge of the platter. Randomly place the tofu cubes over all. Pour the Peanut Sauce over the top and garnish with chopped peanuts.

5. Serve immediately.

continued

Peanut Sauce

Makes about 2 cups

INGREDIENTS

1 cup unsweetened coconut milk

¾ cup smooth peanut butter

1 hot green chile, cored, seeded, membrane removed, and chopped

One 2-inch piece ginger, peeled and minced

One 2-inch piece lemon peel

2 tablespoons fresh orange juice

1 tablespoon light brown sugar

1 tablespoon soy sauce

1 tablespoon tamarind paste dissolved in 1 tablespoon warm water

1 teaspoon minced garlic

1 teaspoon fish sauce

INSTRUCTIONS

1. Combine the coconut milk and peanut butter in a medium nonreactive saucepan over medium heat, stirring to soften the peanut butter. Add the chile, ginger, lemon peel, orange juice, sugar, soy sauce, tamarind mixture, garlic, and fish sauce, stirring to blend. Bring to a simmer, then lower the heat and cook at a bare simmer for about 10 minutes or until well blended and flavorful.

2. Remove from the heat and remove and discard the lemon peel.

3. Pour the sauce into a blender jar. Cover and process until very smooth. If the sauce seems too thick—it should be pourable—add water a tablespoonful at a time.

4. Serve as directed in a specific recipe or store, covered and refrigerated, for up to 1 week. Reheat before serving.

Note: Peanut sauce is excellent on rice noodles that have been tossed with slivered cucumbers, bean sprouts, carrots, or fresh herbs, such as cilantro and mint.

Strozzapreti with Fava Beans and Spring Onions

Serves 6

This is a spring green recipe for me because in the spring, when fava beans just come to the market, they are often accompanied by asparagus and ramps or wild leeks. Ramps aren't cultivated—they grow wild in woods throughout the Northeast and in some of the Atlantic coast states. I generally prefer ramps and their greens, but because ramps are so seasonal and regional, I use spring onions in this recipe. However, this dish is delicious with almost any type of onion.

INGREDIENTS

¼ cup extra virgin olive oil

½ cup finely chopped spring onion

2 cups shelled and peeled fava beans

2 cups sliced asparagus

1 cup vegetable stock

About 1 teaspoon fresh thyme leaves

Salt and pepper

1 pound spaghetti, strozzapreti, or other dried pasta

Freshly grated Parmesan for serving

INSTRUCTIONS

1. Heat 2 tablespoons of the oil in a large frying pan over medium heat. Add the onions and cook, stirring frequently, for about 4 minutes or until just softened. Stir in the fava beans and asparagus. Add the stock and thyme and season with salt and pepper. Continue to cook for another 5 minutes or just until the liquid has begun to evaporate a bit and the vegetables are still almost crisp-tender.

continued

2. While making the sauce, bring a large pot of highly salted water to boil over high heat. Add the pasta and return to the boil. Boil according to package directions for al dente. Drain well and return the pasta to the pot. Drizzle with the remaining 2 tablespoons olive oil and toss to coat lightly.

3. Pour the sauce over the pasta, tossing to coat well. Serve immediately with a good sprinkling of freshly grated Parmesan cheese.

*Beans with Swiss Chard, Olive,
and Sun-Dried Tomatoes*

CHAPTER FIVE

Accompaniments

All types of beans can be found served as accompaniments.
Fresh beans and peas are particularly suitable as side dishes and
are especially delicious during the summer months when they
come straight from the garden. Some side dishes that you will find
here can also move to the center of the table, particularly when they
are combined with grains. How you feature these dishes at your
table is truly up to you.

Green Peas and Lentils

Serves 6

This dish is an interesting combination of the earthy lentils and the sweet peas. I use frozen peas here, as this makes the dish available all year long, but if you have them, fresh peas will shine. Always serve this dish warm, as the warm lentils mellow out the acid in the lemon and vinegar and coax the dressing flavors to sneak into the skins of the peas.

INGREDIENTS

½ pound black lentils

2 garlic cloves, peeled

1 bay leaf

One 13-ounce package frozen petite peas, thawed and patted dry

¼ cup chopped scallion, white and green part

2 tablespoons chopped fresh mint

½ cup extra virgin olive oil

2 tablespoons fresh lemon juice

2 teaspoons red wine vinegar

Pinch sugar

Salt and pepper

INSTRUCTIONS

1. Place the lentils in a medium saucepan. Add the garlic and bay leaf along with enough salted water to cover by 2 inches. Place over medium-high heat and bring to a boil. Immediately lower the heat and cook at a bare simmer for about 20 minutes or just until the lentils are cooked but still firm and holding their shape.

2. Remove from the heat and drain well, reserving a cup of the cooking liquid. Discard the garlic and bay leaf.

3. Transfer the lentils to a serving bowl. Add the peas along with the scallion and mint. Add the olive oil, lemon juice, vinegar, and sugar. Season with salt and pepper and toss to blend well.

4. Serve warm.

Peas with Mint

Serves 6

This dish is about as simple as you can get and still be luscious.

The important thing is to keep the bright green color—if you use fresh peas and cook them too long, they will lose their color and not be one bit appetizing. That is why I use thawed frozen peas here.

INGREDIENTS

Two 13-ounce packages frozen petite peas, thawed and patted dry

¾ cup heavy cream

Salt and pepper

½ cup chopped mint

INSTRUCTIONS

1. Place the peas in the bowl of a food processor fitted with the metal blade. Process until very smooth.

2. Scrape the pea puree into a medium saucepan. Add the cream, season with salt and pepper, and place over medium heat. Cook, stirring constantly, for just a couple of minutes to barely heat but allow the bright green color to remain.

3. Remove from the heat and stir in the mint.

4. Serve immediately.

Risi e Bisi

There is really nothing more classic than a risotto with peas.
It can be used as a side dish or as a first or main course. It is a rich and delicious traditional Italian recipe.

    This exact same recipe can be made using cooked beans or lentils—the flavors and the colors will be different, but it will still be delicious.

INGREDIENTS

Approximately 4 cups hot low-sodium chicken broth

¼ teaspoon saffron threads

3 tablespoons unsalted butter

¼ cup finely diced fennel

¼ cup finely diced onion

Salt

1 cup Arborio rice

½ cup dry white wine

2 cups fresh peas or thawed frozen peas, patted dry

1 tablespoon extra virgin olive oil

1 cup grated Parmesan cheese

Pepper

INSTRUCTIONS

1. Place the chicken broth in a large saucepan over medium heat. Bring to a simmer, then remove from the heat, add the saffron, and set aside but keep warm.

2. Place the butter in a heavy-bottomed saucepan over medium heat. When melted, add the fennel and onion and season with salt. Cook, stirring frequently, for about 3 minutes or just until the vegetables begin to soften. Lower the heat, add the rice and cook, stirring, for about 5 minutes or until the rice is shiny and has absorbed some of the butter.

3. Return the seasoned broth to low heat.

4. Add the wine to the rice and cook, stirring constantly, for about 5 minutes or until the rice has absorbed the wine.

5. Begin adding the hot stock, about ¼ cup at a time, and continue to cook, stirring constantly, until each ¼ cup is absorbed and the rice is creamy but al dente.

6. Stir in the peas and olive oil and cook for an additional 4 minutes if using fresh peas. If using frozen peas, cook for just an additional minute.

7. Remove from the heat and stir in half of the cheese. Cover and let stand for 3 minutes.

8. Uncover and pour into a large serving bowl. Garnish with the remaining ½ cup of cheese and a sprinkle of pepper.

9. Serve immediately.

Sesame Snow Peas

This recipe, redolent with Asian flavors, is a side dish that can be served either warm or at room temperature. It is a lovely addition to a picnic or barbecue.

INGREDIENTS

1½ pounds snow peas or sugar snap peas, trimmed

2 tablespoons low-sodium soy sauce

1 teaspoon sesame oil

1 teaspoon peanut oil

¼ cup slivered water chestnuts

1 tablespoon toasted sesame seeds

1 tablespoon black sesame seeds

INSTRUCTIONS

1. Bring a medium saucepan of salted water to a boil over high heat. Add the snow peas and blanch for about 30 seconds or until still bright green and crisp.

2. Immediately drain and shock under cold running water. Pat dry.

3. Place the soy sauce, sesame and peanut oils, and water chestnuts in a medium frying pan over medium heat. Add the snow peas and cook, tossing and turning, for about 2 minutes or just until warm and nicely flavored.

4. Remove from the heat and add the sesame seeds, tossing to coat.

5. Serve immediately.

Bulgur and Chickpea Pilaf

Serves 6

This is a great make-ahead side— perfect for outdoor gatherings.

You can add almost any vegetable and herb you like in addition to or in place of those in this recipe. Cucumbers, green bell peppers, or jicama are three that work well. You can also use almost any cooked dried bean that pleases you.

INGREDIENTS

1½ cups bulgur wheat

Salt

2 cups cooked chickpeas

¾ cup chopped scallion

½ cup diced red bell pepper

¼ cup chopped cilantro

¼ cup chopped dill

½ cup extra virgin olive oil

3 tablespoons lemon juice

½ teaspoon ground cumin

½ teaspoon ground turmeric

¼ teaspoon cayenne pepper

INSTRUCTIONS

1. Place the bulgur in a large heatproof bowl.

2. Bring about 2½ cups of lightly salted water to a boil over high heat. Add the boiling water to the bulgur, cover, and set aside for about 1 hour or until the bulgur has absorbed all the water. If you are unsure about the absorption, scrape the bulgur into a fine mesh sieve and let any excess water drain off. You want the bulgur to be moist but not wet.

3. Transfer the bulgur to a large mixing bowl. Add the chickpeas, scallion, bell pepper, cilantro, and dill.

4. Combine the olive oil with the lemon juice in a small mixing bowl. Add the cumin, turmeric, and cayenne and whisk to blend. Pour the dressing over the bulgur and toss to blend well. Taste and, if necessary, add salt.

5. Serve at room temperature.

Indian-Spiced Chickpeas

Serves 6

It is appropriate to season chickpeas with the scents of India, as chickpeas and lentils are stars in the cuisines of that country. This is a particularly aromatic dish that can also be used as a main course with basmati rice or other grains.

INGREDIENTS

1 pound chickpeas, soaked

¼ cup peanut oil

2 cups diced red onion

1 hot red chile, cored, seeded, and minced

1 cup peeled and seeded tomatoes

1 tablespoon minced ginger

1 tablespoon minced garlic

1 tablespoon chopped basil

1 tablespoon chopped cilantro

1 tablespoon ground cumin

1 tablespoon garam masala (see Note)

1 teaspoon ground coriander

½ teaspoon cayenne pepper, optional

¼ cup orange juice

2 tablespoons lemon juice

Zest of 1 orange

INSTRUCTIONS

1. Cook the chickpeas according to directions on page 27. Drain well, reserving the cooking liquid. Set aside.

2.	Place the oil in a large heavy-bottomed saucepan over medium-low heat. Add the onion and cook, stirring frequently, for about 20 minutes or until the onions begin to caramelize and turn deep brown but are not burning.

3.	Add the chile along with the tomatoes, ginger, garlic, basil, cilantro, cumin, garam masala, coriander, and cayenne, if using. Cook, stirring constantly, for 3 minutes. Then add the orange and lemon juices and cook, stirring occasionally, for 15 minutes.

4.	Add the chickpeas and orange zest and continue to cook, stirring occasionally and adding chickpea cooking liquid as needed, for another 15 minutes or until the flavors have mellowed and the chickpeas are nicely flavored.

5.	Remove from the heat and serve hot or allow to cool and serve at room temperature.

Note: *Garam masala is a spice blend used in Indian cooking. It is available in the spice section of most supermarkets, Indian markets, specialty food stores, and online.*

Summer Beans

Serves 6

I call these summer beans because that is about the only time you find beautifully crisp, brightly colored yellow beans and fresh lima beans at the farmers' market. Of course, you can make them any time of the year, but I think you'll find that this recipe shines in the middle of summer.

INGREDIENTS

1 pound fresh yellow wax beans, trimmed and cut cross-wise into pieces

2½ cups fresh shelled lima beans

Salt

¼ cup crumbled bacon

1 tablespoon olive oil

1 tablespoon minced flat-leaf parsley, optional

Pepper

INSTRUCTIONS

1. Combine both types of beans in a large saucepan of cold salted water. Place over high heat and bring to a boil. Immediately lower the heat and cook at a gentle simmer for about 4 minutes or just until the yellow beans are crisp-tender and the limas are just beginning to tenderize. Both should retain their beautiful colors.

2. Remove from the heat, drain well, and pat dry. Add the bacon and olive oil and toss to coat.

3. Transfer to a serving bowl. Add the parsley, if using, then season with pepper and toss to coat.

4. Serve immediately.

Lima Beans with Ham

Serves 4 to 6

Lima beans are truly elusive— fresh ones appear for just a couple of weeks in the late summer or early fall, and only at some farmers' markets. You almost never see them in a supermarket produce section—not even at specialty produce stores. They are worth hunting down when they are in season, and I find that their rarity makes them even more alluring. When seeking them out, I try my hardest to pick out the pods that contain pale green, medium-sized beans. The larger beans tend to be starchy and less flavorful, whereas the tiny ones are so small that you would have to buy pounds and pounds to unearth enough for a meal.

In this recipe, the beans are silky and smooth, and the ham adds a lovely hint of smoke. Of course, you don't need the ham, but it certainly elevates the flavor of the finished dish. You could also use any smoked or cured meat you might have on hand.

INGREDIENTS

1 tablespoon extra virgin olive oil

1 small shallot, peeled and finely minced

4 pounds fresh lima beans, shelled

Salt and coarse black pepper

½ cup chicken stock or low-sodium, nonfat chicken broth

3 ounces smoked thinly sliced ham, cut into slivers

2 scallions, trimmed and finely sliced crosswise

INSTRUCTIONS

1. Heat the oil in a medium frying pan over medium heat. Add the shallot and sauté for about 4 minutes or until softened. Add the lima beans and season with salt and pepper. Stir in the chicken stock, cover, and cook for about 10 minutes or just until the beans are tender.

2. Uncover the pan and add the ham and scallions, stirring to blend. Taste and, if necessary, add additional pepper.

3. Remove from the heat and serve.

Succotash

Succotash is a traditional American summertime mixture that has as many versions as there have been cooks. You can use almost any bean—fresh, cooked, or dried—in combination with corn. But the traditional dish demands fresh lima beans, which is the only way I make it. I always add some bacon, but it is not one bit necessary. You can also add 1 cup diced tomatoes, diced bell peppers, chopped onions, or cream if you like.

INGREDIENTS

2 cups fresh lima beans
2 tablespoons unsalted butter
2 cups fresh corn kernels
Salt and pepper
¾ cup crumbled cooked bacon

INSTRUCTIONS

1. Place the lima beans in a medium saucepan in salted water to cover. Place over high heat and bring to a boil. Immediately lower the heat and cook at a gentle simmer for about 5 minutes or until just barely tender. Remove from the heat, drain well, and pat dry.

2. Place the butter in a large frying pan over medium heat. When melted, add the lima beans along with the corn kernels. Season with salt and pepper and cook, stirring frequently, for about 6 minutes or until the corn has softened a bit.

3. Remove from the heat, stir in the bacon, and serve immediately.

Beans with Swiss Chard, Olives, and Sun-Dried Tomatoes

Serves 6

You can use any dried bean you like in this dish—white, red, pink, or black—they will all work nicely.

Don't like Swiss chard? Choose your preferred greens. You also have the option of using any cheese to finish it. The wonder of this dish is that you can truly make it your own specialty. See the photo on page 180 for my favorite combination to serve.

INGREDIENTS

2 cups dried beans of choice, soaked

One 28-ounce can tomatoes, sliced, with their juices

1 bunch Swiss chard, tough stems removed and chopped

1 medium onion, peeled and diced

½ cup sliced Kalamata olives

¼ cup sliced sun-dried tomatoes

1 tablespoon Roasted Garlic (see page 53)

¾ cup extra virgin olive oil

Salt

Red pepper flakes

½ cup shredded Cheddar or other cheese

½ cup bread crumbs

INSTRUCTIONS

1. Cook the beans according to directions on page 27. Drain well, reserving the cooking liquid.

2. Preheat the oven to 375°F.

3. Lightly coat a 2-quart casserole or other baking dish with olive oil. Set aside.

4. Place the beans in a large mixing bowl. Add the tomatoes along with the Swiss chard, onion, olives, sun-dried tomatoes, and garlic, and stir to blend well. Add the ¾ cup extra virgin olive oil and season with salt and red pepper flakes. If the mixture seems too dry, add some of the reserved bean cooking liquid.

5. Combine the cheese and bread crumbs in a small mixing bowl. Set aside.

6. Transfer the bean mixture to the prepared baking dish. Cover the entire dish with aluminum foil and transfer to the preheated oven.

7. Bake for 45 minutes. Uncover and, if the mixture has dried out, add some of the reserved bean cooking liquid, stirring to incorporate. Sprinkle the top with the cheese–bread crumb mixture and return the dish to the oven.

8. Bake for an additional 15 minutes or until bubbling hot and the top is golden.

9. Remove from the oven and serve.

Anne's New England Baked Beans

Serves 6

Regardless of how closely this dish aligns with the classic Boston-style baked beans, it is still classic to me, as it's a specialty from my Irish-speaking almost-daughter, Anne. When she immigrated to the States, we adopted each other through our mutual love of Beans on Toast (page 216). Using a slow cooker, as Anne does, or an Instant Pot makes this a great no-heat-in-the-kitchen recipe for summer cookouts, barbecues, and family get-togethers. These beans are now our favorite topping for beans on toast.

INGREDIENTS

8 ounces salt pork, rind trimmed

3 cups finely diced onion

1 pound dried navy or other small white beans, soaked

4 bay leaves

1 cup pure maple syrup

½ cup ketchup

2 tablespoons Dijon mustard plus more for finishing, if desired

1 tablespoon salt

1 teaspoon black pepper

¼ cup cider vinegar, optional

INSTRUCTIONS

1. Place a plastic liner in the slow cooker (see Note).

2. Cut the salt pork into small cubes and place it in a large frying pan over medium heat. Cook, stirring frequently, for about 7 minutes or until all the fat has been rendered out.

3. Using a slotted spoon, transfer the pork to a double layer of paper towel to drain.

4. Keeping the frying pan on medium heat, add the onion and cook, stirring frequently, for about

5 minutes or just until the onions have softened at bit.

5. Place the beans in the slow cooker. Add the reserved pork and onion along with the bay leaves, syrup, ketchup, mustard, salt, and pepper. Add 9 cups cold water. Cover and cook on low for 12 hours or until the beans are tender but holding their shape.

6. Uncover and remove and discard the bay leaves. If desired, add the cider vinegar and a dash more mustard to give the beans a "lift."

7. Serve as you would any baked bean.

Note from Anne: *Using the slow cooker liner makes cleaning up a breeze. The only trick to this recipe is patience—give the beans all the hours they need to become tender, rich, and delicious.*

Carrots with Peanuts

Serves 6

This simple but very interesting side dish combines sweet, slightly crisp carrots with crunchy peanuts and fresh herbs. If you replace the butter with olive oil or peanut oil, this makes a nice room temperature picnic or barbecue dish.

INGREDIENTS

1½ pounds carrots, peeled and cut crosswise on the diagonal into ½-inch-thick slices

Salt

2 tablespoons unsalted butter

1 tablespoon lemon juice

2 teaspoons honey

1 cup chopped dry roasted peanuts

2 tablespoons chopped cilantro

1 tablespoon chopped mint

INSTRUCTIONS

1. Place the carrots in a large frying pan. Add just enough water to cover the bottom of the pan. Season with salt, cover, and place over medium heat. Bring to a simmer and cook for just about 3 minutes or until the carrots are bright orange and crisp-tender. Immediately remove from the heat, drain well, and pat dry.

2. Wipe the pan dry and return to low heat. Add the butter and lemon juice, stirring to allow the butter to melt. When the butter has melted, add the honey and stir to incorporate. Add the carrots and cook, tossing and turning, for another 2 to 3 minutes or just until the carrots are nicely coated with the butter sauce.

3. Remove from the heat and add the peanuts, cilantro, and mint, tossing to incorporate.

4. Transfer to a serving dish and serve immediately.

Beans Agrodolce

Serves 6

Agrodolce **is an Italian word that translates to "sour and sweet."** Almost all cuisines have some version of a sweet and sour condiment, and this one reflects Italy. This dish goes very well with roasted or grilled meats, particularly lamb.

INGREDIENTS

¼ cup clarified butter (see Note)

2 tablespoons minced red onion

¼ cup dried currants

3 tablespoons balsamic vinegar

2 tablespoons light brown sugar

3 cups cooked dried cranberry, cannellini, or other medium-sized bean except black beans

INSTRUCTIONS

1. Place the butter in a large frying pan over medium heat. When melted, add the onion and cook, stirring frequently, for about 4 minutes or just until softened.

2. Add the currants, vinegar, and brown sugar and continue to cook, stirring, for about 4 minutes or just until the sugar has dissolved.

3. Add the beans, cover, and cook for 7 minutes. Uncover and taste. If the sweet-sour flavor seems well balanced, remove from the heat. If not, add either more vinegar or sugar, a bit at a time, until the balance is reached.

4. Remove from the heat and set aside to cool to room temperature.

5. Serve or store, covered and refrigerated, for up to 1 week.

Note: To make clarified butter, place whatever amount of butter you need in a medium saucepan over low heat. Allow the butter to melt and then continue cooking until the foam disappears from the top and a light brown sediment forms on the bottom of the pan. The melted butter should now be a clear, golden yellow. Skim the clear liquid from the pan and transfer to a clean container. You now have clarified butter, which will not burn when used as a frying oil. It will keep, covered and refrigerated, for up to 2 weeks. It may also be frozen.

Hoppin' John

Serves 6

This traditional dish of the American South, always served to welcome in the new year, can be changed to incorporate slices of meat, tons of onions, garlic, and local hot and spicy seasonings.

I always cook the rice separately and combine it with the seasoned peas when serving. It is all yours to take Hoppin' John into your own family traditions.

INGREDIENTS

2 cups black-eyed peas, rinsed and drained

1 pound salt pork, bacon, or ham, cut into ¼-inch cubes

1 cup diced onion

3 cups chopped collard greens

½ teaspoon dried thyme

½ teaspoon red chile flakes

Salt and pepper

Cooked rice for serving

INSTRUCTIONS

1. Soak, rinse, and cook the black-eyed peas according to directions on page 27. When done, drain well, reserving about 2½ cups of the cooking liquid. Return the peas to the pan.

2. While the peas are cooking, prepare the remaining ingredients.

3. Place the salt pork in a large frying pan over medium heat. (If using a lean ham, add 2 tablespoons of any fat you prefer to the pan.) Cook, stirring frequently, for about 8 minutes or until the fat has rendered out and the meat is crisp. Using a slotted spoon, transfer the meat to a double layer of paper towel to drain.

4. Pour off all but 1 tablespoon of the fat in the frying pan. Return the pan to medium heat and add the onion. Cook, stirring frequently, for about 5 minutes or just until the onion begins to soften and color. Remove from the heat and set aside.

5. When the peas are ready, add the reserved meat and onion to the peas along with the greens, any fat in the frying pan, the thyme, and the red chile

flakes. Add the reserved pea cooking liquid and season with salt and pepper.

6. Place over high heat and bring to a boil. Immediately lower the heat, cover, and cook for about 20 minutes or until much of the liquid has been absorbed but the mixture is still moist.

7. Remove from the heat and let rest, covered, for 15 minutes.

8. Serve hot over or along with cooked white rice.

Refried Beans

Serves 6

This recipe is as close as you can get to a traditional Mexican refried bean recipe. I like to make a batch and keep it on hand for making enchiladas, a quick burrito filling, a tostada topping, or for serving as a side dish. No matter how you end up using your refried beans, they truly are a comfort dish like no other

INGREDIENTS

1 pound dried pinto beans, soaked (see page 27)
1 cup diced onion
¼ cup chopped cilantro
1 tablespoon minced garlic
1 teaspoon fresh oregano leaves
Salt and pepper
1 cup bacon fat

INSTRUCTIONS

1. Place the beans in a large saucepan with cold water to cover by 2 inches. Add the onion, cilantro, garlic, and oregano and place over high heat. Bring to a boil, then lower the heat and cook at a gentle simmer for about 2 hours or until the beans are very soft. The beans should still be liquidy—if not, add water throughout the cooking process. When the beans have softened, season with salt and pepper.

2. Remove from the heat and drain well, reserving the liquid. Place the beans in the bowl of a food processor fitted with the metal blade and, with the motor running, add the cooking liquid a bit at a time. The beans should be a bit rough—do not puree.

3. Place ½ cup of the bacon fat in a large frying pan over medium-high heat. Add the beans and cook, stirring constantly, for about 15 minutes, incorporating the fat into the beans as you stir. Cook until the beans are a bit dry.

4. Remove the beans from the heat and let cool.

5. Then return the beans to the heat and, using the remaining ½ cup of bacon fat, repeat the frying process. You may not need to use all the fat.

6. Store, covered and refrigerated, for up to 1 week. They also may be frozen. Reheat before using.

Note: *When giving the beans their first fry, you may add finely diced onions, tomatoes, and/or minced garlic.*

You can also incorporate 2 cups of shredded queso blanco or Monterey Jack cheese just before serving.

Black Bean Crepes

CHAPTER SIX

Snacks and Sweets

Here you can really have some fun incorporating beans into your meals in unexpected ways. Beans add tremendous nutritional value to smoothies, cut fat in desserts, and make pancakes and crêpes into delightfully healthy treats. Once you have experimented with these recipes, use your imagination to bring beans into some of your favorite family recipes.

Pickled
Black-Eyed
Peas

Pickled Black-Eyed Peas

Makes about 4½ cups

These pickles are best used as a side dish, topping, salad component, or zesty tidbit in a sandwich wrap. You can use any firm cooked bean in place of the black-eyed peas, and you can add hot chiles to the mix if you like a little heat.

INGREDIENTS

4 cups cooked black-eyed peas

1 medium onion, peeled and diced

1 cup white wine vinegar

¼ cup light brown sugar

1 tablespoon minced garlic

1 teaspoon mustard seeds

½ teaspoon red chile flakes

½ teaspoon salt

INSTRUCTIONS

1. Combine the peas and the onion in a heatproof bowl. Set aside.

2. Combine the vinegar with the sugar, garlic, mustard seeds, chile flakes, and salt in a small nonreactive saucepan. Place over medium heat and bring to a simmer, stirring to dissolve the sugar.

3. When the sugar has dissolved and the mixture is very hot, remove from the heat and pour over the black-eyed peas. Set aside to marinate for at least 1 hour before serving.

4. Store, covered and refrigerated, for up to 2 weeks.

Hot and Spicy Chickpeas and Nuts

Makes 2½ cups

It's really a good idea to double or triple this recipe, as these crunchy bites are quite addictive. They are a great bar bite, party treat, or everyday healthy snack.

INGREDIENTS

1½ cups cooked chickpeas, well drained and patted very dry

1 cup hazelnuts or any other nut you prefer

About 3 tablespoons peanut oil

1 teaspoon curry powder

1 teaspoon fennel seeds

½ teaspoon ground cumin

¼ teaspoon smoked paprika (see Note)

⅛ teaspoon cayenne pepper (see Note)

Sea salt

INSTRUCTIONS

1. Preheat the oven to 450°F.

2. Place the chickpeas and nuts in a mixing bowl. Add just enough oil to generously coat, tossing to evenly cover.

3. Add the curry powder, fennel seeds, cumin, paprika, and cayenne and toss to lightly coat the chickpeas and nuts with the spices. Season with sea salt and transfer to a rimmed baking sheet.

4. Place in the preheated oven and toast, stirring frequently, for about 30 minutes or until well toasted and crisp.

5. Remove from the oven and allow to cool before serving or storing.

6. Store, tightly covered, in a cool spot for up to 2 weeks.

Note: *If you don't like heat, replace the smoked paprika with sweet paprika and eliminate the cayenne.*

Adzuki Bean Salsa

Makes about 4 cups

This salsa is a changeup from regular salsas and a very healthy one, too. You can use this as a topping for Mexican dishes, as a dip with chips or crackers, or as a mix with grains for a salad.

INGREDIENTS

2 cups cooked adzuki beans
2 shallots, peeled and minced
1 garlic clove, peeled and minced
½ cup diced tomatillos
½ cup diced onion
¼ cup diced yellow bell pepper
¼ cup diced red bell pepper
¼ cup diced green bell pepper
1 tablespoon white vinegar
2 teaspoons lime juice, more if needed
Salt

INSTRUCTIONS

1. Place the beans in a large mixing bowl. Add the shallots, garlic, tomatillos, onion, and bell pepper. Add the vinegar and lime juice, season with salt, and toss to blend.

2. Cover and refrigerate for at least 1 hour before serving.

3. When ready to serve, taste and, if necessary, add more salt and lime juice.

4. Serve as you would any cold salsa.

Sugar 'n' Spice Peanuts

Makes about 2½ cups

Who doesn't like peanuts? This is an easy recipe that takes the circus nut to new and zesty heights. As long as the peanuts are properly stored, airtight and at room temperature, they will keep for a few weeks. A warning: do not make these on a humid day or they will quickly turn limp and soggy.

INGREDIENTS

2½ cups dried roasted peanuts

1 tablespoon peanut oil

2 teaspoons pure chile powder

2 teaspoons ground cumin

2 teaspoons light brown sugar

1 teaspoon curry powder

1 teaspoon garlic powder

½ teaspoon onion powder

¼ teaspoon cayenne pepper, or to taste

Sea salt to taste

INSTRUCTIONS

1. Preheat the oven to 300°F.

2. Place the peanuts in a large mixing bowl. Drizzle with the oil, tossing to coat well.

3. Combine the chile powder, cumin, sugar, curry powder, garlic powder, onion powder, and cayenne pepper in a small mixing bowl. When blended, sprinkle over the oiled peanuts and then toss to coat well.

4. Transfer the seasoned peanuts to a large rimmed baking sheet, taking care that they are in a single layer. Place in the preheated oven and roast for about 15 minutes or until slightly crisp, dry, and toasty.

5. Remove from the oven and season with sea salt.

6. Set aside to cool before serving or storing.

Instant Pot Boiled Peanuts

Makes 2 pounds

I was introduced to these peanuts by friends from Cairo, Georgia, who loved them and wanted me to like them, too. They have a very distinctive taste and texture that, to me, takes some tries to love. To tell you the truth, I never have taken a deep liking to them—you might need to be a born Southerner to truly enjoy them. However, they fascinate me and I think everyone should try them at least once.

INGREDIENTS

2 pounds green peanuts (see Note)

½ cup salt

¼ cup red chile flakes, optional

INSTRUCTIONS

1. Place the peanuts in an Instant Pot along with the salt and chile flakes. Add enough cold water to cover completely.

2. Place the steamer rack on top of the peanuts to weigh them down and keep them immersed in the water as they cook.

3. Cover and set to Pressure Cook for 90 minutes.

4. Allow to do a natural pressure release for 30 minutes, then open the valve to allow remaining pressure to escape.

5. Remove the peanuts from the cooker and allow to cool slightly before eating. When done, the peanuts are slightly spicy, slightly salty, and soft as a just-cooked bean.

6. Also may be eaten at room temperature.

Note: Green peanuts are a specialty ingredient that, unless you live in the southern United States, will have to be mail ordered. You can start your search for a seller by consulting the Sources section of this book (see page 233).

If you don't have an Instant Pot or slow cooker, you can cook these peanuts in a large soup pot on the stove. It just takes a very long time and careful watching to make sure the peanuts stay submerged in the water. It can take anywhere from 4 to 9 hours in gently simmering water to get the peanuts to the right consistency and flavor.

Beans on Toast

Makes as many as you like

My mom was a first generation American of Scottish parentage, so I grew up eating a cheap and cheerful dish called beans on toast that is everyday fare throughout the United Kingdom. The original is simply spoonfuls of Heinz baked beans (now known as Heinz Beanz) dumped on a slice of brown bread. Of course, over the years, cooks have devised their own versions, so beans on toast can now mean many things from plain to fancy. I always try to use Anne's New England Baked Beans (page 198), but when I want to be true to the original I use Heinz Beanz. If you have a favorite homemade baked bean recipe or a brand of canned baked beans, do not hesitate to use them, either.

I don't always use baked beans to make beans on toast, as I am apt to rely on whatever cooked beans I have in the fridge. In the photo here, the beans happen to be yellow eyes—a bean that could easily replace the standard navy bean used in the recipe for Anne's New England Baked Beans or the traditional New England baked beans. There are no real serving amounts for this recipe; just pile on as many beans as you like. This is my take on my mom's original version—a little fancier, but still homey and delicious.

INGREDIENTS

For every open-faced sandwich:

1 slice toasted wheat bread

Zesty mustard for spreading, more for serving

At least ½ cup warm beans (if the beans are soupy, I let them cook for a bit so I don't end up with a very sloppy joe)

1 thick slice Cheddar

2 slices crisply fried thick bacon, if you happen to have it on hand

Spicy pickles, optional

INSTRUCTIONS

1. Preheat the oven to 400°F.

2. Lay the toast on a cookie sheet—preferably non-stick so you don't have to use any elbow grease to scrape off burned-on melted cheese.

3. Generously coat the toast with mustard. Spoon the beans on top of the mustard and then lay a piece of cheese on top of the beans.

4. Transfer to the oven and bake for about 5 minutes or just until the cheese has melted.

5. Remove from the oven and, if using, crisscross the crisp bacon on top.

6. Serve piping hot, either whole or cut into triangles, with a spoonful of zesty mustard and, if you have them, some spicy pickles on the side.

Sweet Rice and Lentil Packaged Mix

Makes 4 packages

This is an easy "gift from the kitchen" that makes a lovely hostess or holiday gift. It is so easy to put together that even the most harried gift giver can make it look as though it was a piece of cake!

INGREDIENTS

4 cups basmati, jasmine, Texmati, Wehani, or brown rice

1 cup lentils

16 whole cloves

8 black peppercorns

2 cinnamon sticks, broken in half

¼ cup finely minced candied ginger

2 teaspoons toasted cumin seeds

2 teaspoons coarse salt, or to taste

1 teaspoon toasted cardamom seeds

1 teaspoon freshly ground white pepper

INSTRUCTIONS

1. Place 1 cup of the rice into each of four containers. Add ¼ cup of the lentils along with 4 cloves, 2 peppercorns, 1 piece of the cinnamon stick, 1 tablespoon ginger, ½ teaspoon each cumin seeds and salt, and ¼ teaspoon each cardamom seeds and white pepper to each container, stirring or shaking to blend well.

2. When well blended, seal tightly, label, and store in a cool, dry spot for up to 1 month. Each container holds enough to serve 4 to 6 people when cooked.

Note: Always attach a tag with cooking instructions. The instructions should include these elements: For each portion of the rice-lentil mix, bring 2 cups of salted water to a boil. Then add the mix, return to the boil, lower the heat, cover, and simmer for about 15 minutes or until tender. Fluff with a fork and serve.

If you use brown rice in the recipe, you will have to increase the recommended cooking time for whatever type of brown rice you use.

Dal Pancakes

These aren't your usual breakfast pancakes! They make a terrific snack when wrapped around some yogurt and chopped raw vegetables, or leftover meats or poultry. I also like them pulled apart and dipped in salsa, chutney, or just as they are—so much better than chips!

INGREDIENTS

1 cup red lentils or yellow split peas

½ cup low-sodium vegetable broth

½ cup chopped onion

1 tablespoon minced ginger

1 tablespoon minced garlic

1 teaspoon minced hot green chile, or to taste

½ teaspoon ground cumin

¼ teaspoon ground turmeric

Salt

¼ cup whole-fat plain yogurt, plus more for serving

2 tablespoons minced scallions, white and green part

2 tablespoons chopped cilantro

2 tablespoons chopped flat-leaf parsley

Clarified butter for frying (see page 201)

Yogurt for serving, optional

continued

INSTRUCTIONS

1. Place the lentils in a small heatproof bowl and cover with very hot water. Set aside to soak for 1 hour.

2. Drain the lentils and place them in the bowl of a food processor fitted with the metal blade. Add the vegetable broth, onion, ginger, garlic, chile, cumin, turmeric, and salt. Process for about 3 minutes or until well blended and frothy.

3. Pour from the processor bowl into a medium mixing bowl. Add the ¼ cup yogurt along with the scallions, cilantro, and parsley and stir to incorporate completely.

4. Heat a griddle over high heat. Generously coat it with clarified butter. When very hot, lower the heat to medium-high and ladle in enough batter to make a 5-inch pancake. Cook for about 2 minutes or until the underside is beginning to brown. Turn and cook for another 2 minutes. Remove from the griddle and keep warm. Continue cooking pancakes until all the batter has been used.

5. Serve warm with a dollop of yogurt, if desired.

Socca

Makes one 10-inch tart

Socca is essentially a street food sold in the South of France, particularly around Nice. It is also sold in the neighboring Italian province of Liguria, where it is known as *farinata*. Socca is a great cocktail tidbit or afternoon snack. The key ingredient that makes it so unique: chickpea flour.

INGREDIENTS

3 tablespoons extra virgin olive oil

1 cup chickpea flour (see Note)

2 tablespoons herbes de Provence (see Note)

½ teaspoon salt

½ cup cooked chopped onion

Coarse salt and cracked pepper, optional

INSTRUCTIONS

1. Preheat the oven to 350°F.

2. Using 1 tablespoon of the olive oil, generously coat the interior of a 10-inch tart pan. Set aside.

3. Place the flour in a medium mixing bowl. Set aside.

4. Measure out 1 cup of very hot water. Add 1 teaspoon of the herbes de Provence along with the salt, whisking until the salt has dissolved. Pour the hot water mixture into the flour, beating to incorporate.

5. Immediately transfer the flour mixture to a medium heavy-bottomed saucepan. Place over medium heat and cook, stirring constantly, for 5 minutes.

6. Scrape the mixture into the prepared tart pan. Using a pastry brush, generously coat the top with the remaining olive oil. Sprinkle the top with the onion and remaining herbes de Provence.

7. Place in the preheated oven and bake for about 30 minutes or until golden brown and the surface has cracked.

8. Remove from the oven and set on a wire rack to cool slightly.

9. Cut into small wedges and serve.

10. Alternately, you can break the socca into pieces and fry them in hot olive oil for about 1 minute or until brown. Drain on a double layer of paper towel and season with coarse salt and cracked pepper.

Note: *Chickpea flour is also known as besan or gram flour. It is available from Indian markets, specialty food markets, and online.*

Herbes de Provence is a dried herb mixture typically used in the Provence region of France. It can be a mix of thyme, savory, marjoram, lavender, rosemary, or oregano. It is often used to flavor meats and poultry.

Black Bean Crepes

Makes about 16

You can eat these just as they are, sprinkled with some shredded cheese, or as a snack. Or, like in my variation on page 206, you can fill them with seasoned vegetables, fish, meat, or any filling you prefer. The bean puree makes these crepes somewhat denser and more filling than the classic, so they can really stand alone as a snack without a filling.

INGREDIENTS

¾ cup cooked black beans
½ teaspoon red hot sauce, or to taste
Salt
1 large egg, at room temperature
2 tablespoons melted unsalted butter
½ cup all-purpose flour
½ cup light beer
Clarified butter (see page 201) or peanut oil for cooking

INSTRUCTIONS

1. Combine the beans with ½ cup water, the hot sauce, and salt in a blender jar. Cover and process until very smooth. Add the egg and melted butter and process until well incorporated. Add the flour and beer and continue to process until the batter is very smooth and thin. It should be easily pourable. If the batter seems too thick, add water as necessary.

2. Pour into a clean container, cover, and refrigerate for 2 hours.

3. Cut about sixteen 6-inch squares of parchment or waxed paper. Set aside.

4. Remove the batter from the refrigerator, uncover, and test for consistency. You want a smooth batter that pours easily from a ladle. If necessary, add warm water a bit at a time until the desired consistency is reached.

5. Heat a 6-inch nonstick skillet or crepe pan over medium-high heat. When hot, using a paper towel, lightly rub the interior of the pan with clarified butter.

6. Pour about 2 tablespoons of the batter into the center of the hot pan, tilting the pan to lightly and evenly cover the bottom with a thin layer of the batter. Lay the pan back on the heat and cook for about 1 minute or just until the edges are browning. Using a small flexible spatula (or your fingertips if you are willing), lift up the edge of the crepe and carefully turn it over. You may have to use your fingers to do this as crepes are very fragile. Cook for another minute or just until set.

7. Carefully lift the crepe from the pan and place it on a square of parchment paper. Top with another square. Continue making and stacking crepes until all the batter has been used.

8. Serve warm with any topping or filling you desire.

Protein Pancakes

Makes 10 to 12

This pancake is not at all what you would think of as a pancake.

However, unusual though they are, they are tasty and full of good nutrition. I like them served with melted butter and jam, and sometimes with peanut butter and jelly. You can use any type of sweetener in the batter that you like, but maple syrup gives the pancakes a nice morning flavor.

INGREDIENTS

1 cup split mung beans (see Note)

½ cup rolled oats

½ cup plain Greek yogurt

3 tablespoons pure maple syrup or other sweetener of choice, plus more for topping, optional

Pinch salt

1 teaspoon baking soda

Peanut oil for cooking

Butter for topping, optional

INSTRUCTIONS

1. Combine the mung beans and oats in a medium heatproof bowl. Add 2 cups of very hot water and stir to blend. Cover and set aside to soak for 20 minutes.

2. Uncover and transfer to a blender jar. Add the yogurt, maple syrup, and salt and process for about 3 minutes or until a thin pancake-like batter has formed.

3. Pour into a medium mixing bowl. Whisk in the baking soda.

4. Heat a griddle over medium-high heat. Lightly coat it with a bit of peanut oil. When hot but not smoking, ladle in the batter, about ¼ cup at a time. Cook, turning once, for about 3 minutes or until golden brown and cooked through.

5. Serve warm with butter and maple syrup, if desired.

Note: You can also use whole green mung beans instead of split ones. If so, they will have to be soaked for a minimum of 2 hours. However, you can put them to soak the night before to save time in the morning.

Mocha–Black Bean Smoothie

Here's an easy, tasty, and very healthy way to get beans into your diet. If you're not a coffee drinker, eliminate the coffee powder—you will still start the day with a smile. Any bean can be used in a smoothie, but I prefer black beans in this mix as they greatly enhance the color.

INSTRUCTIONS

1. Pour the milk into a blender. Add the banana and beans and process to blend. Add the cocoa powder, peanut butter, honey, coffee powder, and vanilla and again process to blend. When well blended, add the ice cubes, a couple at a time, and process until smooth and icy.

2. Serve immediately.

INGREDIENTS

1½ cups milk of any type you prefer

1 medium frozen banana, cut into chunks

¾ cup cooked black beans

2 tablespoons cocoa powder

1 tablespoon peanut butter

1 tablespoon honey or other sweetener of choice

1 teaspoon instant coffee powder

1 teaspoon pure vanilla extract

Approximately 1 cup ice

Mom's Peanut Rolls

Makes about 18

My mom made these frequently when I was a child, but I had forgotten about them until I found an old recipe card of hers. These are a terrific kids' snack, as they aren't too sweet and have the nutritional power of peanuts.

INGREDIENTS

2 cups sifted all-purpose flour

7 tablespoons sugar

1 tablespoon baking powder

½ teaspoon salt

2 large eggs, at room temperature

½ cup milk

¼ cup unsalted butter, at room temperature

¾ cup chopped peanuts

INSTRUCTIONS

1. Preheat the oven to 350°F.

2. Line a baking sheet with a silicone liner or parchment paper. Set aside.

3. Combine the sifted flour with 1 tablespoon of the sugar along with the baking powder and salt. Sift again into a medium mixing bowl.

4. Separate one of the eggs, reserving the white for the filling. Combine the egg yolk with the remaining whole egg in a small mixing bowl. Add the milk and whisk to blend well.

5. Add the butter to the flour mixture and, using your hands or a dough blender or pastry cutter, cut the butter into it. Add the egg mixture and, using a wooden spoon, stir to just combine.

6. Combine the remaining 6 tablespoons sugar with the peanuts and reserved egg white in a small mixing bowl. Stir to blend well and set aside.

7. Lightly flour a clean work surface. Place the dough in the center and knead it for 1 minute.

8. Using a rolling pin, roll out the dough to a rectangle about ¼ inch thick. Spread the peanut mixture over the top, then using your hands, roll up the dough in jelly roll fashion into a firm log.

9. Using a sharp knife, trim off each end to make even. Cut the roll crosswise into slices about ½ inch thick.

10. Place the slices on the prepared pan. Transfer to the preheated oven and bake for about 15 minutes or until golden brown around the edges and cooked through.

11. Remove from the oven and transfer to a wire rack to cool slightly before serving.

White Bean Pie

This pie is right up there with pumpkin pie and sweet potato pie as a great fall and Thanksgiving dessert. If you cut down the sugar to a smidge, it also makes a terrific luncheon dish with a tossed green salad on the side.

INGREDIENTS

2½ cups mashed cooked white beans

1¼ cups light brown sugar

2 tablespoons cornstarch

2 teaspoons ground cinnamon

½ teaspoon ground nutmeg

½ teaspoon ground ginger

¼ teaspoon ground cloves

3 tablespoons unsalted butter, at room temperature

4 large eggs, at room temperature

One 13-ounce can evaporated milk

1 tablespoon lemon juice

One 9-inch unbaked pie shell

INSTRUCTIONS

1. Preheat the oven to 450°F.

2. Place the mashed beans in a medium mixing bowl. Add the sugar, cornstarch, cinnamon, nutmeg, ginger, and cloves. Using a handheld electric mixer, beat until the sugar is well incorporated into the beans. Add the butter and continue to beat until well blended. Add the eggs, one at a time, and beat until very well incorporated into the beans. Add the milk and lemon juice and beat to blend.

3. Pour the mixture into the pie shell. Transfer to the preheated oven and bake for 10 minutes. Lower the heat to 350°F and continue to bake for about 40 minutes or until the pie is set in the center.

4. Remove from the oven and place on a wire rack to cool slightly before cutting into wedges and serving.

White Bean–Orange Cake

Makes one 9-inch Bundt cake

Beans add a lot of moisture to this cake and, of course, some extra nutrition. The beans replace some of the usual fat required for a cake, and they make a dessert that keeps well for a few days. When using beans in dessert recipes, I always try to combine them with a strong flavor, as beans can be bland. For cakes, flavors like chocolate, citrus, or sweet spices do the trick. The orange in this recipe really takes it above and beyond!

INGREDIENTS

3 cups all-purpose flour

2 teaspoons baking powder

1 teaspoon baking soda

Pinch salt

2 large eggs, separated, at room temperature

¼ cup unsalted butter, at room temperature

2 cups confectioners' sugar, sifted

1½ cups white bean puree

1 cup buttermilk

¼ cup plus 1 tablespoon fresh orange juice

1 teaspoon pure vanilla extract

2 tablespoons orange zest

1 teaspoon whole milk

INSTRUCTIONS

1. Preheat the oven to 350°F.

2. Lightly butter and grease a 9-inch Bundt pan. Alternately, spray it with nonstick baking spray just before filling.

continued

3. Combine the flour, baking powder, baking soda, and salt and sift into a medium mixing bowl. Set aside.

4. Place the egg whites in a medium mixing bowl and, using a handheld electric mixer, beat until firm peaks form. Set aside.

5. Place the butter in the bowl of a standing electric mixer fitted with the paddle attachment. Beat on low for 2 minutes or just until the butter is very light. Add 1 cup of the sugar and continue to beat until very light and airy. Add the bean puree and continue to beat for about 4 minutes or until well incorporated.

6. With the motor running, add the egg yolks, one at a time, beating after each addition to blend completely.

7. Begin alternately adding the dry ingredients and the buttermilk, beating until well incorporated. Beat in ¼ cup of the orange juice along with the vanilla.

8. Remove the bowl from the mixer and fold in the beaten egg whites along with the orange zest,

mixing to blend well. You don't want to do this with the mixer, as it will deflate the egg whites and the zest will stick to the paddle and not get incorporated into the batter.

9. Scrape the batter into the prepared Bundt pan. Transfer to the preheated oven and bake for about 50 minutes or until a cake tester inserted near the center comes out clean.

10. Remove from the oven and set on a wire rack to cool for about 15 minutes. Then invert the pan onto the rack and turn the cake out. Allow the cake to cool on the wire rack.

11. While the cake is cooling, prepare the icing: Combine the remaining 1 cup confectioners' sugar with the milk and remaining 1 tablespoon orange juice, mixing with a fork until well blended.

12. When the cake has cooled completely, drizzle the top with the icing. Allow the icing to set before serving.

13. Store, covered, at room temperature for up to 2 days or refrigerated for up to 1 week.

SOURCES

Many of the sources that I recommend also sell heritage grains, organic products, and specialty foods. Almost all of them supply information about using their products, plus recipes. They are also quite helpful when answering any bean-related questions you might have. They all have online stores, with the exception of those organizations supporting bean growers.

Alma Gourmet
Dried Italian beans
Website: www.almagourmet.com
Alma Gourmet Ltd.
39-12 Crescent Street
Long Island City, New York 11101
(718) 433-1630

Anson Mills
Southern peas
Website: www.ansonmills.com
Email: info@ansonmills.com
1922 C Gervais Street
Columbia, South Carolina 29201
(803) 467-4122

Bob's Red Mill
Dried beans, peas, and lentils
Website: www.bobsredmill.com

13521 Southeast Pheasant Court
Milwaukie, Oregon 97222
(800) 349-2173

California Beans
California bean information/recipes
Website: www.calbeans.org
California Dry Bean Advisory Board
531D North Alta Avenue
Dinuba, California 93618
(559) 591-4866

Camellia Beans
Dried beans and Southern peas
Website: www.camelliabrand.com
Email: info@camelliabeans.com
L. H. Hayward & Co., LLC
5401 Toler Street
Harahan, Louisiana 70123
(504) 733-8480

Elegant Beans and Beyond
California-grown dried beans
Website: www.elegantbeans.com
PO Box 578
Clarksburg, California 95612

Hope and Harmony Farms
Raw peanuts
Website: www.hopeandharmonyfarms.com
509 North County Drive
Wakefield, Virginia 23888
(800) 233-8788

Kalustyan's
Dried beans, spices, international foods
Website: www.foodsofnations.com
123 Lexington Avenue
New York, New York 10016
(212) 685-3451

Kandarian Organic Farms
California-grown dried heritage beans and peas
Website: www.kandarian-organic-farms
.myshopify.com
1288 Second Street #1/2
Los Osos, California 93402
(805) 528-4007

North Bay Trading Company
Dried beans and lentils
Website: www.northbaytrading.com
13904 E. US 2
Brule, Wisconsin 54820
(715) 372-5031

Purcell Mountain Farms
Dried beans, peas, and lentils
Website: www.purcellmountainfarms.com

393 Firehouse Road
Moyie Springs, Idaho 83845
(208) 267-0627

Rancho Gordo
Dried heritage beans
Website: www.ranchogordo.com
Rancho Gordo New World Specialty Food
1924 Yajome Street
Napa, California 94559
(800) 599-8323

Red Hill General Store
Bulk dried beans
Website: www.redhillgeneralstore.com
1035 Sylvatus Highway
Hillsville, Virginia 24343
(276) 728-3456

The Bean Institute
Bean information/recipes
Northarvest Bean Growers Association
Contact web manager: adamv@communiqueinc.com

Zürsun Idaho Heirloom Beans
Idaho heirloom beans
Website: www.zursunbeans.com
PO Box 558
Twin Falls, Idaho 83303
(877) 767-2626

Italics are used to indicate illustrations.

For information about permission to reproduce selections
from this book, write to Permissions, The Countryman Press,
500 Fifth Avenue, New York, NY 10110

For information about special discounts for bulk purchases,
please contact W. W. Norton Special Sales at
specialsales@wwnorton.com or 800-233-4830

Manufacturing by Versa Press
Series book design by Nick Caruso Design
Production manager: Devon Zahn

Names: Choate, Judith, author. | Pool, Steve, illustrator.
Title: The mighty bean : 100 easy recipes that are good for your
    health, the world, and your budget / Judith Choate ; photo-
    graphs by Steve Pool.
Description: First edition. | New York, NY : The Countryman
    Press, division of W. W. Norton & Company, Independent
    Publishers Since 1923, [2021] | Series: Countryman know-how
    | Includes index.
Identifiers: LCCN 2020049389 | ISBN 9781682686379 (pbk.) |
    ISBN 9781682686386 (epub)
Subjects: LCSH: Cooking (Beans) | Cooking (Legumes) | Quick
    and easy cooking. | LCGFT: Cookbooks.
Classification: LCC TX803.B4 C47 2021 | DDC 641.6/565—
    dc23
LC record available at https://lccn.loc.gov/2020049389

The Countryman Press
www.countrymanpress.com

A division of W. W. Norton & Company, Inc.
500 Fifth Avenue, New York, NY 10110
www.wwnorton.com

978-1-68268-637-9 (pbk.)

10 9 8 7 6 5 4 3 2 1

PHOTO CREDITS:

All photographs by Steve Pool unless noted below.

Page 4: © FotografiaBasica/iStockPhoto.com
Page 41: © Thyra Parthen/iStockPhoto.com
Page 59: © etorres69/iStockPhoto.com
Page 81: © NataliaBulatova/iStockPhoto.com
Pages 83 and 189: © ALLEKO/iStockPhoto.com
Page 89: © barol16/iStockPhoto.com
Page 106: © SharonFoelz/iStockPhoto.com
Page 118: © ivanmateev/iStockPhoto.com
Page 135: © jenifoto/iStockPhoto.com
Page 137: © DeniseBush/iStockPhoto.com
Page 141: © OksanaKiian/iStockPhoto.com
Page 151: © jmillard37/iStockPhoto.com
Page 163: © Frank Angeletti/iStockPhoto.com
Page 199: © grandriver/iStockPhoto.com
Page 205: © Paul_Brighton/iStockPhoto.com
Page 223: © Quanthem/iStockPhoto.com
Page 229: © PJjaruwan/iStockPhoto.com